500
1

turned completely now + off its hinges.. And then telling was from one who said she was "a very old lady":- but that her father was Professor Morse whom I mention in the first installment.. She wants me to tell me that , and also told me that his biography has just been published?.. She was trying to make out who I was, too - she said) she didn't remember me....& wondered when I lived ..

Harriett writes me that a lot of old ladies in Salem keep calling her "where 'bouts in Salem" ! used to live + what my father looked like... Apparently they're all reading] the Atlantic Monthly ... Ranie writes me the other day + said that what she calls my Atlantic has been kept under glass in the Radcliffe college library, with other recent publications by old Radcliffites ..

THE JOURNALS AND LETTERS OF
THE LITTLE LOCKSMITH

Also by Katharine Butler Hathaway

THE LITTLE LOCKSMITH

MR. MUFFET'S CAT

KATHARINE BUTLER HATHAWAY

The

Journals & Letters

of

The Little Locksmith

Illustrated by the Author

COWARD-McCANN · INC · NEW YORK · 1946

Manufactured in the United States of America.

VAN REES PRESS • NEW YORK

Contents

FOREWORD ix

1. I OFFER MY HAND 3

2. A PERSON IN LOVE WITH A HOUSE 7

3. THE SEARCH 53

4. THINGS JAPANESE 70

5. PARIS 113

6. INTERLUDE IN THE HAUTE SAVOIE 163

7. DANS NOTRE PÉNICHE 218

8. MR. AND MRS. MUFFET 231

9. BACK IN MAINE 275

10. FROM THE JOURNALS 343

Illustrations

1. Woman Reaching   21
2. Girl Writing   33
3. Catharine Huntington   59
4. Dennett's Wharf, Castine   73
5. Woman's Head   96
6. Elliot Paul   118
7. Woman   137
8. Camille Paul   151
9. Young Man   176
10. Paris Window   244
11. Kittens in Drawer   256
12. Apple Tree, Blue Hill   279
13. Girl   307
14. Elizabeth Keats Butler   339
15. Flowers   347
16. Flowers   391
17. Flowers   393

Foreword

KATHARINE BUTLER HATHAWAY had a reckless appetite
for life. Within the limits of her physical capacity, she
was an artist; but the main medium of her art was not
paper or pencil, but her life itself. She was imprisoned at
first in a fateful physical predicament; her story is one of
her continual battling to be free. At times of critical decision and action she felt the strong sense of some inward
force impelling her toward an unknown goal, and, since
she obeyed this instinct, her life, like a plant or tree, took
on organic pattern and shape, and grew around and over
the obstacle. "A man's life of any worth is a continual
allegory," said Keats, "and few eyes can see the mystery of
his life." Katharine's was a life of such worth. Her eyes
discerned its mystery. She believed goodness and happiness to be the same. She denied a moral distinction between flesh and spirit. Through audacity her life became
rich, and in gratitude she began an autobiography as her
"bread-and butter letter to God."

In her book, "The Little Locksmith," preliminary things
were told, but the rest was left waiting. She intended the
volume as an introduction to the tale of her Island Years,
which were years when a desperate need drove her beyond the confines of the complacent life of her family
to the heights and depths of experience, and "changed
everything that went before and everything that came

ix

after." The Island Years coincided with her possession of her house in Castine.

While she was getting this house ready to live in she dedicated it to three secret wishes. She wished it to be a house for children, a house for artists, and a house for lovers, because these three classes of people seemed to her to share a common need for sanctuary from the hostility and indifference of the world. She wanted her house to serve as such a sanctuary. Her first actual summer there was disillusioning because of amiable summer visitors, who failed to comprehend her purposes, and unconsciously thwarted those purposes by laying an unimaginative conventional surface over the intended life of her house. But after the last of these guests were gone, and she was alone in the house—during that first embracing cold Maine winter—she began to feel a sense of wonderful well-being, with a surge of confidence in the success of her scheme.

She became an intimate friend of the artist, Philip von Saltza, and his wife, Beata. Philip's house was furnished with ancestral Swedish possessions and he had converted his barn into a studio. The Japanese artist, Toshihiko, came to Castine the next year and settled in a ramshackle house at the crossroads, and began to paint. When Philip and Toshihiko began conversations about paint and painters at Katharine's house, and especially after her little nieces and nephews came for the summer and were fascinated by the diminutive foreign artist, and they all were so free and light-hearted and merry together, Katharine felt that the first two secret wishes were beginning to be fulfilled.

Toshihiko's appearance in Katharine's house revived for her the special atmosphere of her childhood when she had been intimate with Japanese things. During those years, her grandfather, James F. Almy, the Salem merchant, had opened a Japanese goods department in his store and gifts of Japanese porcelain, prints, tiny curio boxes, bamboo handled brushes, and thick rice paper were brought to her room. Lying in her bed the child avidly seized every treasure that floated within her reach, and the textures and odors and sight of Japanese things became part of her life.

Katharine had been confined by a rigid mechanical apparatus which was designed to prevent the curvature of her spine by a tubercular infection. It was not until ten years afterward that she was pronounced cured and rose from her bed. She was never taller than a ten-year old child. Her curvature was slight. Her head was handsome and low in relation to her shoulders. Her shoulders were wide, her hips narrow, and her legs and hands finely slim and beautiful, so that when she half-reclined she looked like a mermaid. She never breathed nor moved easily. Even her intimate friends didn't know that she suffered from the consciousness of any deformity. Yet the fact is that she was horribly shocked when she saw herself for the first time in a mirror. She felt as if a wicked fairy had put some hideous disguise upon her life, and that she was disqualified forever for love, which she thought was the greatest of human experiences. Being debarred from expressing her great ardour in any of the usual physical ways, she turned to the sublimation of art. The long impasse which followed was not broken until years afterward when she bought a house in Castine.

What followed was "like the Japanese fairy tale of a man who visited a lady in her palace under the sea. It is romance, and it becomes legend. As one looks back upon it, it comes to seem like an allegorical tale. One recognizes it as the true heart of one's life, for without it one's life would have been empty."

Toshihiko talked to Katharine about herself more under-

standingly and frankly than anyone had ever done before.
He spoke intimately about his own life and about Japan
and it seemed even more fascinating to her than it had
in childhood. Toshihiko belonged to a family which was
prominent in commerce and concerned only with wealth
and power. He had been asked by his father and uncles
to prepare himself for business; but he chose instead to
be an unconventional artist, and to free his life from all
the ceremonial and rigid repression of his class. As she
listened to him Katharine began to learn that Japanese
repressions were a great deal more terrible than any New
England repression and that repression heightens one's
sensibility. She discovered in Toshihiko an awareness of
delicate tones of feelings and meanings which matched
her own. These he symbolized by the Japanese word
nonbili. Katharine and Toshihiko were set apart by this
perceptivity, and they found a magical island under the
sea, where the old spells might be released. When she
made her third wish—that her house might be a refuge
for love—it never occurred to her that it could be for
herself; but now she fell in love with Toshihiko, and the
fulfillment of her love made her life another life, the life
known by normal human beings.

Toshihiko went to Paris to paint and Katharine found her
house intolerable without him. When she knew that she
couldn't endure it, she locked the door and fled to New
York.

She was still in an emotionally vulnerable state when
Taro stepped into her life. Taro was Toshihiko's friend
and cousin; he too had left Japan in order to be an artist.
He was Katharine's frequent companion that winter, and
in the spring she took him to Castine. Taro asked Katharine to marry him and live in Japan. She was in love
with him and passionately wanted to throw away her old
life to live with him in Japan. At the end of that spring

Taro went home to Japan to inform his family and to arrange the wedding. But the influence of his family was too strong for him and after many weeks of silence he cabled her that he had married a Japanese girl.

Katharine took the news numbly, but thawed out into despair, and sailed to France. Toshihiko was still in Paris. She needed his help but discovered him changed, cruel, and perverse; and suffering from some neurotic torture of his own. In any event he was impressed and surprised by the new drawings that Katharine was beginning to make.

These drawings were extravagantly praised by Elliot and Camille Paul, and Camille had slyly taken Katharine to the Louvre to incite her further accomplishment and the device worked, for Katharine's hand began to come amorously alive when she drew. She stared with adoration at the flowers and still-life objects as her hand lay tracing them.

Katharine looked at flowers and said, "Draw plants and trees from the root up. You can't grow them from the top down." In saying this, Katharine was akin to the Chinese painters. The alive feeling in her hand when she drew was what made her draw. She was careless afterward of what she had drawn.

Her startling happiness at drawing made her suddenly realize, by contrast, how overclouded and poisoned her winter had been by Toshihiko's disturbing, vexing presence. She wrote to a confidante, "I am not as brave as you think. I am a baby. I want to cry." She made up her mind not to see Toshihiko again, and brought the Japanese cycle to its close, and took almost random flight to the Haute Savoie. She cast in her lot with French workmen there. She became an outcast from her own world of convention and appearance, and tossed her life away in order to find it.

Among simple mountain people she shed the garment of her identity, the troublesome disguise of pride and shame. She had shed it before in Castine in the company of her nieces. She had tried to shed it with artists and lovers. Her early dream had been of anonymous love, unpossessed and unpossessing, not a personal relationship with another person as much as a yielding to some divine and universal force—an entry into the Garden of Eden. She imagined that all the other misfits of the world must have her same longings for a love without guilt, responsibility, or shame—for careless love. The Japanese associations had been acts of despair. Every one seemed imprisoned, nearly every one in the world, each in his own predicament—like a bird in an empty room, which seeks to escape, and flies back and forth, and can find no way out although all the doors and windows are open.

In the Haute Savoie, Katharine's first sight of plowed fields, blossoming trees, and the mountain slopes blue with gentians were like her childhood's magical hills of Vermont. She left the stuffy inn where she stayed at first and took a peasant's house and moved in with the workmen. A simple subtle person among simpler sensuous ones, she acted out a mountainside idyll of love. Then it all ended in a coil of deception, and she confronted her deceptors in the first battle royal of her life. At the same juncture a cable arrived which announced her mother's illness. It was with a new clarity that she sailed for America where she arrived pale and wrung, but healed.

In the following spring of 1932 she met Daniel Rugg Hathaway, at Catharine Huntington's house in Boston, and married him in September. She returned with him to Paris under quite different stars—happy and pleased as a child. When she married Dan, she sold her house in Castine, and by that symbolic act brought her Island Years to a final close. "One reaches the island, is tossed ashore and stays one's allotted time, and one leaves the island in the end. One leaves it, but the island floats there still, separate from the rest of one's life, foreign and almost incredible. . . . Some fortunate lives unfold without obstruction or flaw, and these do not need islands."

Katharine's life began to flow back again into the quietness in which it began, and she felt in Paris a fierce nostalgia for America, which her expatriate friends did not seem to feel. She longed for the soil where her roots belonged. She restrained herself and wrote and sold her book, "Mr. Muffet's Cat and her Trip to Paris," and then with the proceeds returned to America and bought the brick house in Blue Hill which she describes in "A Person in Love with a House." This Blue Hill house (which Dan, by his care, made his) hadn't its windows open and its curtains blowing in and out of them like the first house in Castine. It was a refuge from storm, and contained the studio where Katharine composed "The Little Locksmith."

"Un labeur courageux muni d'humble constance
Resiste à tous assauts par douce pacience."

She felt after that only an occasional recurrence of her old mad longings; but the functioning of her heart and lungs, because of lack of room in her chest, became increasingly difficult. After "The Little Locksmith" appeared in the Atlantic, she was able to breathe only when she crouched on her elbows and knees like an unborn child or a snail. She returned to Salem by ambulance in that embryonic position, and died there on the day before Christmas in 1942.

This book is composed of the unfinished manuscripts, letters, journals, and notes which she left. In one of the notes she wrote:

"In telling the whole story why not very simply tell the truth . . . Don't pretend to be better than I am . . . the arrogance of people who pretend they are not human. This book will try to express Christianity and without malice—without revenge—the badness which is inside of all of us. I have done bad things and yet I am not a bad person. You can see that I am a good person—What is the harm in telling these things?—This is a plea for honesty and innocence—one has to break through with frightening honesty and innocence."

The arrangement of the book is this:

First Katharine introduces herself to the reader by narrating her encounter with a gypsy which revolutionized her conceptions of honesty. She describes herself, next, as a Person in Love with a House—with two houses actually.

Then the book goes back to 1912, and begins the contemporaneous account of events. Some material is retrospective, some of it is finished and some of it not yet finished. It is Katharine Butler Hathaway's direct experience of life, told without conscious art. A lifelong correspondence with Catharine Huntington furnishes the chief thread of sequence.

The final chapter includes beautiful Blue Hill scenes of flowers and the water; but it is chiefly valuable because it illuminates Katharine's spiritual destination. Notes for it were gathered from the mature years when Katharine wrestled with truth as deperately as Jacob wrestled with the angel and cried out, "I will not let thee go unless thou bless me!" The return of an ordinary spring seemed to her like a catclysm of nature. A human renascence was like the spring, only more violent, more living.

Terrible forces, destructive of things past, were surely powers of Eros as well as powers of Death. Such cataclysm must be followed by some transformation of the world as in those classic times when philosophers first examined human conduct, or like the Renascence which freed men's minds, or the democratic revolutions, a century and more ago, which promised to make America the New Testament of an Old World. Indestructible living ideas had to be planted over and over again in the particular idiom of each great century.

In retrospect she wrote: "At first little K. was not going to be like the locksmith—She was lucky and safe ... but is anybody? If there is a little locksmith, everybody must be him too ... It can't be for one and not for another ... The panic fears of then and of now!—the suspicion of cruelty, wickedness, danger, accident, hatred, evil!—But if I make my bed in hell, lo, thou art there,—even the little locksmith is safe, the soldiers, sailors, lost children, the torn and broken. If these things *are*, why only try to avoid and escape them one's self, why not share them and give help?"

"I can't deny it or pretend it's not so," she scribbled, "mine was a life of failure—one thing after another—like most lives ... but that is all right, it is universal, it is the great human experience to fail."

THE JOURNALS AND LETTERS OF
THE LITTLE LOCKSMITH

1. *I Offer My Hand*

WHEN I was young I was very certain of my talent and my future, and then I lost my certainty, and yet even then I used to be startled by the look of my hand. I would stare at it and feel as if it were separate from me. It awed me because I saw in it a look of force and talent which were more than anything I had ever manifested. The hand didn't look as if it had any of the shyness, doubt, and diffidence that I had come to know so well in myself. I thought I saw in it a mystical joy, a crowd of hidden powers—a power to make things, a power to love, and to know and understand much that was beyond what I myself knew. Yet it looked at that time as if its powers were sleeping. Their hour hadn't come yet when they would be aroused and play their part. My hand seemed to be asleep then, and for that reason all the more mysterious and wonderful and promising to me. When it was awake, what would it not do? I had believed once that I would achieve something and make myself famous, but I had not. Yet there was my hand, even when I was past thirty, still having that look of being able to do almost anything it wanted.

It has not fulfilled the promise of that look. It is an amateur still. It is an intricate, sensitive tool because it was made that way; it is a knowing, ingenious, construc-

3

tive workman. But it has never awed me by doing something beyond myself. It hasn't reached, or come anywhere near reaching, its consummation—and mine—the final unimpeded flow of accomplishment when the whole self is fused and mature at last and working in a pure passion of release; when at last all childishness and amateurishness and pretention are shed away. The possibility was there, born in the hand, but there was something wrong in the body or the head that the gifted hand unluckily belonged to.

Yes, at this point turn the hand over, idly and absent-mindedly as if by second nature, as people do, in order to examine the network in the palm, looking for what signs of talent may be there and for some indication of what may have been wrong, to cause delay and unfulfillment. But, first, I'm wondering if you despise palmistry and don't believe in it. I love it myself because it is so human and ridiculous, and so old. It is like the fortuneteller's own old pack of cards, dirty and dog-eared from having been used over and over for the benefit of such an endless procession of ignorant, hopeful, superstitious hearts, including the rich and the poor, cheating them all yet comforting them all in their pitifulness and their trouble so they can go home and sleep. Palmistry is a toy left over from the childhood of our race, which we shamefacedly hide whenever anyone is looking. Although we may despise it with our superior minds, it is older and nearer to us than our minds are, like sleep or tears, as even the best of us demonstrate when we are unhappy. When a desolation suddenly hits our lives and we don't know which way to turn, or when we are heartsick from having had to wait too long for the letter, or the footstep, or the voice, it is strange how easy it is to abandon temporarily the superior intellectual attitude and slip into the credulity in which all of us seize hold of the least hope that a gypsy

4

may find for us as we spread open wistful palms for her to see.

I don't care how proud and secure you may be now, or how completely you may have dismissed and forgotten it, if you have ever had any experience of heartbreak you must have listened to a fortuneteller at least once with every nerve of your body at attention, even while you carefully pretended not to believe a word of it. If you have not done that once in your life, then your turn hasn't come yet, that's all.

I love the fortunetelling profession because its clients all are people who are at that stage in their lives when they want more of life than they are getting. Instead of asking just to be quietly spared any more experience, as most of them probably will sooner than they could possibly believe, they are at that stage when they are only too willing and eager to live at almost any price. They are all hungry and amorous and softhearted and pitifully vulnerable, just from carrying around with them day and night such a fantastic load of wishes. The old and secure and contented never bother with fortunetellers. People who have got everything they want are not the ones who push their way into gypsies' tents and wear out the doorbells of card-readers' and crystal-gazers' lodgings. It is only the people who are at the impatient, feverishly loving, and unsatisfied stage, which is like a sickness that everybody must pass through sooner or later, who keep these trades alive.

Once when I myself was in the throes of that sickness I stopped beside a field at sunset where I saw a gypsy camp. I got out of my car, and a gypsy girl came toward me in the pink sunset light and took my hand to read my fortune. She sensed my trouble and began to talk to me about it as she stared into my palm. She spoke with a kind of fierce emphasis, as though she'd seen at once that my case

5

was serious, and in all gravity and earnestness she was doing her best to help me. I felt a tremendous commotion inside me as she brought everything that was most intimate and poignant out into the light of day there between us, two strangers standing on the edge of the field.

She was not like an ordinary fortuneteller, who is usually a listless being with a personality that one is not conscious of and can ignore, while one takes what she has to give as if she were only a mouthpiece. This girl was different. Her mind was wide awake at the same time that her clairvoyant powers were working. She understood and knew so keenly the importance to me of what she was saying that she embarrassed me.

And when she looked at last up at my face, to drive home what she was telling me and to search my eyes with real concern to see if I understood, something infinitely silly and snobbish in my training made me think I couldn't allow an ignorant gypsy to look into me as she was doing and see my real self, usually so carefully hidden from strangers and now naked and humble before her in the trouble that had driven me there. And so, instead of meeting her gaze with the honesty it deserved, I laughed in her face and pretended I had only listened to her for a joke.

She flung my hand away from her. "Do not laugh! Do not laugh!" she said angrily. She was young and beautiful, but her face became terrifying in its severity. She frowned as she rebuked me, and her straight black brows were very dark and threatening.

"You laugh with your head, but in your heart you do not laugh," she said. The scorn and loathing she put into that clairvoyant sentence, and the way she looked after me as I went away, made me ashamed as I have rarely been ashamed, and suddenly revolutionized my conception of honesty.

2. *A Person in Love with a House*

1

APPARENTLY I am susceptible to houses as some people are susceptible to other human beings. Twice in my life I have fallen in love with one. Each time it was as violent and fatal as falling in love with a human being. The first time it happened was ten years ago, and that experience caused as much of an awakening in me as another person's first human love affair. I bought the house, and it changed the whole of my life. Marriage could not have done more.

Before I had seen my predestined house, I had been restlessly wandering and hunting for something. I was thirty years old, rather frail in health, and not married when the search began. I thought I could never marry or have a job, and so a kind of sturdy peasant instinct began to work in me and made me want to attach myself to something solid and earthy instead of drying up like an empty bean pod.

In following this instinct I was very hard to please. I spent two or three years peering at one house after another and rejecting them all. I became aware of houses as a man is aware of women, who cannot help seeing every one who passes by and sensing her possibilities. He observes the humble ones as searchingly as he does the haughty ones, and he understands them all intuitively. I became like that toward houses. I became a connoisseur of houses, judging according to some inexpressible standard of my own. But, delightful and appealing as many of them were, my instinct kept telling me to go on. Not one of them roused any desire in me. So I went on, and it became a habit, a seeking that began to seem as if it had no purpose and would never end—as if I were noting and cataloguing houses simply as a pastime. It began to seem a little futile. If I had been collecting snuffboxes or old fans, I would have had something to show. Obsessed by houses, I rejected them all. I maintained an absolute virginity, thus preparing myself for complete surrender when the terrific impact of first love came. And then it came. The miracle happened. It was love at first sight, unforeseen and erratic as lightning. It was not the kind of house I had dreamed of choosing, but I had met my fate.

It was a large square house built in 1800. It stood on a hillside overlooking a Maine harbor on a historic wooded peninsula which had once belonged to the region called Acadia. To say that I adored it tells nothing. I cherished it with an unutterable tenderness—unutterable love. It became a part of me. I could not imagine my life going on without it. It was alive, I felt, and I loved it as much as one can love a person. The thing that made it alive was the particular feeling it gave to me and to the other people who came there. It seemed to have a tutelary spirit that watched over it and cast over it a magic spell, an unbroken mood of marvelous tranquillity in which there was a center of pure joy. It was as if a little of the early morning joy of the world were contained there in a deep, invulnerable serenity, like an ecstatic laughing infant held in its mother's benign hands. It seemed as if our tutelary spirit were one who has looked at all human experience and smiles because she knows that all is well. She has seen the

8

most horrible things that can happen to us, and the most fortunate things, and in her smile is the mingling of utmost compassion with utmost serenity, out of which the only true joy can spring. I once saw a statue of a Japanese god whose face had that same look. It was an imperturbable face with a dreaming half-smile.

I do not know why my house was blessed with such a guardian, but I swear it was so blessed, and others will swear the same. People said there was something magic there. Everybody felt it. The magic reached its fullness every year toward the end of the month of August, the time when the taffeta skirts of the aurora borealis appeared and disappeared in the dark north sky above Windmill Hill, rustling and flouncing back and forth in their mysterious ballet—the same time, at the end of the month of August, when people told us wide-eyed that they had heard the ghost of the drummer boy. Then, at that full moment of August, a deep, deep stillness of sun and sea and timelessness gathered and lay like harvest riches within the house and without—heavy purple dahlias in bloom against the shutters, doors and windows open to the divine air, crickets chirping on a brick path. And over it all a spell.

I called my place Sellanraa because I had been reading *Growth of the Soil*. It did not occur to me that there was a great discrepancy between the Sellanraa of Izak and Inger and my Sellanraa, in that mine was owned by a woman alone. I was the hare-lipped Inger, and there was no Izak to do a man's work on the place and to bring it to its proper fulfillment. I was an old maid all the time while I owned and lived in Sellanraa. I was an aunt there, and a daughter, and I was alone. It was when I was alone there that I was really wedded to Sellanraa and found my true delight. I was not aware of the lack of Izak because Sellanraa itself was my beloved.

9

2

In the first place, before I could begin to work at all on my dreams, I had to attend to the practical necessity of finding servants for my house. My mother said I would never find anybody to go to such a faraway place. She said she didn't see what I had bought such an enormous house for anyway, when I was not strong enough to do any work in it myself and it would need at least two maids if not three to take care of it. But I would not let anybody dampen my faith. I believed that my house was different from other houses. Secretly I knew that the whole enterprise had been born in mystic joy and therefore was blessed and loved by the gods, and that the problems most people made so much of would almost solve themselves for me. I didn't know, any more than my mother knew, why I had bought that large house. Any action whose reasons and explanations can all be contained in a few smooth practical sentences, and which arouses a unanimous chorus of approval from all the family and relations, may well be suspected of not being a living, deep-rooted action at all and scarcely worth pursuing. Because the thing I had obeyed was something that was beyond my understanding, I dimly recognized it for one of those acts which are to become an organic part of one's destiny, and I clung to it as if it were life itself. If it was to be defeated at the very beginning by my not being able to get servants, then my own destiny was also to be defeated by the same trifling cause, which I refused to believe. Besides, I knew that that house was magnetic, as love is magnetic. There would be no difficulty as to people, servants, or anyone else not wanting to come there. "Come, leave the world which errs and which reproves, and come and be my guest, for I am Love's." I wanted it to be like Chekhov's house at Yalta.

10

A Person in Love with a House

And to begin with, sure enough, I had Kathleen up my sleeve. Kathleen was an Irish girl we had found two years before in Gloucester where we had taken a cottage for the summer. The foolish, uncalculating devotion that is born in some people welled up in her for us, whom she scarcely knew. It was her nature for her to be happy and exhilarated only when she could work her hands to the bone for some lucky person whom she considered far above her in education and refinement and delicacy of health. It wasn't enough for her to work her hands to the bone for her pretentious bullying husband and two children. Six years before, when she was a self-respecting maid accustomed to working in the nicest families, she had left a frail old lady's comfortable house in order to marry the young man who began almost immediately to throw his shoes at her head. She was a devout Catholic and a submissive wife, but her marriage destroyed in her all personal happiness and filled her with a tremendous reverence and regret and nostalgia for the gentle people she had served and for their safe orderly houses. The best she could do in this bad situation was to become very subdued and reticent and apparently submissive to her husband and mother-in-law, and within herself to build up daydreams and secret ambitions for her two children. She had the wonderful and not unusual idea in such circumstances of transferring to her children the romantic devotion which she had to give to someone. But she could not give her true romantic devotion to her children until she had contrived somehow to set them up above herself. So she came to work for us that summer in order to earn money for their first music lessons, which in her eyes was the first step toward refinement and superiority.

She was happier with us than she had ever been since she got married, she told us later. It was the first time her husband had let her go out to work. He thought of noth-

11

ing but his own comfort, she said, and was afraid he would be neglected. But she had persuaded her mother-in-law to take care of him and the children for a few weeks, and so she had got back a little of her long-lost freedom and independence. From seeming at first reserved and sad, she became almost too eager and devoted. We had brought books with us to the cottage, and we sometimes talked about them, which, as she glanced respectfully at them and overheard our talk, gave her the joyous surmise that we had had wonderful educations. My mother and I were not very strong and seemed used to being waited on, which meant that we were superior and fragile and refined. These things constituted her highest ideal of what employers should be. Her romantic fancy did the rest.

According to her fancy we were used to living in the greatest elegance, and therefore the very best she could produce every day would not be too much to keep us satisfied. She seemed to take a solemn delight and pride in assuming that we would expect at least four courses for dinner every night, served punctiliously. Puff paste, cream of mushroom soup, oyster bisque—these were everyday occurrences, and she cooked and served single-handed. Before she went home in the evening she ran upstairs to turn down our beds and fill the carafes on our bedside tables and lay out our nightgowns and slippers. She even looked everywhere the first day for the small decanter of old rum which she took for granted we owned and would expect her to bring in with our tea. It was a shaky little seaside cottage made out of an abandoned boat-house. There was damp straw matting on the floors, and no plaster or paint on the rough board walls and slanting ceilings; but Kathleen made our life there something to dream about long afterward. She treated us as if we were royalty in exile.

12

A Person in Love with a House

I felt that she was a sort of miracle, as any person is a miracle who for some unknown reason yearns to achieve perfection, only to lay it at the feet of indifferent strangers. And a human miracle of this kind is like a delicate machine—it needs somebody near at hand who understands such things, to watch over it and see that it is correctly taken care of, or else it will surely come to grief. I was the one, as a fellow artist, I thought, who understood what Kathleen was and how she should be treated. I insisted that we must seize hold of her lovely fancy of the kind of supine, pampered ladies she thought we were and live up to it with every atom of our strength and imagination. We must let her remain convinced that if she did not turn down our beds we would be much too refined and helpless to do it ourselves; that we would be fatally insulted if she ever dreamed of giving us less than a four-course dinner with fingerbowls; that we would almost faint if she put any but the correct doily on the tea tray. There was no other way for us to be worthy of such an artist, I said.

But when it came to playing this part my mother and sister succumbed to great apathy. They were definitely opposed to being grand if it meant being any different from their natural selves. They even had a terrible tendency to destroy the miracle by laughing. Because Kathleen's achievements were so astonishing and so elegant, they sometimes struck my mother and sister as being funny, and so they received them with a ridicule that was subtly and fatally destructive. Or if they happened to like them, they hailed them with childish whoops of excitement—not calculated to preserve Kathleen's idea of solemnly elegant ladies, and all too likely to bewilder and confuse a single-minded artist.

"But what if we don't *want* all those elaborate frills?" my mother pleaded, almost hysterically laughing at me

13

for my tyranny when I tried to make her behave better. "And it is *silly* to let her turn down my bed at night when I much prefer the way I do it myself!"

"But she can do it any way you want her to if you will only explain it to her," I said, my soul tormented and groaning. "The way you treat her, making jokes about everything, you just bewilder her; and pretty soon something marvelous will be all ruined. *Please* explain it to her, and let her do it for you!"

"No, I don't *want* to explain it!" she said willfully. "Nobody can do it *exactly* the way I do it myself. I don't like to have anyone *touch* my bed!"

So I myself had to work all alone very hard at being grand to make up for my mother's and sister's lack of cooperation. I was fragile and helpless and refined all that summer for Kathleen's sake, and Kathleen repaid me with her foolish, ignorant love. We were partners for art's sake, and it united us.

Then I discovered that, according to her fancy, the elegant lady who graciously accepted her devotion would in return take a sort of benevolent feudal protecting interest in her and her children. With many apologies and hesitations and a becoming humility, she began to confide in me about her own life and her children and to ask my advice. I know she expected me to commend her when she told me how hard she tried to protect her children from the vulgar talk and ignorance of their father and grandmother. She told me with a kind of humble smugness that she never let her children play with other children because the others in her neighborhood were all so common. She asked my advice about the proper age to send them to dancing school. She could not wait to begin to plaster on the refinement. She told me how she gave them, a boy and girl, their baths back to back in one bathtub because she could not afford the time to give them

14

their baths separately, and of how well they obeyed her rule that they must never turn around and look at each other. She said proudly that she could go out of the room and be perfectly sure that they would not peek. When she told me this, I know that she expected me to praise her for upholding standards which she implied were my own.

But that was heavy work even for me. I began to feel an inexplicable distaste for her children as I began to be drawn deeper and deeper into the role of Kathleen's fancy of a benevolent patroness, and I would change the subject hastily and selfishly to rhubarb tarts. But nothing daunted Kathleen. Nothing could change her idea of me. And if I could not feel the warmth toward her children that she thought I did, she never noticed or suspected it. And it certainly did not prevent her from showering her own warmth and adoration on a child of my flesh and blood. When my little eighteen-months-old niece Ranie came to stay with us, Kathleen's devotion instantly reached out to embrace the coming generation in our family as well as our own. In the afternoon when her other work was done, she became the perfect nursemaid, sitting out on the sea-wall with little Ranie while the rest of us were sleeping. When little Ranie took her first step, clinging to Kathleen's rough hand, Kathleen's delight and pride made it a historic moment which seemed to weld Kathleen into our family permanently.

Yet when September came we had no plans for the future, and we parted from Kathleen with only the most apathetic sort of promise to come back the next summer. So that great gift of generosity and ardor was thrown back on her when we were through with it as if it had been nothing of great particular value. And, being inconstant and volatile, as people must be who do not own a house, we did not take the cottage the following summer, and more than a year had passed when I wrote and

15

told her about my house in Maine. She wrote back with characteristic ardor. She asked me to let her come and work for me and bring her children. She said she would work for almost nothing to make up for my letting her bring the children, and the farther away it was the better. It could not be too far away from her husband and mother-in-law. We arranged a rendezvous and the bargain was sealed. Each of us was amazed by the piece of luck that had fallen to her. It was the very stuff that Kathleen's dreams were made of. And mine, too.

We had wonderful conferences on the subject of kitchen utensils and uniforms and dotted muslin caps and aprons. Kathleen made out a long list of the things we *must* have. She was an ardent and romantic list-maker. I remember the pastry brush, the egg slicer, the special tins for baking very tiny cakes and muffins, and the three sizes of white enamel pitchers. We bought seeds for the salad garden she was going to have beside the kitchen door. I even dreamed of our making cheese and butter and wine. We would copy the life of the old country estates in Sweden or in Imperial Russia. I would mark every piece of linen with a little cross-stitch symbol, the device of Sellanraa. A cricket would be our mark. I spent that winter in a characterless hotel apartment, but I scarcely saw its walls or knew where I was because my heart and imagination were at Sellanraa, building a rich new life.

When at last the spring came, Kathleen and I met at the Salem railroad station one night in early April to take the night train to Bangor. There was not much style about us that evening. Kathleen and her children looked like immigrants, Kathleen carrying cardboard suitcases and lumpy packages wrapped in newspaper. The children were done up in hideous sweaters and mufflers and unbecoming woolen caps out of which peered their sour

16

little complaining faces, which it happened that I had
never seen before.

3

The next morning we were met at the Bangor station
by Joseph Dennett, of Dennett's Wharf, Sea Street, Castine (Autos and Boats for Hire, Sail Loft, and Yachts
Watered). He seized our luggage with his beaming, reassuring smile and packed us into one of his large, rumbling, comfortable limousines. Since the yachts and
pleasure boats had begun to disappear from the harbors
of Penobscot Bay, the Dennetts had shifted the emphasis
of their business from sea to land, and on almost any fine
summer afternoon their large dowagers' cars were to be
seen along the road to Bar Harbor or Blue Hill, carrying
small parties of those ladies who owned (and had owned
for years) cottages at Dice's Head—middle-aged and
elderly Philadelphia or Hartford ladies who always wore
long white serge coats and rather jaunty white felt hats
with veils. They carried large summer pocketbooks of
white or pale pastel linen, and their silvery hair was done
in impeccable marcelled waves.

Their expeditions were not purely frivolous and pleas-
ure-seeking. There was usually an important errand that
had to be done—there was a very special (and very expensive) knitting wool that had to be bought at a certain
shop in Bar Harbor, and afterward they would go to tea
at Jordan Pond; or there was the weekly appointment for
the scalp treatment by the French hairdresser. So they
would go, sitting up very straight, with all the windows
shut and little silk curtains drawn if it was a very sunny
afternoon, while the stately, rumbling car carried them up
and down the fabulous wild mauve-colored hills and
round the edges of harbors fabulously blue.

17

Joseph Dennett was the man who could be trusted to take such fragile, delicate, and important ladies anywhere at any time, and avoid all the jouncy places in the road, and wait reliably outside the hairdresser's or the teahouse, no matter how long. He was a real man; he was not like those solemn, false chauffeurs whose masks hide all sorts of mean and mocking thoughts about their helpless, inept little employers as they help them in and out and take their trembly orders. Joe Dennett was not that kind. He joked and laughed with his ladies, he even laughed *at* them and made jokes about them to their faces, while his round blue eyes beamed on them mischievously. Even while he laughed at them he was tenderly careful of them, and the most brittle and austere of them was always ready for a joke with him.

I had become one of his most dependent customers during my two summers at the boardinghouse, and because when I came I happened to be on terms of intimate friendship with one of the earliest established families in the summer colony, he treated me almost as if I too belonged to the highly respected class of those who owned their own cottages, instead of being merely a fluttering, transient, negligible boarder. Also, I was a fragile one during those summers; and, just like the breakable old ladies, I had to call up the wharf and get Joe whenever I wanted to go anywhere; and I had to be handed in and out like them; and, moreover, I was distinguished by an infirmity that beat any of the old ladies'. On account of a temporarily disabled heart, I had to be carried up the steps of the movie theater, and Joe was the one who carried me. The white serge coats went to the movies also, and scandalized lorgnettes were raised among them when I went laughing up the steps at a horizontal angle in Joe's arms and then was set upright and disheveled beside the ticket window. When I bought my house he was one of

18

the first to congratulate me, and I knew that if ever I got into any difficulties in my newly adopted town there was one person who would help me out. So, of course, it was Joe who was waiting at the station platform on that wonderfully early cold April morning to take me and my retinue over the last forty miles of our momentous journey.

Those miles between Bangor and Castine are magic miles. The car soars up and down the high hills that tower above the slow-moving broad Penobscot—the road soars along beside the river like a sea gull, going eastward, going out into the Bay, headed straight for that tip of rock and fir trees where the bell buoy of Dice's Head swings in the waves and clangs mournfully and romantically. It was on that ride, on my first return to Sellanraa, that I first began to see this northern maritime land, so cold and dark and blue and luminous. I saw a land of curves infinitely varied and repeated—curves upon curves —the great sweeping curves of the hills and valleys, the curved shapes of the round wooded islands, the solid roundness of boulders and rocks, the circling coves and crescent harbors. The shapes of hills and bays and inlets endlessly unfolding as we flew along gave me a continuous shock of surprise and wonder and delight; they lifted me up to ecstasy, they sang to me. It was not only the shape of the land itself that stirred me so. It was also the houses scattered along the road at intervals against the magnificent sweep and contour of hills and inlets and meadows sloping to the river and the weirs. It was those tender little painted wooden houses grown into the earth —chalk-white ones, yellow ones, chocolate ones, red ones. It was the small gray weather-beaten sheds and henhouses and barns and stone walls. It was also the silver tin cans in windows, with red geraniums growing in them; it was the tropical shells on doorsteps, the small raked flower

19

beds, wells and well-sweeps, the solitary cats pausing in open barn doors. Each separate object in that wonderfully lucent, ample air seemed to exist in its own clear-cut intensity—alive, separate, important, yet at the same time delicately, poignantly, unutterably humble. Each four-square, deep-rooted little house, each red chimney, each soaring elm existed in depth and solidity and mystic joy.

Rolling up and over the great curving hilltops and speeding now past plowed fields and now past beaches that shone blue-black with mussel shells like wet iridescent silk, our car seemed to be the only thing that was moving in that world. The figures of men working, here and there a woman standing in a doorway, two or three children beside the road—all were motionless, faces turned toward us as we passed. Each person, like each inanimate thing, seemed to exist in the inviolable serenity of his own completeness and satisfaction. A person cannot move so slowly or stand so still in a vast and peaceful landscape, I thought, unless he himself is tranquil and satisfied through and through. They turned toward us faces singularly clean of irritation, or of glum introspection, or of malice and discontentment, or of the look of chronic unconscious sadness which is the most typical of all the marks of its poisons with which the city distorts the faces of its inhabitants. They looked as if they knew something I didn't know and would like to know; as if they were acquainted with a fundamental richness of life that was altogether pleasing and satisfying. They looked as if they would not exchange their way of living for any other. They had the air of leisure and completeness which only the fortunate few in cities can afford to wear. They turned and smiled at us, and waved a hand.

At last we came to the beginning of Ten Mile Square, then Miles Gardner's Corner and the little gray house with moss on its roof that used to stand there, then down past

Warren Hooper's beautiful old mansion, and across the British Canal, we soared up the last hill, the long, dark, fir-topped flank which is the gate to Castine. As we rolled over the top of it beside the faded red windmill, the town, the harbor, and the islands lay suddenly before us. And with a lover's quick, jealous eyes, my house was the only thing I saw. It stood just below us beside its big horse-chestnut tree, against the blue harbor. This was my first returning. This moment could never be repeated. I felt the same shyness and agitation and exquisite delight that two people feel when they meet each other again for the first time after they have become lovers.

4

In the spring when Kathleen and I arrived the house was in such disorder we could barely push our way through the rooms, for in the autumn past my dreams for my house and the men's work had been stopped abruptly by winter weather before the painting and papering were finished. There were stepladders and pails and rolls of wallpaper standing in the rooms, all mixed up with my mother's antique furniture and barrels of china and boxes upon boxes of books.

But my house! There it was, like a boat at anchor in the spring sunshine. Those calm, kind rooms made it seem a good deed that I had done in bringing all our family possessions to rest in such a place. The sunny terrace reassured me, and the two old apple trees, and the harbor's mesmerizing blue. All would be well. Such rich material was in my hands and such exulting creative desire in my heart that I was happier than I had ever been in all my life before.

Kathleen and I fell to work, preparing the house for its great opening summer. She unpacked dishes and kitchen

things and washed them and arranged them on cupboard
shelves. She scrubbed floors, washed windows, made beds.
The painter came, the saturnine, black-browed Mr. Per-
kins; and in the quiet house we could hear the reassuring
monotonous slap of his brushes.

We all worked in different parts of the house. I could
hear Kathleen when I wanted to, but I could forget her
too and be essentially alone if, as often happened when
I was kneeling over an open trunk or a box of books, my
hands stumbled upon an old letter or some little lost treasure I had forgotten the very existence of, and the dead
past came to life and unfolded like some great flower and
enveloped me. Since I had grown up and ruthlessly cast
off my childhood, I had been notoriously unsentimental
about the past and ruthless about personal possessions
and inanimate objects of any kind. Now these family
mementos lived for me for the first time, and what they
told me sometimes made my throat ache with the *lachrymae rerum.* I found myself handling them with a tenderness and awe that was most strange and unfamiliar to me.
During the interval of five years since I had last seen our
things, something must have matured within me.

One day I found in my hands the manuscript of a poem
in my father's handwriting. He had died when I was only
fifteen. We had been in love with each other ever since
I could remember, but he had died while our minds were
still separated by my immaturity. He had gone before
I was capable of recognizing him. Now, while I knelt on
the floor in my new house in that April stillness twenty
years after, he came so close to me and with such a swift
poignant cry that I found the tears streaming down my
face. The poem must have been written just after he had
been told that he was mortally ill, and the poem said he
could not bear to die. In that moment I knew him; we had
reached each other at last—not as a little girl and her

23

father, but as a man and woman who love each other, looking into each other's eyes. That moment made my house truly my own. The room where it had happened could never be strange to me any more. It must belong to me and to my life ever after.

5

There were two square living rooms, one on each side of the wide hall. In the one on the left I put my father's tall bookcases. I spent hours in my arrangement of the books. As an aunt, planning an aunt's house, the thing I took special delight in was making the lowest shelves into a nieces' and nephews' library. There I ranged all that were left from our own childhood. Until then our children's books had been tumbled about and scattered or discarded and ignored as if they were not worth bothering about any more. Now I took each one in my hands and dusted it with love and remorse and gave it a salute of honor and placed it in its own indisputable place in the Nieces' and Nephews' Library of Sellanraa, there to stay as long as Aunthood was in Flower. Oh, my *Child's Garden of Verse*, illustrated by Robinson, its flyleaf all lovingly scribbled up, and *Grimm's Tales* illustrated by Walter Crane. Walter Crane's *Baby's Opera* and *Aesop's Fables*, and his book of English ballads with the tunes done with so much of his favorite Pompeian red and blue. Boutet de Monvel's *Jeanne d'Arc* and, greatest favorite for its marvelous illustrations, *La Civilité Puerile et Honnête par l'Oncle Eugène*. A dear *Alice in Wonderland*, green covers faded and worn in a very businesslike way and back rather loose, and darling Mrs. Molesworth almost equally faded and threadbare, Carrot's *The Cuckoo Clock* and *Sweet Content*. And Mrs. Ewing—*Jackanapes* and *Daddy Darwin's Dovecot; Little Women,* back and covers

24

shattered almost beyond belief by my own maudlin and
excessive love. And not far away, near enough so the
children's hands might touch it by chance, I put immortal *Cranford,* illustrated by Hugh Thomson. Also
bordering the Nieces' and Nephews' Library, half belonging to it and half to the grownups, I placed four tall green
volumes which my parents had bought for our summer
home in Vermont long ago—*The Insect Book, The Mushroom Book, Nature's Garden,* and *The Butterfly Book;* also
other smaller handbooks of birds and trees and flowers.
These four tall green books had magnificent colored plates
in them which I hoped to see my perspiring little nieces
and nephews gazing on, solemnly and learnedly identify-
ing specimens they would have found in the domain of
Sellanraa. I wanted to add much more to this department
of my auntish library. I wanted to buy all of Fabre, and
Maeterlinck's *Life of the Bee* and *Life of the Ant;* I wanted
books about shells and sea creatures, books about the
heavens and about the earth, about weather and winds
and tides. I wanted also to buy a handsome great globe
of the world, and a microscope and a barometer.

I put the piano in the same room with the bookcases. It
was a ninetyish upright piano, ornamented with curlicues
and fretwork. No interior decorator would have permitted
it to stay in the house. But I could not see it with a
critical eye; none of us ever could. We could no more
have thrown it out of the house on account of its looks
than we could have thrown out a member of the family.

None of us knew how to play it except my mother, but
my sister could sing to my mother's accompaniment. She
never sang except for my mother and me, and it was a very
private, unpretentious kind of singing. She had not sung
at all for us since she got married and left us, and since
our piano and all her songs had been buried in the warehouse. And I wanted this room at Sellanraa to re-create

25

that which had been lost—the sight of my mother sitting forward a little fussily on account of her bifocal lenses, and pretending that she was clumsy and rheumatic and old and could not really play properly any more, while her hands moved with surprising accuracy over the keys. I wanted to see my sister standing beside her, the way she always used to stand when she sang, easy and young and uncritical, resting one hand on the back of my mother's chair.

When my mother was ready—pretending to have a struggle with the opening bars—my sister would begin to sing, and a shiver went over me. Her voice sounded as if she were walking barefoot alone on the side of a mountain in the early morning, and singing the way peasant girls are supposed to sing, artlessly and freshly, because they are young and it is morning. Like a peasant girl's, her singing was effortless, and it expressed her own natural feelings. She never bothered to talk very much to anybody about anything, and especially she never seemed to be troubled by the desire that compels most people to confide in someone about their emotions. Everything that she wanted to tell about her feelings she seemed to tell when she sang. Her repertory was not very large because I always wanted her to sing the same songs over and over, and she was always willing to humor me. They were the ones that she liked best too. I always wanted her to sing *"Maman, dites à moi ce qu'on sent quand on aime,"* and "I sowed the seeds of Love, in April, May and merry June," and "Greensleeves was all my joy, and who but Lady Greensleeves," and "The Bailiff's Daughter of Islington," and "O Mistress Mine."

Now I had a new song that I wanted her to sing. I had heard it just before I came to Sellanraa, and I liked it so much that I bought the collection it came in to bring with me. While I was arranging the Nieces' and Nephews'

Music Library, I used to stop quite often and take out my new book and play my new song with one finger until I had learned it and learned all the words. I did not know exactly why it seemed to me such an amusing, playfully romantic song, but I liked it very much. I could hear it over and over and never grow tired of it. So it became for me the special song that belonged always to Sellanraa. It was called "The Song of Transformations."

Among my own possessions which came along with the other household goods there was a cheap little golden-oak victrola, the kind that Sadie Thompson carried on her travels, the kind that is most disreputable-looking, companionable, and human. I had two records sung by Edmond Clement which plaited themselves into the poignant stillness of that first spring. During those first days I used to feel an almost unbearable sense of inner excitement which those romantic songs, *"Le Roi d'Ys"* and *"Le Rêve"* from *Manon,* used to release and let pour through me. I felt a dark, exultant poem of experience coming up all around me, being woven magically round me and possessing me. And something stronger than myself seemed to be rejoicing because of some sort of knowledge that was to dawn on me but was still hidden.

There was a mirror hanging over the front hall table. I used to stop and look at myself as I passed by with this exhilaration on me, feeling so strange and wonderful and alone and new to myself in my strange house in this new land. I stared into the mirror, and the reflection I saw looked like a portrait of an artist by himself. I did not see a woman. It looked more like a very intelligent gifted young boy. Nor did I see my deformity. It was not there; it had been canceled, wiped out, forgotten. There was an exultation in me so powerful that it canceled everything personal and limiting. What I saw in my reflection was the debonair, unsmiling look that you always see on the face of the artist when he is looking at himself and painting. It is an intimate, naked scrutiny, yet impersonal. And behind that look something always burns and glows and triumphs; it is the artist's joy at work and in its prime— that fierce joy, that delicately calm and still and humble joy, that unassailable joy. My reflection made this kind of a portrait because as I looked and saw what I was, that matchless joy came flooding through me, promising me everything, promising to unfold as long as my life lasted, if I would be faithful to it. I felt in myself a ferment of growth and transformation as great and revolutionary and inevitable as that which makes a green stalk unsheathe itself and rise up into the air. I was glad I was not expected to function as a woman. I was humbly grateful that I could be impersonal and unhampered and dedicated wholly to that life-giving, fruitful joy.

In my awareness in front of the mirror it was only the *Anima*, quite mature and wise, who looked forth, not yet the *Persona*. The poor stupid *Persona* who was still asleep, unconsciously waiting to be released from the spell that bound her. Yet I had an insatiable thirst for those two songs of human love, and I kept playing them over and over in the stillness and solitude.

6

It was wonderful to be there in the early spring alone during the long April stillness, busy like a child who is lost in a deep, happy absorption. Planting certain books here, drawing materials there, games there, blankets and linen in that cupboard, tea things on this shelf, this chair here beside this table, I felt as if I were laying out a design for a garden, planting seeds in a certain pattern out of which I hoped that the customs and habits, the manifold occupations and amusements, of Sellanraa would grow.

My partner, Kathleen, was also inventing and establishing customs. She had laid down boundary lines for her children. We agreed that after the family and guests began to arrive Marian and Cecil were to be kept out of sight except when they were invited to appear. This rule was necessary to Kathleen's sense of propriety; and it was also, I had to admit, necessary to mine. But that rule made me feel guilty. I felt as if I had betrayed the whole race of children by not allowing the children of my cook the same freedom as my nieces and nephews. But Kathleen seemed to be wonderfully immune to the maternal vanity which usually makes this kind of a domestic arrangement full of tension. At first, when we were still living informally among barrels, the rule was not enforced. Marian had been put into the village school, but Cecil was too young to go, and all day long I could hear Kathleen stop her work to go to a doorway and shriek at him and jerk him into the house and scold him for playing in the brook or getting into the Douglas's manure. I noticed that whatever happened his expression never changed. His expression, I soon observed to my discomfiture, was one of fixed pugnacity and ruthlessness. He had hard, staring, cruel blue eyes. He never whimpered or cried, he never laughed. In every sort of mood he only stared. He stared in obstinacy, in hatred, and in inquisitiveness.

Sometimes he wandered all over the house when Kathleen's back was turned. I could hear his threatening, hard little shoes clopping through the still bedrooms, coming nearer and nearer to the room where I was busy and alone. The next moment from the doorway I would feel his hard stare hitting me like a rock. I soon realized that I was afraid of him—a four-year-old child standing in a doorway, staring at me. He was only a ridiculous little male snippet

29

who wore the smallest silly buttoned boots and black ribbed cotton stockings wrinkled and lumpy over his drawers, and his short trousers were usually soaking wet in the middle. He would advance into the room where I was unpacking and arranging things. If any fragile little treasure were lying in sight, he would stare and clutch simultaneously; or if there was a rug to be kicked up, he would kick it with his hard, blunt, contemptuous little foot, and if there was a pale-colored silk chair-cover to sit on he would sit on it, his wet urine-smelling seat and legs pressed tight against it.

His sister Marian was the opposite in her behavior. She made up for his lack of diffidence and shyness by an unnatural self-abasement. She was a clammy little girl. Although she was spotlessly clean, somehow she always smelled of a stale moisture. Her hands dangled heavy and moist at her sides from thin red wrists. Her body was too small and thin for her age, and yet it seemed to be heavy with some inexpressible stagnant dumbness. She would come and stand beside me in an unchildlike mood. She would smile at me, and it was a manufactured smile, painful to see. It was the smile of a person who is stupid enough to believe that his servility will please you, and not merely please you but win you over to him in spite of yourself. I never knew what to do about a smile like that. I could not smile back again without smiling falsely myself, and if I looked glumly at her, as I seemed to have to do, she only grew more cringing and artificial in her efforts to propitiate me and win me.

7

Perhaps it is not necessary to describe the features which were so inextricably associated with the haunting spirit of my Sellanraa. It really cannot interest anybody to be told what another person's beloved looks like. Yet I do feel that mine was more beautiful than most.

There was the brick path leading from the road to the door, to the beautiful door that had a fanlight over the top and fluted carving on each side. And there at the end of the brick path where the roses knocked against the sitting-room windows, the fields fell away down and there was the panorama of water and islands. It filled all the southern side of my horizon, the round soft fiery blue of the harbor, framed within a circling rim of little round dark hills. Against this, the peaked roofs of fishermen's houses along the bottom of my field, their shingles glistening fresh against the blue, and sometimes smoking in the hot sun after a foggy night. Besides the picture that Sellanraa looked upon, there was the body of Sellanraa itself —the sloping field, the young orchard, the screen of Balm of Gilead trees, the grass terrace where we had breakfast on summer mornings, the old brook bed and gaunt willows. There were the square peaceful sitting rooms, the wood fires in wide fireplaces, the many-paned windows, the square bedrooms with their fires and old mantlepieces; and there was the west wind that always began to come blowing across the links in the middle of summer afternoons and always made the hall mirror knock against the wall, and sometimes blew over a vase of flowers on the hall table. There was the woodshed and the secret stairs up to the great porch that had a high roof like a barn roof. The porch was really the upper floor of the ell that had been stripped of its partitions and ceiling and made hollow like a barn, with windows all around its walls. It faced the east, and it received the pink light of sunrise like a vast shell.

This was the body and spirit of Sellanraa, and there was another part also. It was the web of experience that was continually being woven out of the body and the spirit and was inextricable from them—the life, the enchanted life, of Sellanraa. There was each separate summer that made, when it was done, a pattern of its own, distinct and different from every other summer. There were two winters, never-to-be-forgotten. Every year there was the marvelous moment of arrival, and then the continual coming and going of the friends of Sellanraa—cars standing in the dooryard, overflowing with excited newcomers, big and little. There were the three little sisters, Ranie and Kitty and Ann. There were Harriet and Libby and Jonathan. There was Tony, young and grave, who adored Sellanraa with the poetic devotion of a boy just wakening to the beauty and torment of life. There was my brother Warren and my brother Fergus. And there was Tony's mother, who sometimes caught her breath and heaved huge sighs because she could never express what she felt about Sellanraa. She knew that there was magic there. She heard it like an undertone, like the trill of tiny insects in the grass, inaudible to some—or the faintest rustling of silk. She loved to come back to it after a solitary autumn drive over the hills, coming in by the kitchen door very quietly and with cold hands taking cold red apples out of her pockets and putting them on the kitchen table. In that sumptuously beautiful country, solitude was as thrilling as love. To us who had had enough experience to feed on, solitude at Sellanraa was a rich romantic dream. And yet at the same time it was true that people and intercourse had a charm there that was unknown in ordinary places. People who came there discovered that their hair grew more curly than usual, their jokes more sparkling, their personal attraction more irresistible, their love more surprising. Simple songs that were sung there had a terrific hauntingness that they did not have elsewhere. Conversations were crazier and more inspired than in other places and sometimes lasted all night. Breakfast went on forever.

People lay on the floor, talking and dreaming in an atmosphere that can only be described by the Japanese word *nonbili.* And there was always the divine inherent solitude of Sellanraa, waiting at the top of a secret flight of stairs, or just outside the door where the fog was blowing. There must be a million memories all told, locked away in the heads of all the people, great and small, who once, so short a time ago, were sheltered by the body and spirit of Sellanraa. As much as with any other part of it, I was in love with the magic stuff of its life that continually grew.

8

After I had been wedded to my house for eight years, I came suddenly to an impasse. Necessity can be as inexorable as death, and I sold my house. I felt as if something were dying in me, and that I had killed it. That same summer I got married—this time to a human being—and we went abroad to live. I thought I was very fortunate to be able to go away and see strange countries. I thought I could not have borne it to stay in the same land with my house after it had ceased to be mine. We expected to live abroad for a long time. I was always dreaming that after we had made our fortune we would come back to that New England azure coast and buy Sellanraa again.

We made friends in Paris. There was a Frenchman who lived in a studio near ours with his American wife. They became our friends. The husband owned a place in the country just outside Paris. It was a small pink plaster house and a strip of land on the edge of the Marne with poplar trees growing on it and an orchard and a garden. I saw that he felt the same about his place as I had felt about mine. He used to stroll up and down his garden path and stare about him in a kind of madness of adoration. Once he had made quite a long visit in America. I

34

asked him if when he was far away from France he had not found that when he felt homesick it was his own strip of land that he longed for more than for all of Paris, although he adored Paris like all good Parisians. He said yes, that was true. One day I happened to find a photograph of my house that I had not seen for a long time. Our French friend looked at it. "You mean to say that you sold this beautiful house!" he exclaimed, as if a dreadful tragedy had happened. I felt guilty and grief-stricken, and we both cried, mourning for Sellanraa.

I have met American expatriates in Paris who said they had no feeling of belonging to America. They spoke resentfully as if it were America's fault. They said there was nothing in America that could interest or satisfy them. They seemed to me like children who had been horribly wronged. I felt sure that their parents must have brought them up without letting them know the earth, some special piece of the earth that was their own. In France wine is thought of as food, so necessary to life that nobody is too poor to go without it, whereas to us it is luxury. In the same way, by a standard of values older and more knowing than ours, a plot of ground of one's own is thought of as a necessary part of life by the humblest, while with us it is not unusual for both the poor and the rich to live all their lives almost entirely divorced from the earth, knowing no surfaces except concrete and brick and metal ones. Therefore it is not strange that Americans more than most people are able to go and live in other peoples' countries without ever learning what it is to be homesick. If only there were some little acre of land that each remembered from childhood, they would not be able to go and expose themselves and the pitiful barrenness of their family life and the poverty of their emotional inheritance in such a deplorable way to home-loving foreigners. It would not have to be an acre, it could be half or a quarter of an acre if only it had belonged to their parents—and not merely belonged to them, but been tended and cherished by them, made fruitful, made orderly, made beautiful, so that the children would have acquired the same sense of making and tending and cherishing.

9

After living for three years in Paris we came home in the spring. We had not made our fortune, but we had found out that it was not there for us to make. On the train from Paris to Antwerp the April morning when we started home, I felt hungry-eyed, looking out of the train window as we sped through Normandy and saw the amazingly beautiful green earth. We had been for three years in a Paris studio, and never at all in the real country. The sight of that luxurious emerald plain with its marvelous embroidered squares and oblongs seemed to melt my heart after some long rigidity. I saw a stone farmhouse deep-rooted in the midst of the fields. A little garden with delicate stitching of fresh green against the rich brown furrows was enclosed by a lilac hedge. The orchard at one side was all in flower. Two or three old willows separated house and granary, garden and orchard from the wide fields. The spring morning sun slanted into the little green enclosure. An old woman and an old man stood there as the train went by. That momentary glimpse has stayed like an image in my memory. It was a sign for me of how man can make the earth blossom, and how in doing that he is taking part in a miracle and living the most beautiful life in the world. All the way across the sterile ocean I was dreaming of green fields. If we have nothing else in America, I thought, we must have a house and a field of our own.

When we got home we hovered as near as possible to

our families whom we had not seen for so long. We were happy living in a little rented Victorian mansion in our home city while we were orientating ourselves. But I lost no time in sending for a catalogue of farms for sale which I saw advertised, and I read its items over and over until I knew them almost by heart. The farm catalogue became my prayer book which I kept beside my bed at night and picked up whenever I had a moment of leisure during the day. It charmed me so much that I read aloud from it to my visitors, thinking that they also would be charmed. I read them about the trout brooks and the rich black loamy tillage; the spring-watered pastures, and the apples, plums, and cultivated berries; about the cool cellars, sheds for tools and chickens, mail and groceries delivered, the "good neighbors, near enough." The catalogue with its colored cover design of two sweetly sentimental horses' heads looking out of a window was intended for practical people who were looking for a real investment, where honest work would bring in a living. But there was something else that got into the descriptions, a naïve enticement entirely unlike the snobbish enticements of other realtors, and to me it was irresistible. They would mention a trout brook or a river bordering the farm, or Christian doors with old-time latches as an afterthought after telling the really important things first, such as "good barn 36 x 51, 8 ties, hay fork, 2 cows, heifer, farm tools thrown in."

During May and June I read these luscious things over and over, savoring each item—the wood lots, the blackberries, the springs—and my husband and I decided to use the catalogue as our guide and sometime during the summer take a little tour through the neighboring New England states and visit at leisure the towns where our favorite numbers were to be found. It encouraged us to see for how little money we could buy any of the most alluring little properties, even with trout streams.

In July a heat wave came. Everything went out of my head except a craving for the north. In my mind's eye I saw my cool azure coast, the bay, the islands, the roofs of the fishermen's houses. In great haste we answered an advertisement in the paper of a farmhouse on that coast to rent for the summer at a price small enough to fit our purse. "Stay as long as you wish," the advertisement said. "Plenty of dry wood at the back door." It was about eighteen miles away from Sellanraa in a town I had often driven through, other summers, other years.

We left the city of Salem at seven in the morning and drove north. In midafternoon we reached the Hancock Bridge which connects the high wooded banks of the great Penobscot River at Bucksport. Once across that bridge I was in my own country, the country of Sellanraa. I had a strange guilty feeling when we reached a certain familiar corner and did not take the so-familiar road which, as we flew along it faster and faster, had always meant the poignant, swiftly mounting excitement of return after absence, one's imagination leaping ahead in an ecstatic rush to fling open those doors and lean out of those windows, and gaze again in a sudden stillness of recognition at the particular view which was not exactly like any other view in the world. Instead, we did not take that glamorous and happy road to Castine, but took one which skirted carefully outside my town and joined another one beyond, which took us up and down what we had always called the roller-coaster hills, and along high ridges and deep into a little forest, and at last out into the town where we were to find our rented farmhouse which we had never seen.

It was while we were making that detour that I began to discover that in terribleness and fatality one's love for a house can be like one's love for a person—like romantic love. I felt then, for Sellanraa and for the road to Sellan-

38

raa, that rigid sort of silent, speechless pain that is so well known to anybody who has ever suffered in a love affair. It is a sickness not only of the heart but of the whole body. When we took that wrong road I felt as if, on account of some nightmarish misunderstanding, I were avoiding the person who had meant the most to me in the world. Sellanraa had given me the most poignant experience of my life, and part of me was and would be forever there, haunting and clinging to the place like a poor crazy ghost whose infatuation will not let her lie still where she belongs, out of sight and forgotten.

After the first waves of this emotion hit me and almost swamped me, I fought them off. I ordered myself smartly to sit up straight and join my husband in looking for our rented farmhouse as we drove along the route we had been told to follow. Very soon it appeared ahead of us at the bottom of a gently sloping hill on the right-hand side of the road, while on the left hand lay fields along the shore of the bay—fields and blue water and Mount Desert Island looming grandly out of the blue reach.

10

Our farmhouse was not a very old one—it belonged to the eighties or nineties—and it had the sharply pointed roof and the little gimcrackiness over the front door and the neat little piazza with turned posts which give a house an air of tasteless perkiness and a barren sort of smugness. It is a type which seems to express, more than it expresses anything else, the feeling that it is just as good as its neighbors no matter how grand they may be. It represents an attitude which was apparently very prevalent in rural America at one time. Upon the porch eaves was nailed a neat, well-printed little sign that said Mountain View.

The present owner's wife was standing in the front yard waiting for us. Cheerful and talkative, she unlocked the door and ushered us in. I took a furtive glance into the parlor. I saw the patent rocking chair, the parlor organ, the stuffed armchairs, the stuffed rocking chairs, stuffed side chairs, the huge gimcrack gold-framed mirror, and the enlarged framed photographs of relations hung so high up on the walls they nearly touched the ceiling, the stiff coarse white lace curtains and dark-green shades, the thin woolen carpet in a yellow floral design. The formula of the rural New England parlor is very well known, and most people just laugh. But when one is in a particularly sensitive mood it can make one's heart sink horribly. It made me feel desolately sad and waiflike to look at it that day.

The house grew much better as we went into the back part of it where pretentiousness disappeared. The kitchen, of course, where the family had really lived, had a worn human coziness, and the woodshed was a sweet place, packed almost to the roof with beautiful short lengths of firewood. We stepped out from the soft chips and sawdust into the rich blue-green grass behind the house. The house ended at the woodshed, and across a little space of thick grass stood the weathered barn. Our landlord's wife pointed out a little door in the back corner of the barn which she told us was the privy. Beyond the privy lay a spear-shaped field which seemed to thrust back the en-croaching shadows of a deep wild wood that came up all around the edges of the field.

Before our landlord's wife left us, my husband asked if he might move some of the furniture, rearrange it a little according to our taste. She gave her permission laughingly. It meant nothing to her. The old people were dead, her husband's folks whose house it had been, and she didn't care what we did with the furniture, she said.

40

A Person in Love with a House

So during the next twenty-four hours I was aware of a
colossal heaving and gasping and pushing and lifting,
and now and then a most portentous and fatal-sounding
bump and a yell telling me it was all right. These sounds
were accompanied with a rich mixture of sweat and
curses, and they ended eventually with the final banishment of most of the furniture into the attic. We retained
only the parlor organ and the patent rocking chair, because the organ was a source of entertainment and the
chair was amusing in its awfulness besides being comfortable. We prepared to live in austerely empty rooms,
with only a few wooden chairs and tables, a bed and a
dressing table and a chest of drawers.

In spite of my husband's touchingly buoyant and brave
work during our first week at Mountain View, in his attempt to make the place more human, I was haunted by
an exile's thoughts. Every time I went out of the woodshed
door and walked on that soft mown grass I smelled the
sweet Maine smell, which really is not like any other
smell. To me it was the smell of Sellanraa. There was a
little bronze-colored pond next to the house surrounded
by tall grasses and elder bushes. At dusk I heard a bull-
frog twang his G-string out there in the pond, and I saw
fireflies dancing all over the back field. I suppose everybody's memory is like a box of old discarded keys. If you
looked through the boxful you wouldn't know what locks
half of them ever belonged to. But when you least expect
it, and by some wayward chance, every once in a great
while you find one of those old keys in your hand, and
before you know it and against your will it has unlocked
a door that you had closed and forgotten long ago. I
didn't know until those hushed Maine evenings came that
the voice of a frog and a silent moving constellation of
fireflies were keys that unlocked for me the most secret
and magic doors of my lost Sellanraa, and that they could

hurt me so. They could raise around me the phantom walls of my house, and the feeling of the unutterable spell it had woven upon my life. They could make me suffer anew from a loss that seemed unbearable.

The alien perky little farmhouse, the woodland, field, and pond filled me with a wild dismay because they were like and yet so pitifully unlike the matchless thing that their frog and their fireflies conjured up for me. It was like having some foolish person chatter to you about your lost beloved and by chance hit upon certain of your most intimate and precious recollections of him which you could not have brought yourself to speak of aloud.

So then I knew for sure that I was a person desperately and eternally in love, and that it was incurable. It was one of those things that last through a whole lifetime and about which there is no choice but to be faithful. I felt as if I should strike out madly and hurt anyone who offered to console me with any compromise. To hell with the trout brooks and the dark richly loamy tillage of unknown, unloved places! To hell with Mountain View! To hell with all the houses in the world as far as I was concerned—except one.

11

When I sold Sellanraa, I did not sell it to strange people, but to friends who had known and liked it through coming there as my guests. Therefore I knew that an inevitable result of our return to America would be an invitation to go there, and I thought of it with dread. Drawn irresistibly back to the haunting country of Sellanraa, we had come nevertheless very clandestinely and furtively, and we hoped that for a little while, at least, nobody would hear of our coming. But we had been there less than a week when the new mistress of Sellanraa drove into the dooryard of Mountain View.

A *Person in Love with a House*

I felt as if I were a deposed princess who had gone into seclusion and self-imposed exile in a neighboring kingdom, and that now, my whereabouts having been discovered, I was receiving a gracious surprise visit from the reigning princess.

We greeted each other with the ardent affection of polite princesses. There had always been a feeling of kindliness and friendship between us which had happily not been impaired by the fact that she now possessed my palace and lands. She had not stolen them from me—far from it. My treasury had become so depleted that I had been forced to find a successor in order that I might abdicate honorably and pay my debts, and I had been very thankful indeed that it was a friend rather than a stranger who had come to the rescue and was now occupying the place I loved. Therefore when she graciously condescended to seek me out in my seclusion and to plead with me to go back with her and make a little visit, we were precisely in the mood of the two princesses—I shrinking from and resisting her invitation with the natural sensitiveness of fallen royalty and with a stubborn, proud grief which I had not wished her or anyone else to see; while she, seeing and fully understanding the real pain behind my diffidence, pretended not to see it and skimmed and played over the surface of it with a lighthearted and gentle cajolery, like a very adroit fisherman trying to catch a despondent fish who is sulking on the bottom of a deep pool. Her manner and her method of dealing with me in this difficult moment touched me and charmed me so much that I soon rose to the surface and said I would go.

My own former chief lady-in-waiting, now hers, had accompanied her on this excursion to Mountain View, and we had fallen into each other's arms with tears of joy. My husband and I showed them our humble peasant's dwelling, our parlor organ and patent rocking chair. They

43

played the organ and rocked in the rocker with exclamations of delight, and somehow, somewhere, I began to feel assuaged and comforted and not so much like an exile. So I said good-by to my husband, who promised to come and fetch me the next day; and, wedged in between the bantering yet benevolent princess and the lady-in-waiting on the front seat of the royal roadster, I went submissively over the hills with no detours and no evasions straight and unswervingly into the heart of the town which held Sellanraa. But as we drew very near I could not conceal the sad panic of my heart and the quakings of my poor spirit, and I begged them not to make me see the house that day, but to let me spend the night at the lady-in-waiting's cottage on another street. It seemed as if it were enough merely to sleep in that very haunted and long-dreamed-of town again.

It is not an easy experience for two people to be forced by external circumstances to break away from each other after being passionate lovers. And it is not easy for them to meet again after a period of years when their love has not changed or diminished an atom and the circumstances are still such that there is no hope of their being reunited. The meeting is certainly not a happy one, but simply a piece of torture. All I remember of the next day and our short afternoon visit at Sellanraa is that it is not an exaggeration to say that it was like that kind of a meeting. All the morning as the minutes passed, bringing it nearer and nearer, I shrank from it almost as if it had been the scaffold I was going to. Just before we went I was fortified with a burning stirrup cup, and as soon as we arrived our compassionate host and hostess produced a tray of very strong cocktails, so that a soft cloudy curtain was drawn across an experience which in its true nature would have been nearly unbearable. But it was only a thin transparent curtain and I had to be incessantly on my guard in order

44

to look politely about me without *really* seeing, and to keep my normal perceptions forcibly smothered in order to sit there without *really* feeling the presence of Sellanraa around me.

In the early evening my husband and I said good-by and drove home over the roller-coaster hills, home to Mountain View. The road that goes over those hills is like a huge swing. First you fly up in a great thrilling toss, and then you fly down, up and down, up and down, while your headlights climbing up ahead or pouring down again are the only lights to be seen in those dark hills and valleys except the small squares of yellow lamplight that shine out here and there from the farmhouses.

The night ride over the roller-coasters is best of all when a thick fog is blowing in and you can see only the smothering white veils that stream across your headlights, veil upon veil, and condense on the glass and keep the windshield wiper clicking. You cannot see the hills and valleys then; you only feel them, like a marvelous lullaby, as the huge swing wrapped in fog tosses you up and down, up and down, while your motor purrs and thunders alternately.

That night the hills and a dense blowing fog and the smell of Maine lulled me with a wonderful sweetness. A burden had been lifted and a dread had gone out of me. I realized for the first time how, ever since the day I had left my Sellanraa, knowing that I could never come back to the same Sellanraa again, I had felt, like a weight half-hidden in the back of my mind, the dread of the inevitable day when I should have to come back and let my eyes look there and my hands touch again the thing that could no longer be a living part of me. I had feared and dreaded that day more than I could possibly tell anybody, and more as each year had passed. Now it had actually come and was over. I had gone through it in an armor of numbness, but I had gone through, and it was over. I felt as if now, after long weariness and exile, my poor infatuated ghost could lie still.

The next morning I began to feel very happy at Mountain View. Wonderfully, it did not dismay me nor torment me any more. It was no longer a distorted copy of something else; it was just itself now. With the immense relief that had come to me the day before, I began to feel a kind of amused and fond contentment as I looked around that morning. I began to like the little bronze-colored pond. It seemed strange and wonderful that day to see four bronze butterflies that matched the pond, all alike, poised among the tall weeds where the old lady's flower bed had evidently been and was now all but vanished. I liked the hayfield across the road and the mowing machine that went clacketing drowsily back and forth in the hot sun drawn by a pair of brown and white oxen, against the blue bay. It was not love, as I had known love, and it never could be; but it was fondness and gratitude for an anonymous little hiding place that had some quality about it that was very touching and sweet.

12

On the afternoon of that happy day, when we drove into the town as usual to get our newspapers, they had not arrived and we had a little time on our hands. My husband suggested that we go and look at the brick house. I didn't know what house he meant—we were always noticing and peering at and discussing houses regardless of whether or not we were thinking of buying one, or could if we wanted to. After he spoke I remembered the For Sale sign that we had noticed at the entrance to a driveway that went between very tall thick cedar hedges, and I remembered that we had caught a glimpse of an old brick house within, mostly hidden by the hedges. It was on the edge of the village, near by, so we went to look at it while we were waiting for our newspapers.

We drove in between the thick dark walls of cedar and stopped the car in a small round dooryard in front of a brick house with faded turquoise shutters. The dooryard was all enclosed by the high hedges, and they embraced also the two front corners of the house, so that the front of the house was hidden from the world, while all the rest of it lay full in the sun and looking down over the harbor.

The door was standing open, and we walked in. First, a little hall with a hook in the ceiling to hang an oil lamp from, and a small narrow staircase. Then we opened a door on the right and went into an empty room where the shutters were all closed. The shutters and the hedge outside made a cool green darkness, but we could see the unspoiled woodwork of the fireplace, the deep recesses of small-paned windows. That room opened with double sliding doors into another. They were old-fashioned double parlors, each with its fireplace. The shutters were open in the back room, and oblongs of sunshine lay on the bare floor. There were four windows, deeply recessed. Two of them were on the southern side of the house with a fireplace between. A huge lilac bush grew against the first window, and the second one looked out on fields, the edge of a cove, a corner of the village. The other two windows were on the back of the house, the eastern side.

As soon as we stepped into that sunny empty room, I began to feel the strange thing which I had believed could never happen to me again. It was a sudden warmth and tumult inside me, as if a great bird were asleep inside me and had suddenly awakened and begun to lift and beat his wings in great strength and joy. This feeling came simultaneously with a feeling of portentous stillness, as if all of

47

me, except that strange inhabitant of my breast, were hushed and darkened so that I could hear and feel what his meaning might be. In that instant it was as if I could hear and feel things behind and under ordinary things. I moved around the room unable to speak. I felt weak and awe-struck. It seemed more than I could possibly deserve—to find a second love after having known a first that seemed matchless. And having found it, I wondered weakly and humbly if I had it in me to respond a second time with the ardor and the sustained devotion that such an opportunity demanded. But that is the kind of thing I never doubt very long.

It was like a house one goes into in a dream, a house already familiar and loved although one has never seen it before. It had also, with all its sense of familiarness, the romantic strangeness and surprise of a house found in a dream.

I did not have to look out of the back windows or step to the back door and look. It was a poem whose words I already knew. I did look, of course, and I saw that everything was there—the old apple trees and a sunny eastern slope that ran down to the water, and on the north side a ravine with a brook bed and gaunt willows. It was composed of the same parts and orientated according to the same diagram as Sellanraa.

And, like Sellanraa, it seemed alive. It immediately invited, even in neglect and emptiness, a richness of life that was akin to me—something deep and tranquil and fruitful. It invited a life that could be both elegant and homely, indolent and yet charged with hours of intense work, a severely and utterly secluded life at certain seasons and at others blossoming into the most wonderful celebrations and parties.

As I was standing in that southeast corner room I saw it

48

as it would look in midwinter, as I had seen the corresponding room at Sellanraa so many times—a wood fire burning, and the smell of snow, and the gorgeous winter sun of the Maine coast pouring through those windows, and the world outside and the figures in it like a Breughel winter painting—a jovial human and animal gaiety and movement against a background of Arctic purity and beauty, a world carved out of a sapphirelike intensity of cold and stillness.

While I was absorbed in this trance, my husband was evidently no less struck with the place than I. I looked at him, and I knew by the intent quick way that he opened doors, peered sharply down cellar stairs, glanced up at ceilings, and rapped walls to discover hidden brick ovens that he also had picked up the scent of our elusive quarry and was tracking it down. While I was dumb and almost paralyzed by my prophetic sense that this was the house we were going to spend the rest of our lives in, his awareness of the same thing made him go at the house in a fury of eagerness, and he uncovered its secrets with lightning speed, like the hero of a detective story. At the end of fifteen minutes he knew that at some distant period in the past the kitchen had been made smaller, the position of the stairs had been changed, and the hall made narrower; but he had not been able yet to determine the meaning of a patch of brickwork in the closet of a small downstairs bedroom, or the reason for the curious way certain boards were laid in the kitchen floor.

Taken all in all, his explorings only strengthened our first wonderful surmise that this house was fated to be ours. He said there was no electricity and he was glad of it. He had always liked oil lamps better than electric ones. He said there was no water supply except a cistern in the cellar with a pump in the kitchen, and of course no plumbing at all. There was no furnace, thank God, he said. He had no use for central heating. Airtight stoves and coal grates and a nice kitchen range were healthier and cozier, and much less destructive than furnace heat to the old French furniture we had brought home with us. I agreed with him eagerly. We were both delighted by the fact that neither of us was daunted by the lack of modern conveniences, and we hoped it meant that the price of the house would be within our reach. France had trained us and given us an un-American sense of values. Living in a dignified old house in Paris which had not been modernized, we had been astonished and delighted by the feeling of emancipation that comes when you cast off the superstition that bathtubs and hot and cold running water and electric lights are essential to a civilized person. It had seemed a kind of triumph to escape from the slavery of that superstition, and to find out that if it is done with a little system and forethought, which soon becomes a habit, one's toilet can be performed easily and even luxuriously by using tall tin pitchers of hot water and a large basin and plenty of towels. By submitting ourselves to this humble and yet really cozy arrangement in Paris, we had been able to buy some very beautiful books and furnish our apartment with a certain elegance. What is intolerable to a civilized person is the very poor imitation of modern conveniences which one so often finds in foreign countries —running water that doesn't run, furnaces that do not heat, gas stoves that are out of order, electric lights that go out every three minutes, leaving you helpless on a pitch-dark, unknown staircase. It is the meanness and dishonesty of this kind of thing that make Americans so impatient of primitiveness and so attached to their own faultless machinery. But really simple and honest primitive methods, which most of us have so completely and quickly forgotten ever existed, can produce a comfort and pleasure that is equal to what is achieved by the method of perfect machinery. Just as hand-woven cloth is as fine and more beautiful than the best that can be made by a machine, hand-wrought domestic life can be as comfortable and beautiful, if it is made by an artist in that medium, as the domestic life which runs so smoothly by machinery.

I could never have lived in this primitive and perfect style alone either in America or in France, lacking, as I did, the physical ability to lift and carry. But a new era dawned for the solitary Inger of my Sellanraa the day that Izak appeared, an Izak who had all the Robinson Crusoe qualities, and not only a remarkable talent for making fires burn, kettles boil, and ovens bake under the most desert-island kind of circumstances, but a talent for making transplanted trees and flowers flourish and grow and old furniture take on a luster—in fact, for creating order and a beautiful elegance out of the most disheartening material. The value of this kind of creative and manual skill in husbands was suddenly recognized in America when in 1929 so many men of the type which had been until then the most envied and imitated—the great financiers and business geniuses—turned into helpless babies and shot themselves or jumped off penthouse roofs because they did not know anything about living.

Maybe it was the exultant joy in the prospect of using this ability of Dan's which made the brick house seem so thrilling a house to have fallen in love with. The usual American tool, money, was lacking. We could not order a terrace and make out a check to pay the mason and gardener to build it. We had something much more interesting to do than make out checks. We had to put ourselves into this house, and not merely our signatures.

Sellanraa, my first love, the moment had come. I was saying farewell to you. You were magical. Our intercourse was perfect in a way that no human intercourse can be. You were to me more like a sylvan temple than a house, and your crickets and your dahlias and your northern lights were only a few of the treasures that had been made miraculous by your haunting spirit. I was the votary who humbly tended your treasures and guarded your sacred fire and learned in solitude what your spirit could teach me.

But surely Sellanraa was not a suitable name for such a place. It dawns on me now that I never told anyone that I called it Sellanraa. It was only in my own thoughts of it that I found myself calling it by that name. I think perhaps this secrecy shows that it was not the right name, but that it was an unconscious prophecy. Perhaps the first Sellanraa was not really Sellanraa at all, but a sort of phantom and a foreshadowing and a preparation for the real Sellanraa that was to come—the Sellanraa of true fulfillment, where Izak and Inger would work together in the partnership that makes the earth blossom. Perhaps it was with this end in view that our wise and subtle Mother Nature made me, a little spinster, fall so desperately in love with a house when the idea was so firmly rooted in my head that I could never marry or be anything except a vestal virgin. It is just beginning to dawn on me now what the old woman was up to. Thus she worked by slow stages of enlightenment, through devotion and grievous separation, upon a blind and erring child until now at last she has landed Izak and Inger together on the threshold of the brick house and the rediscovery there of the most ancient and happiest way of living ever invented.

3. *The Search*

[To Warren Butler]

January 7, 1909

You seem to be playing the part of the airy moth yourself
this week. You seem to have lighted in Salem for a second
or two and then taken to your wings, forgoing the delightful pleasure of a dance. And they said sadly, "He
seemed bored." Moreover, you have not written to me
about the tea which Glovey and I are coming to with
pleasure—which was a bitter blow. I honestly miss your
letters horribly when you send them all in other directions
than mine.

If I had written down all that I feel this week, I should
be able to send you a great volume of essays on various
interesting subjects. But there was nothing very tangible
that I could harpoon with a pen, sad to relate. It has been
simply a long-drawn-out mood, and a very pleasant real
one, full of philosophical and poetical reveries—partly the
result of a glorious dose of Stevenson and partly of my
being in bed with nothing to do but consider my own
future, etc., and partly of a strange foggy night when I
did not sleep because I had been struck by one of those
spells when your spirit simply gazes awe-struck and
dumb at the heavenly beauty and wonder of things. I feel

as if I *must* get out under the stars in the night or in the thick heavy fog of nights like these when only a dim yellow light or two light the streets. I would like to run through it, close to the earth and all around and over the hills through the dark. I feel as if I did not really *know* life in the least, and I am overcome by a crazy yearning desire for experience. I, of all people, am ill-fated by being made with that instinct plugged into me—I who can hardly walk up Conant Street pinned in hard by this dastardly brace, without puffing and smothering like a porpoise.

Good night. I am sleepy.

February 25, 1910

AN explanation is due you, though I had almost forgotten, because since that fine flood I have been absolutely happy.

It was just that I was horribly downhearted with no reason except that I had been missing you immeasurably for weeks. You had not seemed to need me or to think of me (except sarcastically and lightly) for so long that I thought you never would again, and as you have taken for me the place of my most dear father as much as anyone could and the place of all the lovers any girl could dream of (rather exceptional duty for a brother), you see it meant unbearable loneliness to think that you were going on without me. To see you so happily arranging your future knocked me half crazy with a realization of my own terrible helplessness, visions of inexorable spinsterhood, etc., and more than that a great longing for a father who would make things clear.

But this all seems morbid and impossible now. Instead, I humbly thank the stars that govern me that I have known you and that we both have known Glovey. In the last three days or so I feel as if I had grown up and acquired sense and a clearer sight. Everything seems good, and I thank the Lord I am so happy—that we all are. Glovey had a mother's blessing bestowed on her last night. It was the highest comedy I ever saw, and everybody felt great. I truly never was more glad of anything. I have always loved her very much, and I have known her especially well this year, and now I know her and love her better than I ever did before.

I see I can't write a decent letter, but I think that your intuition will make it clear to you.

May, 1910

O WARREN, Warren, Warren dear, please write to me, please help me. I am so sick of myself and of my life, and I am all alone. I can see numberless possibilities of joy, but I am powerless to reach them. And it is such exquisite, perfect joy, perfectly in tune with my own soul. I am so inexorably bound in alone with myself, and now a hideous fear has possessed me lest I should forget how to talk and lose my way to everybody.

I refuse to be blinded by this foggy sorrow. I am going to stop writing such an insane letter.

I *am* strong, and infinitely powerful. I can overcome everything. My soul *can* transcend my body. I know it. There is eternal youth in me, and I will not be afraid of my utmost longing and desire.

O God, help me, help me! I would rather see the stars and break my heart with longing for them, than be blind.

Write to me, oh, please write to me!

May, 1912

APRIL NIGHTS

Night is drooping under the rain,
    Drugged with the dreams of Spring

55

Heavy she lies in exquisite pain
Pain of the unborn, beautiful thing.

She is dark and old and she slumbers long,
Heavy with sleep and the sound of rain.
But when Spring shall arise from her,
young and strong,
Night shall be robed and jeweled again.

SONNET

I sought Truth on the pinnacles of earth,
And standing on the coldest, clearest height
My spirit shook, exultant, at the sight
The endless-wheeling stars wherein the girth
Of Time was writ, beginning with God's birth.
But when my soul, in her Icarian flight
Came to where Death sat in a blinding light,
I fell a-weeping, sick for mortal mirth.
Now to a deep, deep vale have I withdrawn
The stars shut out, I play awhile with words
And weave in gentle sounds the whir of birds
In soft-winged parley round my house at dawn,
But though I fill my ears with sweetest phrase
I hear Truth step along my fringed ways.

August, 1912

SUMMER

I

In the city streets the old and the young are dying,
Struck by the sun, their faces purple and red.
White children in the high windows are lying
A woman in travail screams from a foul bed.

56

The Search

With burning body I pray that there be no morrow
  With desperate soul I curse the creator of sorrow.

II

The sick, sick dream fell from me, and awaking,
  Here am I in a lonely boat on the cool sea,
And the wind and the sea and the sun are silently taking
  My sad, reviling soul away from me
Until I long of yesterday to borrow
  And bring my soul back in a dream of sorrow.

[To CATHARINE HUNTINGTON]

March 6, 1912

THIS wild life, this tearing back and forth between Cambridge and Boston, is tiring me and I don't see any reason in it. I shall be so glad indeed when the day comes for me to go to Lexington and live a tranquil life with you.

The horrible academic atmosphere and all the complicated mixture of people and their ideas, and, worst of all, their feelings, make me very tired.

At this time of year it's all I can do to keep quiet—it seems as if I must go away to Jamaica, or some still, free place where it is summer and where Cambridge was never heard of.

June 3, 1912

THIS morning I woke feeling rather young and incompetent and spiritless. How horribly unpleasant! But now, in a pleasant mood, I have sworn off on "temperament" and tea on my mother's request. I shall always be nice to everyone, not enthusiastic and ecstatic about everyone and never changing. Never unpleasant or tigerish—always

57

explainable. I've decided this is the ideal life. So when you get letters written like this you will know that an infinite placidity has settled on my soul:

Dear Catharine,

What a pleasant day it is! I have been darning stockings all the morning and reading "The Outlook." I read Thomas à Kempis every evening.

I'm wearing out a beautiful and very durable plaid dress that I had when I was nine.

Quite fondly,
K. B.

My letters grow worse with my increase in age. Everything about me grows worse also.

We have just been having a family discussion upon the subject of summer. It appears that Mother and Warren are going to the Pacific Coast in July and stay until September or October, which leaves me and Lurana to arrange ourselves as we like in Danvers. Unless all my friends decide that Danvers is too hot a place to come. But what difference does "place" make anyway? I'd as soon live in a slum as anywhere else. I've decided to take everything that happens like a true sport. I shall write immortal poems while the children yell in the street and the blacksmith over the way curses. He has a favorite phrase that I should love to repeat to you if I had his raucous voice and pleasant, affectionate way of handling oaths.

July 6, 1912

I AM sitting at the dining-room table—the coolest place —and before me is a jar of crimson ramblers and beside me an empty glass wherein a faint aroma lingers of grape juice and ginger-ale—a great mixture, by the way. And as

the noble and beautiful
Catharine Huntingdog
by KBH
July 25, 1942
at Blue Hill.

CATHARINE HUNTINGTON

I sit I think of you and of heaven and Jehovah and the great Himalayas. I have wide rambling thoughts, inconstant ever. The blue bowl on the sideboard makes me think of the horizon when one is fifteen hundred miles away from America and fifteen hundred away from Liverpool. If I were only there! If I were only in England or France!

September 12, 1912

I HAVEN'T written a real letter for months. Here on the Maine coast one feels too healthily inarticulate to be able to write. I haven't had any communication with my state of mind for ages past. Here we are out of doors all day, eating blueberries and blackberries—everything that grows on the roadside—cooking bouillon an hour or two after breakfast in a vacant schoolhouse. In the schoolhouse one draws on the blackboard portraits of all one's friends. I shall go sailing soon, I'm hoping, and deep-sea fishing. In the evening we sit around a long dining-room table lighted with numberless oil lamps and read *The Black Cat* and the *Blue Book* and the *Red Book* and play the mandolin with the accompaniment of a seraphic parlor organ—our music is chiefly temperance songs.

My purpose in life is rather shaky still. Lucia and her father, Dean Briggs, talked to me about certain admirable English courses at Radcliffe, and the next evening after I was in bed with the light out, Lucia talked to me about the social duties of college, and altruism, and running the magazine. She is most lovable. She advised me fully, and insistently and seriously, but I am not altogether won. I might go to Radcliffe unwon though, and wander through another year, without keeping my eyes on the altruistic possibilities of my presence there. Idiotic! I'm exciting folly. The hour is late and it seems that any word, no matter how sensible, is not worth writing when one looks out of the window and asks oneself the baffling questions of night. A midnight letter is a maudlin thing at best, but you *may* strike a glistening word or two that will show you my pitiful aspiration.

September 18, 1912

I AM the most unhappiest thing you know. For no reason at all I am in despair. Indeed, I cannot write anything which I should not later regret.

In deep gloom,
K. B.

September 19, 1912

HERE is a letter fresh from this morning's mail written to me by Rollo Ogden, a New York critic and editor, father of Winifred, and this letter is pretty thrilling: it contains his opinion of my literary chances. Would you like to learn from him a method for exciting your theme writers, making their young hearts beat like triphammers and their brains burn with ambition and wide flowing thoughts? When I see you I'll show it to you, if I can manage it with the proper nonchalance. I cannot decide whether to go back to Cambridge or not. I incline first one way, then the other. Mr. Ogden says in his letter, "My advice would be to read all you can and to look into your heart and write." I think I'll wait until Monday morning, and then whichever side of the question just strikes me when I wake, I shall cleave to.

A violin downstairs strives with Dvořák's "Humoresque"—I am in a state, half adoration and half despair.

September 21, 1912

I THANK you for your letter. It was generously written and beautiful, better than Thomas à Kempis because it is not too insistent upon things which are impossible to us. I cannot draw myself away to the realms of joyous angels. I am too much in love with the earth, even its woes and ugliness. I have always had a haunting distrust and fear of comfort and warmth because they seem to me a coating, a crust which quickly makes one dull to the reality of *real* things—like death. It seems to me that the true proportion of realities is that which one must see in the hour of death. If I could only constantly keep that proportion in my mind, I think life would be much greater.

But this is hardly better than the sentimental, religious babblings of some old ladies I know. This year I think I will study some philosophy—history of ancient philosophy —and really know a little about it.

It was good of you to remind me of my youth. I *have* felt as if I'd lived forever. There is nothing better than the encouragement of a good friend.

September 24, 1912

I LONG for you. This room is deserted—only one or two stragglers. They've all gone down to the Copley Plaza. I came here because I was alone, though it is not particularly cheering to one who is solitary. The music plays still, delicately insisting—then loud and cruel. *Ma chère, ma chère, que je vous désire!* I've been sad all day thinking of you. In Cambridge there was the usual first day excitement, but I couldn't decide on any courses, and I didn't seem to belong there. I went up to the Magazine Room where the dust of the Cambridge summer made everything desolate. There was a pile of old manuscripts on a shelf, and the mark of your hand was on it—your comments on things. So alive it was, and personal I almost ached to see it.

There is no person here whom I know, and in the

general desolation of this place I fear that everyone has grown beyond me, gone out into a different world, somewhere intent, absorbed in some fine thing.

O my dear Catharine, the greatest consolation in this moment is that I have you to write to, of any thought or emotion at every hour of day or night.

Do come back soon.

December 6, 1912

I LOOK out the window and I see horrid graduates go by with bony faces, hard faces, and unpleasant hair. How I hate them! And how I hate everybody—the dirty, tired, shrieking, poverty-rubbed intense, bourgeois mob in the lunch room.

Yours viciously,
K.

December 26, 1912

THE dangerous period has come round again when I must burst every bond and go to the Hebrides or Paris or Jamaica. This life is losing its flavor. I can't sit still any longer. If I do, I shall never be able to move again. Will you go? Will you help me excite the bored people of the earth by crying through the streets some new fanaticism, or bombarding a European throne, anything? The terror of it is that *this*, that we are doing now, is being young, supposedly the choicest part of life, and we aren't taking much advantage of it. We're learning to control our impulses and trying to live properly by the rule of three meals a day and getting up and going to bed— And it is going! And then where will we be? In a minute it will be all over, and Heaven knows whether we get another chance or not.

This is a silly thing to tear one's hair over, though, because tearing hair uses up valuable time, and if you realize too acutely how heavenly valuable time is, you are too paralyzed to do anything. As it is, I'm reading French history and French literature, and trying to work on my magazine contributions, which are many-leaved.

January 12, 1913

WINIFRED was so very charmed by your hospitality. As for myself, knowing that it was for me you did it, I am in that wholly despicable mind-wandering mood of marveling humbly, crawling in the dust, as it were, to think that you should wish to be so good to such a poor, foolish, awkward creature as myself. Those words will pain you, yet I feel it so sincerely. Why do you? I don't grace your table either with wit or beauty. You don't need the flattery of my admiration. Only occasionally when we are alone, wandering out of doors in the spring, or sitting through the night by your fireside, is it possible for me to free myself in the least, and then how gracelessly! never, never hitting the thing itself, but blundering along in the dark!

March 19, 1913

I'VE been reading tonight *The European,* by Henry James, which seems to me pretty clever probing into the manners of poor good old New Englanders. I find myself so stilted and full of conscience that I can hardly feel at ease in my own company. Really I think it is vitally necessary that we leave this place immediately. I've had a letter saying that Mr. Ogden thinks I can get a good job in New York next winter. I wish you would go with me. What a golden era it would be! You could write dramatic criticisms and I could write streetcar advertisements and occasionally an editorial for the *Post*.

April 25, 1913

THERE is, I believe, a kind of superstition that I am to see you tomorrow, but in my earthly mind skepticism overcomes the occult in this case. I do not pin my faith to fantasy. Hence I write you a letter that our communication may not wholly cease.

I've been thinking of a poem you wrote about the table of life when you entertain certain guests, where in your capacity of hostess you cannot permit any one guest to get drunk. The idea seems to me most valuable. I am having difficulties with my guests. They are getting into hot discussions, they are glaring at each other and calling names. There is wine spilled and the cloth is all rumpled. How am I ever to create union between them? I simply cannot tell which is right and which wrong. I am beside myself, distracted, and I have quite lost my own appetite.

July 10, 1913

I AM finishing that old story about Cape Cod—the innocent boy who fell in love with a bold, bad, beautiful woman who affects a costume rather like Caroline's. The first day that I wrote on it, I had a gorgeous time. It all seemed so real and vastly interesting, and I thought I was a real novelist. But today it sounds like Mrs. Barclay, and I shudder at it. Wouldn't it be unspeakable after writing and writing away so seriously and clapping one's head in one's hand, to find that it was all a huge travesty of what one had intended, that it really was no better, no different from Mrs. Barclay? Do you think this could happen? Is there any such fiendish power that could turn all one's gold to base unreality?

July 23, 1913

NONE of my works have appeared in the Woodland Journals. Most of them float like mirages in the sky far out of reach, though I feel constantly in the presence of poems by myself, and am almost content to let them float, if I may only see them. I shall never write much, I think. What I write will be done at rare moments. I get a fragment now and then, never any volume. I love planning large things, but it seems impossible to keep up the necessary vitality for really composing them. I can't write page after page. I can never say what I mean the first time. It must be rewritten over and over until I uncover at last what I'm looking for.

August 12, 1913

I AM full of problems, the same old difficulties. I wander about restlessly looking for diversion or peace, and there still follows me a restless weaving, weaving, weaving in my perfectly foolish brain. It is all, as I know well, the fruit of too much introspection. Yet if I could ever clear myself I would gladly look out instead of within. One must commune with one's self in planning a course of action. The difficulty is that "myself and I" come to no definite conclusions. I wonder if that is my particular curse. I observe it in everything that I touch. I look at things, but have no convictions in regard to them.

Much of the problem is the question of using myself to the best advantage. Whether I can write well, should I go at it with a deliberate intention, etc., or get some different sort of job and turn to writing for a change and a diversion. These questions are useless. Instead of asking them any longer I'm going to write something. Some day I shall have a great deal of advice to give to a young person of my temperament and inclinations.

The Search

I think the secret of much of the unrest and dissatisfaction with one's self and longing for a more vivid, expressive existence is the thing planted deep in everyone—turning toward the sun, the love of a virtue and splendor that must be adored. One has an inward sense of harmony. I mean one recognizes, by instinct, the celestial harmony and must try to adjust one's natural discord and dissymmetry to match it. One is always trying to tune one's self to an unheard perfection. In this day everyone writes helpless articles about the Modern Unrest and advises sociological cures: everything from a material point of view, whereas what is needed is a few penetrating words from some St. Francis.

I'm sorry I disappointed you. In writing of the pinpoint theory, I was speaking from a psychological point of view. Of course, speaking in a philosophical way, minutes aren't anything separated from each other. The meanings of things grow and become visible after long, long years of gathered thoughts, surely. I—the person, am not wholly visible—and even then shall not wholly be—until death. But except for the lacking proportion to come in the future, I am just as dead now, except for this second—as I ever will be.

July 6, 1914

WHEN I came home on Friday night, June 26th, I found a large part of Salem in ruins, still smoking, or rather still blazing in some places, and several of our friends and relatives terribly broken up by their losses. But the real part of Salem is untouched—the Museum, Essex Institute, Witch House, Seven Gables, Chestnut Street, and the Common. The Pews had a narrow escape with their house, I believe, but they saved it. A number of fine old houses went, through Warren Street and Hawthorne, near the upper end of Chestnut, and more than half of South

67

Salem. Lafayette Street is simply nonexistent. Everyone who wasn't burned out has been working at the various relief stations, giving out clothes to the refugees. Several troops of the State Militia have taken charge of the town. On a golf course by the sea in South Salem there is a large encampment of French refugees, guarded and fed and taken care of by soldiers. Lurana and I went down there this morning with some supplies for the Red Cross nurses. The people seem to be having a most happy time. In the evening they sometimes are cheered by a band concert, and they sing their own old French songs, our Marlbro' and such. It is said to be quite entrancing to see and hear.

It is a prodigious piece of work to put these thousands of people on their feet again, who have lost houses, clothes, money, and often the mills where they worked. And there isn't enough money to do it with, although help has come from all over New England. Now that the horror of the fire is not so much in our minds, the business of rehabilitation obsesses everyone. I don't consider myself at all good at this sort of thing, but it is simply impossible to think of anything else. At the Relief Station one fits a laboring man out with clothes in the most matter-of-fact way. One takes an anxious interest in the size of his neck and his feet and the width of his shoulders that would amaze you until you found yourself doing it. They come to you in such a trustful way, the foreigners particularly, you feel you have missed your destiny if you give him a blue shirt when he should have had a more practical black one.

Our French nuns were burned out. I have looked for Sister Alexandre at the encampment of the French, but have seen nothing of her. They raised a wooden cross there by the sea and say their masses out of doors. When the orphan asylum was burning the firemen desperately tried to find the orphans to get them out of the building.

They were nowhere to be found until someone discovered them all out behind the building kneeling in neat rows all over the lawn with their little orphan hands up, praying for deliverance—the little dears—the Roman Catholic form of fire drill.

You will think I am mocking. I'm not, dear Catharine. My first instinct, surprising even to myself, when a second fire broke out the other night, making the whole sky red, was to get on my knees like the little orphans.

August 22, 1914

I TREMBLE to think of what you may be experiencing. I was so glad indeed to get your letter written at Windsor and to know that you were safely off the continent, but it is all terrible beyond belief. Now that the great horrible forces are set going, Heaven alone knows where or when they will mercifully stop. For my own sake I wish you were nearer home.

We are quite hopeless of getting true or prompt accounts of happenings. I hear tonight that the German Army has swung past Brussels and is aiming for Ostend, the nearer England. I cannot bear to think of it and the poor Americans who are caught in the net of it, who are, you say, so completely horror-stricken! We are all going about our business so quietly, so much as usual, with no power to help, or even to know what is going on. And out of this conflict what tremendous change shall come! It is unimaginable—the glittering armies of the earth sweeping upon each other—in this day!

4. *Things Japanese*

JAPANESE things: I knew instantly these things were mine in spirit, at least partly even though they were so foreign. The Japanese love of paper and of microscopic things was already right up my street, and their habit of noticing and admiring small things, of having crickets for pets in tiny bamboo cages.

Toshihiko in Castine. Winter evenings. I try to teach him to bank his fire, regulate his inspiration. He reads art magazines all night, gets excited, sits up all night, is dead the next day and horribly depressed because he can't work. In the evening I try to make him play dominoes, pass the evening without excitement. He is physically small, has intensity, playfulness, agility, wit, appeal, femininity as of a poet—*not* feminine however—strength, intimacy, confidingness. I think of my first meeting with him—my embarrassment and stupid, unseeing, grown-up eye, as looking at something unpleasantly queer.

In my house I feel happy and satisfied at last when Philip and Toshihiko sit and discuss painting; when painting is going on in the house, I feel at home at last. The house is functioning. Then the relatives, nonartists, family life—their superficial amiability.

Japanese language and manners uncover a layer of consciousness we are not aware of. If I am suddenly in a room

70

talking with Toshihiko my susceptibilities instantly become sharper and more sensitive. We are very sloppy and noisy and unreal. Japanese have words to express things we do not express, microscopic moods, *nonbili,* tea-drinker's colors. The Japanese language can teach us to see and to feel things we have not been aware of. If there is no word to express a certain mood or impression, it scarcely exists in our consciousness. At least it doesn't exist with anything like the authority and clearness that it exists when it has been classified and given a name.

Toshihiko has a sixth sense, the sense of movement. Such exquisite sympathy, intuitive understanding, emotion make occidentals seem like great thick-skinned boors. Toshihiko said he knew that when he came home his mother would stay in another room for a day or two just hearing his voice: control of feeling. Japanese letters do not say the things which are the most important—those are understood. They cannot say, "I love you." Japanese poem: "The fisherman's coat is wet but not so wet as my sleeve with tears." The song is minor. Singing, lying on the floor in the firelight, the black bench, tea tray—sometimes I have a lonesome feeling when I see it go down, as if a part of myself is going down there.

Looking at pictures in the evening is marvelous; looking at the *Arts,* over and over, books from Japan, Japanese magazines; playing dominoes on the floor; Mrs. Olsen coming in and stepping over and around him—laughing.

Toshihiko tells me to be a submissive woman. He wants a woman to be sometimes feminine and sometimes very masculine, think like a man.

We go driving on cold snowy nights: side-curtains on, mittens, fur caps; going to movies or to Bangor, to Thanksgiving celebration.

Japanese feeling about talk: useless American polite talk.

Wistful gaiety, the winter evenings. Toshihiko, things he loves and wants.

Lindbergh crossing the ocean—E. E. Cummings published—*Rio Rita.* "Blue Heaven." Mrs. Bertrand Russell's *The Right to Be Happy.*

The Japanese hook and ring game, and the other Japanese game, everybody sitting on the floor in a circle. The English historical game with Philip and Beata. Michigan with P. and B. and Toshihiko at the Pierces. Our kitten, Feather, or Hokus Pokus.

"Blue Heaven" and other popular songs, the atmosphere they convey and what they mean to Toshihiko and what they mean to those dumb, anonymous, dark crowds in movie theaters. Wistful desire for a sweetness in life, charm, delight, and something very personal, your own difference, your own feeling and situation.

I had known for a long time that nobody could ever fall in love with me, because of my being like the little locksmith. I say I knew this, although I never had asked anybody if it were true, and nobody had ever told me that it was. Yet I believed that I ought to believe that it was true. It was their silence, not words, which made me believe that I was expected to believe this. No words ever were spoken, not a single word of enlightenment to help me solve and endure this inhuman predicament. Nevertheless, I thought I understood lovers, and I wanted to protect them.

The Italian elevator man: Toshihiko makes me aware of servants as human beings, opens a new layer of consciousness. Before I looked at them without seeing them or realizing what they were in their own right. To me they were mechanical, although I had a sort of amiability toward them.

DENNETT'S WHARF, CASTINE
Illustration from *Mr. Muffet's Cat*

Breathing, casual, significance of life, not mental, sensuous, conscious, alive, effortless, profound quality of reality. The development; slow, endless—ebb and flow of life, coming and going, the tide, the moon, misunderstandings *toujours*.

October 23, 1927: Glittering day, warm sun, slightly stirring wind, marvelously blue bay. I meant to work because I felt newly born, but I sat outside against the house after breakfast and then Toshihiko came out and ate his breakfast outdoors, and then we sat there until 12. I was reading *Go She Must,* and admiring it and enjoying it very much. And he brought his dictionaries and we talked about words. I have immortal longings on me...

June 1, 1928: Night—We are going away tomorrow. I am in bed. It is still. I can hear one frog's chirp outdoors. This

73

afternoon was beautiful. I was rather tired, but in a dream of ecstasy. It is too beautiful, peaceful. I was thinking of a story about an old woman going to bed—alone—going to sleep, then the imprisoned being, her past being, creeps out of her breast, the young spirit—amorous—eager—alive.

The moon was almost full tonight. It shone above the apple trees in the sky that was still pink with sunset. Rich green grass—Mr. Bridgham working in his garden bending over. Later I drove out to Lille Mem, taking Edward. I realized my restlessness; excitement is partly due to a climax of health and freedom, gained at last after so long —such long patience—the thing has come at last—thanks to Toshihiko.

Because of love Castine has become impossible— Love did it and drove me away from the house, made that house too intensely beloved to be endured without Toshihiko.

Intimacy is necessary in Castine, intimacy with house, with Toshihiko. He especially showed me a degree of intimacy which makes ordinary occidental relationship seem superficial. Some people, many people never in their lives experience intimacy. A person capable of it should not be frustrated in it. I am sometimes.

The island prepared the way for the good life. I sometimes return, desire to go back to the wild, restless, crazy time.

Something out of Nothing: God in the beginning I believed in theory, but it takes a long time to learn to practice it. *Enfin*, it is a long, tough way to learn something very simple. The Will of God. Every generation has a different language, and can't learn what former generations knew until it has been translated into their words. Something out of Nothing requires humility and more humility, to accept limits and work within *limits*.

How supernaturally brave *l'amour* can make a per-

74

son. Now I am quite scared to go around alone, and I shudder to remember the daring reckless things I have done. I think it was nature sending me. How could my family have allowed it? Because they were as ignorant as I was, ignorant as most educated and well-bred people are.

The terrific *malaise* at Castine, this *malaise* because my dream of an abstract life had been thwarted by the dominating personal life of family, etc., all against what I had wanted the house to stand for.

Rain, and a soft wind, and I think of the wind, terrible wind in Castine. Those nights which T. said roused him intolerably. Intolerable seems to be my word now. The way we used to talk about words, and his dictionaries, and sitting out there on the side steps one morning—all the morning instead of working when I was reading *Go She Must*—and then we talked about words. Hysterical, he explained to me how I excited him—I didn't know before—that night when he came and sat down beside me on the floor and he said, "Let's mourn," and he began to cry or pretend to cry and he said under his breath, "Something is going to happen tonight." I put my hands on his face. He got up suddenly and went to the front door and stood there a long time and then came back and wrote a letter to Taro, or somebody in Boston, saying he wouldn't come to Boston, but had decided to stay in Castine.

He said once I made him creative and he began to draw—drawing those pictures last winter—the one I liked and the one I drew of him—dead—death and love—you never realize death until you realize love. I realized then for the first time how your desire to be one with another person may be answered by the creation of one out of two.

Today a picture in the paper of the Japanese girl, Setsui Metsadaira—her Japanese dress. In Castine, looking at the Sunday papers, he used to say he hated the way the Japanese women look in modern dress. Oh, those long conversations, so charming, so lovable—about his childhood and clothes he wore and going to the country with his father and in the hospital and I went with him to the dentist in Bucksport and that night he said, "I was going to wait until two years from now to tell you this, but I'll tell you now—I think it was very sweet of you to go to the dentist with me." P. Wadsworth there in Castine. Cigarette lighter and blue shirt and T. putting the bracelet on my wrist.

The night we came home from Joe's and we said it didn't matter—it would be jesting. In Boston he said he didn't understand what happened in Castine, the last two months because he wasn't in love with me. Sitting at the table in the Armenian restaurant where he had been coming a great deal because Julia happens to like that kind of food—I couldn't eat and he didn't like it. That night before we left Castine, eating the chicken with such joy—Mrs. Olsen and Edward. Mrs. O. said she missed him so when I went back in May. Writing the letter to the steamer and my sweet little cat running along the road. "Feather," P. W. named her. The way T. looked—his eyes got so dark and reminiscent when he saw her in Auburndale. And in Auburndale, when he called me Kitty Devneux and I said I left K. D. in Castine. And two mornings when he was so upset—all covered up under the puff—sleeping late and so depressed.

Somebody is singing now, and I think of the way his throat and chin looked when he sang and Catharine and I so disturbed and upset by his singing Japanese songs. It is unbearable. "The fisherman's coat is wet, but not so wet as my sleeve with tears." Next day at Penobscot I waited for him to paint—with the car and he was so exhausted and went to sleep in the car. Damn! I feel very wickedly resentful toward my mother for all she did without meaning to which makes me so afraid.

[To Toshihiko]

July 9, 1928

Are you singing in Japan? Shouting very loud, ever? Or is such behavior impossible in the position of young master, with the necktie tied very straight? Is your young brother very polite to you, afraid of you? Do you go solemnly tiptoeing about, bowing, rubbing hands together with that overwhelming manner of an ancient hermit? I don't seriously expect to get any answer to these questions. If I wish really to know how you are, I will visit the crystal-gazer. Still, I really do want to know if you can sing now.

I wonder which part of your manifold consciousness is most awake now? I hate this business of sending arrows into the air, because I know so well how very dumb you can be if the wrong arrow comes at the wrong time. But if you are dumb, that is your misfortune, not mine. Of course, there are moments now when you ponder on your destiny, if you are still alive you are doing that, and so I beg you for the sake of your destiny, whatever it may be, read Count Keyserling's *Book of Marriage*. I think it is absolutely necessary for every civilized conscious being. They probably sell it at the nearest bookshop in Tokyo, translated into Japanese.

You are so far away. It is hard to know much about you, even from your letters. I am sure you must be making some progress with your parents or you would leave. Your last letter, that came today, troubles me, because it sounds like the song in *Pagliacci*. The way you used to say it made you feel—somebody pressed against a wall. Are you that way? You sound as if they were crushing you. But perhaps I am wrong. I hope you are getting through all right. Don't stay in the cage too long, though. Oh, don't! ! !

Such a large ocean and such a large continent are between us now that I can say anything I want to. I can remind you that you have a person in me who having once, whether on account of the solitude or the wind, no matter what, held you and been held by you in a very close embrace, can never quite forget you, or in a way can never be separated from you.

I am quite near to you tonight. I can almost touch you. Can you remember me at all? Somehow you never really knew me, only in moments, then you knew me better than anybody, but that didn't matter. I didn't care.

I have just been reading the letter you wrote me from the island. You told me about Julia. I remember the time when you said you were a little boy at a fair teasing his mother to give him a certain toy. You said I was the mother, and Julia was the toy. It makes my heart break the way it would make the mother's heart break.

July 28, 1928

On this lovely pink paper I feel like telling you that I am enjoying life. My effervescent creative happiness keeps bubbling up in me like a spring, making me quite silly, in fact, silly in my *beaucoup joie de vivre. Est-ce que tu comprends français? Je suis absolument heureuse parce que* this evening is so charming in the midst of level fields. Three large blue convolvuluses, or convolvuli, are sleeping on their twisted stems outside my window. Crickets are chirping. I have been having some delicious adventures, and learning *quelques choses.* I have been reading a lovely book called *The Dance of Siva,* by Ananda Coomaraswamy. I have been in a most sweet little cottage at North Truro, also visiting in Provincetown—watching three large blond German aviators experimenting on the moors by the sea with a motorless airplane, calling to each other in rich gutturals. They wear the most beautiful, costly, and careless tweeds and soft sweaters in colors you would praise and Mexican hats with tassels round the brim. They have the wonderful German vitality, and fresh look.

Now a few delicate drops of rain are falling on the leaves. My room is on the ground floor, so I can even hear the grass stir when the raindrops come and the crickets climb up and down the little hills under the grass.

Are you all right? Please remember this thing. That I don't expect to get any letters from you. I've seen you too often struggling to write letters. I don't want you to do any of that for me. And it would be a hundred times as hard to write letters from Japan. Give me credit enough to know that. Give me lots of credit anyway. My credit is increasing, it is flexible. Something marvelous has happened to me.

YOUR letter that came a day or two ago, after you received Van Gogh, made me feel very badly. You are not the one to stay in a cage, at least not any longer than is necessary for you to understand what that suffering is. And surely that didn't take long. *Please* don't stay in the cage. Oh, *don't*! I feel like going there and creeping in like a burglar to unfasten the door for you. Over and over last year you told me not to let you get stuck there. Is there nothing I can do?

Nobody but you can do it really. I can remind you of something, though. You have a place in America; the brick path leads you into the place.

79

30 Warren Street, Salem

I wish you weren't so far away. I wish I could talk to you. My desire to write has gone out of me as completely as if it had been removed by an operation, through the potent action of love. I imagine it could not affect a man so, because art really belongs to a man as it doesn't belong to a woman. I feel now that it is a great mistake, a great sin against nature for my sex to seek fame or even without the desire for fame to give a life's devotion to any art except the art of living. Do you think I am mad? I feel terribly strongly tonight the presence of *lachrymae rerum*. This rain slowly dripping on the tin roof and somehow summer melancholy of this meaningless little place, Salem.

Just as I write that I feel wicked to say it, and I feel the wistful charm existing everywhere where there are human beings. Nevertheless, you will understand what I mean.

I did what you told me. I went up to Castine, to prove to myself that I could go back, and then I turned the key and came away again. Now I am roaming about, visiting here and there, with my car always my slave, my dearest friend, my alter ego.

Oh, New England, I'm sick of it.

Please don't think I'm unhappy, because I'm not, and I'm not trying to make you unhappy. I know what I'm really like; and, what's more, I know that you know—we're not fooling ourselves. But what you're really like I don't know; and that doesn't make me unhappy either: I don't care. I know part of you and I'm glad. As a matter of fact I'm rather proud. I think I know a great deal—for instance, if I ask you something, you won't mind. And if my asking hurt you, I wouldn't care—I'm like that; it's me. I'm glad everything's over: because I've loved you very much.

I'm glad there'll be nothing except memories. You know
what I liked best about you, what I will always like and
will always remember. It's your hands. You know that
and I tell you. Tell me something. Because it doesn't matter and you're going, tell me one thing. Tell me (as if I
were dead and you were talking to someone else with
your hands on her breasts) what there was, once, about me.

I am your second mother, whose hand you pulled at the
fair because you wanted me to let you have a toy. I did
let you have the toy, and it broke your heart because it
wasn't what you thought it was. I am your old nurse, and
your young sister, and I am the one who loves you forever,
because you came to me to help your cosmic loneliness.

July 29, 1928

It is a very hot night, and I can't sleep—I am lying on
my bed, writing down certain impressions I had today,
and I am reading a book by Havelock Ellis called *The
New Spirit*. It has in it essays about certain people, including Walt Whitman, Heine, and Tolstoy. After I
finish reading it I think I might send it to you. The only
trouble being that I borrowed it, so I suppose I have no
right to send it so far away as Japan. I like so very much
everything about Whitman; more and more I think he is
the great person of America.

This room I am in tonight has no windows facing toward Long Island Sound—I am at an old village called
Lyme. Tomorrow I am going over to Black Point, a few
miles from here—a summer resort on the Sound—where
there are white houses, high green hedges, and windmills,
where the New York family called Burlingham live in the
summer, the man who says he is my publisher—waiting
for something to publish. They have always, for some

reason, liked me and been generous to me—but they do not know at all what I am, and I think perhaps it is time for me to break off the friendship, which is really not founded on reality.

After I had your letter I dreamed about you—I saw you on the ground, crying—I wanted to be one of the blades of green under you. This means I want to be the one you don't know—the mother, like the earth. You mustn't worry about me—for any reason. Whatever was, was inevitable. If you made me suffer it was inevitable—my fault. Two people whose inevitable action on each other is more happy than unhappy.

It feels like spring today—there is the pity of spring in the streets. I saw a white wolfhound and I am the wolf-hound. I am your dog, Tan, that ran after you and got run over. When you saw what was going to happen and you couldn't do anything. But I am killed now so I ought not to be able to speak, or write this. But I could just look at you with my eyes before I died. You were standing be-side me. I knew about automobiles, but I forgot because I forgot everything except following you. Do I hurt you writing this? It's only my eyes are looking at you now the last time. Do you understand me better now? I am alone now and I want to be alone. People are alone when they die. Maybe you can't bear this, but I can bear it, so you can.

This afternoon is almost over. I have a light beside me on the little black table which is beside my bed on the sleeping porch. But it isn't really dark. Turning my head I can see the mist and whiteness of the river and the sky and the pale substance between, which is Brooksville. It is a spring day of utter stillness and mist. When the trees, some of them quite bare of leaves and some of them gold and red, are, it seems, alive—marvelously conscious in this wonderful stillness.

Even old barns one sees along the road seem alive and conscious, waiting. When there is no wind moving the surface of things you seem to feel the fundamental movement more. I mean the infinite variety in the molded shapes of hills and valleys. Ecstasy—secret.

The Thimble is waiting for your return—yet the sense of waiting is so joined to the eternal waiting and eternal movement by Nature that it is all the same if the desired one returns or doesn't return. Do you understand? Yes, joy and grief *are one* and the same.

[To CATHARINE HUNTINGTON]

October 8, 1928

I'VE written to Phyllis to get me a housekeeping room in Patchin Place, and there I hope to live, taking with me a few domestic trifles to make it seem cozy. I can't keep my car in New York, I suppose. But let's go down together on the boat, anyway. I haven't heard from Phyllis. I *think* in my letter I suggested an exchange. I offered her this house in exchange for her place—but probably that isn't sensible. But she is slow in answering, so perhaps she is considering it. I hope she is all right.

I am impatient to have you come. I will try to treat you as kindly—as lovely, as you treat me. I can't hope to do so well. But you really *will* like the room.

November 7, 1928

THIS is a night when I simply cannot sleep. It is 2:30 A.M. It is quite useless to turn off the light because I get so bored listening to the incessant mad motors that rush past the window, carrying a thousand people as if they were going to a fire. I have just been to the kitchen and eaten a saucer of canned raspberries and some crackers and cheese, and I have been reading the *Dial* without any pleasure. So now I'll pass the time much more pleasantly telling you that today I got a very cute apartment in 4 Patchin Place on the ground floor (two rooms, bath, and kitchenette). Electricity, bath, coal grates, fresh paint, gas radiator, hot-water stack for fifty-five per month without any lease. Caroline says she will lend me a fine large table and some other things, possibly a bed. I think it is very thrilling—that's what I really want, and what I saw in my mind's eye in Castine—that very apartment. It just happens to become vacant now.

December 31, 1928

I ALWAYS seem to be in such a hurry. I am continually waiting to have time to write to you, and instead of writing to you I am darting from the sink to the coal bin and back again, or throwing on my clothes with insane haste to rush uptown to my psychoanalyst. It looks as if I would have to make time, as they say. Margaret Fairbanks is visiting me while here on museum business. She goes back tonight on the midnight. Next I believe Emily is coming. But tell me when you will come back again to our little blue heaven. At last, yesterday, I bought some material for the bed in the back room. And Margaret gave me four cocktail glasses yesterday and a cocktail shaker. Isn't that a good beginning? Her young friend, Stephen Barr, came to dinner with me last night. Anne came to dinner with me the night before—she is fascinating. Caroline likes M. Fairbanks very much.

And all this time I haven't thanked you for the delightful, expensive, Parisian wooden bracelet. The most charming present, my best. Did you know I wanted a bracelet? And tomorrow I have an engagement with Charley James, who is going to make me a purple hat for almost nothing because he likes the architecture of my head and he says *wants* to make a hat for me. So it will go with the bracelet and I shall be a knock-out.

January 6, 1929

My life is primitive. My hands are black all the time from heaving coal, and rough from washing dishes. I have no time for what we called the exquisite things in life.

I really feel the pressure of coal and food vs. lampshades and screens and pillows. It is a frightful conflict. I am a coal miner and a boudoirine combined, so all the class antagonism is fighting in me: coal-heaver wishes to be recognized by the one who sews ruffles, and the rufflemaker resents intrusion of coal-heaver. Now I have to get up and placate the fire, give it food.

January 10, 1929

Our dearest Toshihiko. I had a letter today and a Xmas card like yours. He sounds sad, pressed against a wall, subdued. I wish he would leave, but he thinks he will accomplish something in time.... interval....

Brooding over T. Y.'s letter, and tears and a wild feeling I haven't had for a long time, like the time on the stoop at Hadley when I bumped my head against the blind during a crying spell. Then I went out, just now, to the delicatessen to buy some eggs. The man, a middle-aged German, told me with distress that he sleeps alone. He said, "It's lonesome, sleeping alone. Do you sleep alone?"

"Yes."

"It's lonesome, isn't it!" I said, "Yes."

"We might sleep together then."

I said well, I didn't know; rather weak answer but pleasant.

I said I have a friend that comes to stay with me often, (thinking of you), sort of pretending I didn't know what he meant.

"Then does he sleep with you?"

"Oh, it's a girl!" I said, feeling silly.

"Oh, that's no good. It's no fun," he said.

"No! of course not!" I exclaimed with a very warm sympathetic look as I went out.

Then I felt like laughing and crying at everything—my wild feeling over T. Y. mixed up with amusement and pity toward the solemn lonesome German. I like people who go straight to the point, in a way, quite honest.

Have a good time! We are only human, after all, as they say.

Silly one! I mean myself.

Be not too sad—gently merry—never mind conversation. That's no good.

February, 1929

I HAVE just finished my dinner and am now lying on the pink pansies sucking a lemon drop. It seems such a novelty to have made a dinner alone that I think I must have not had dinner alone very much. I don't mind it at all. I don't even mind getting quite a nice meal for myself. I had a really exquisite one, with sausages, baked bananas, sweet potatoes, and a salad made of an alligator pear, toast-erettes, and a glass of milk. I am sleeping a great deal in the day. Yesterday I slept all day long, with a splashing rain in the back yard and the sound of the old man chopping wood, and crooning pigeons. Taro came in the later afternoon to say good-by. He had been here late the night before which caused my long sleep and

86

other nights the same. Caroline has cruelly, ruthlessly, wickedly put Dudley Murphy out of K's studio in order to put Taro in. Taro is enchanted. He is coming back next Monday or Tuesday to stay three months, March, April, and May. Those are my Uranian months. Do you suppose there could be any connection? I don't think so.

Taro did devote himself to me, as you said. We rode in a great many taxicabs and had meals in all kinds of places. Once in the middle of the night or early morning we went into the back room of the moist-eyed German who cooked eggs and bacon for us and glanced at me very coldly; because of Taro, I suppose.

February 23, 1929

PEACEFUL loneliness, small hot fire, a meal just finished of six raw oysters, Italian bread, milk, and cheese. Beautiful peignoir, just finished and on—in bed luxuriously all day without dressing at all—after a late night with Taro.

I had a nice time with him. He went back to Boston today, but he says he is coming back soon. Saturday evening we had a very nice time. I made a lovely-looking arrangement for dinner with Taro—white linen sheet for tablecloth, the one you once slept in, all washed by Georgette—and pink plates, blue glasses, and little orange coffee cups from the five-and-ten, and a large bottle of port with Spanish label, also bowl of beautiful grapes.

J.C.P., Phyllis, Stephen Barr, and Taro made a very nice party.

Sunday Taro took me to afternoon Symphony Concert and came back here and stayed late again.

Last night Caroline took us to Harlem where we heard and saw the thrilling Africans until about 10:30 and then T. and I came down to the Grove Street Theater because Susan Smith had given me admission for two to dress

87

rehearsal. We saw the end of it and we weren't terribly thrilled.

You can see that I am now sort of convalescent from night life. We met so many people, it was rather nice the way it happened.

March 10, 1929

I AM so glad to hear from Minna Geddes that you are coming back to New York this week. Even if you are staying with somebody else, I need you in the same city. And I cannot understand those who, to refer to your last letter, do not devote their whole lives to appreciating you at your full value. You *shall* be appreciated.

When we are all dead and lying in our graves we will be remembered and thought of a little bit, maybe. Something to look forward to. I feel fierce and sad today and I feel like writing an angry autobiography, very passionate and beautiful and stirring and truthful. Kind of a revenge.

I'd like to see the Geddes play again with you when you come. I took Dorothy Harvey to it. We liked it very much in many ways. But I am obsessed with a new, or rather an old, song which I heard Walter Byrnes sing at Dorothy's. It is called "Careless Love." I am going to buy an instrument, some kind of a little Irish harp or lute, or something, so I can play tunes like "Careless Love" and "Frankie and Johnny" and break the hearts of my hearers as well as my own. You would like that, wouldn't you? You can maybe help me find some such thing? It sounds rather sapphic. Maybe it will end in a cliff. I feel rather cliff-drawn today.

April 11, 1929

I DO hope that when the favorable stars come we won't forget our crazy sufferings and we won't get too sleepy and contented. Thank God for French people!! Today and yesterday for some reason I was in the *extremis.* I couldn't cook anything, like you. I was sick in the night, throwing up hysterically, and all day today I ate nothing and I felt myself utterly inconsolable, when at last Marthe came in, and she was like the most healing balm, like the painting by Van Gogh called *La Berceuse,* which is the kind of a woman who is the eternal cradle of man—quite homely, not young, not romantic, but everlasting. It was really voluptuous, sinking into Marthe's being in a kind of daze of relief while she made a meal for me. Then she said with a worried look she was afraid something was going to happen to her. I thought she must have some bad symptoms, cancer or something. But, no, she had dreamed all her teeth had fallen out, and that means a death, she said. If she could be with me always I would be all right. But you see she also has her horrors.

I am in love with your new red-haired friend. Are you going to be in love with him? If not, please let me be in love with him. I have never seen him, but your description roused me. I want to take him to Castine and take care of him. May I?

I saw a beautiful production of *The Sea Gull,* but I don't think any better than yours in Boston. Phyllis and I are going to see it again tomorrow.

Now I am stopping to listen to the sounds Marthe makes, handling things and making things neat. It makes a kind of delicious hypnotized feeling steal all over me. And yet she dreamed about teeth! and that is bad! she says.

I wish you could be listening to Marthe too.

I went a second time to see *The Sea Gull.* I have a craving to see it again and again. It is a beautiful performance, and such a beautiful play! It is enough. It is perfectly satisfying.

89

The Journals and Letters of the Little Locksmith

This is such a nice Sunday, or else the stars are kind. Intrinsically it is a dreary, cold, damp, cloudy Sunday, but the stars must be affecting me kindly because I am able to enjoy the long leisurely feeling of sleeping until twelve, getting out of bed at one, making lovely breakfast, smoking a cigarette, turning over and over the Sunday papers, as they say, then washing dishes, lovingly polishing the teakettle and the delicious new coffeepot, laboriously building a fire, rearranging objects, gloating all the time over the charming appearance of the room. Gloating over a little copy of *The Sea Gull* I bought, gloating like a still-life painter over four little calendula buds in a tumbler, gloating over a new painting which is standing on the mantelpiece, and most of all gloating over being alive and the romantic sense of all that has been and all that is to come. Whatever it is.

April 24, 1929

My mother would think it strange and cruel of me to devote myself to somebody in my house when she is delicate and loves me so and might like to be with me. But alas! alas! alas! The image of Toshihiko is too alive in that house for me to exist there as a self-sacrificing daughter carrying around a buried memory in a rapidly wilting body, because the body *would* wilt. Nature doesn't seem to like those daughters, and the sun doesn't shine on them. I couldn't leave my psychoanalysis with Dr. de Forest before June 1, I am afraid, although I will talk to her about it. It is going so well now I don't dare to stop.

I will be in the depths of aloneness, just to show her, and maybe I will pull some treasure up out of *The Well of Loneliness,* not anything Lesbian, I hope. Last night I

90

had a passionately horrible dream of bedbugs, whatever
it means.

April 25, 1929

I AM having a quiet evening sewing. Caroline came for
dinner last night, and she launched me on the "lounging
pajamas" made of silk. They will be beautiful, and I will
wear them sitting on the terrace in Castine or even driving on hot days. Just this makes me long to go and I am
singing, "Over beyond my aunt's, where the deep waters
flow!" . . . We must, if you allow, take your lute. O lovely
cycle of sweetness in Castine, once more! And where is
my child, my Toshihiko? I can't see him and I can't hear
him. But he says he is calling—"It's me! It's me! Will you
watch me?" Tears, O tears, my sweet one—

Forgive me, dearest, dearest Catharine. You're the only
one who quite feels it—bless you! Happiness to you, I
pray.

[TO TOSHIHIKO]

May 2, 1929

Dark spring rain falling—
Every day, every night—
Splashing in the back yard—
Divine—Such strange
Happiness—Lilies of the valley!
Lilies of the valley!
Stillness and tears—

Now it is really a strange hot day—sudden spring. One's
consciousness seems to come suddenly out of its sheath—
like a bud buried in a stalk that suddenly comes out and
there is a flower—wide open. You are connected, in my

mind, with all these things that are the beauty of spring: sudden flowers. You said you wondered how pain changes to pleasure. What about pleasure changing to pain? or it's all one at the same time. Perhaps that's what you meant by strange pleasure. It's in all the sounds today, and in soft faces of children—so hot they take off their coats in the street.

Edith is playing her violin. All day I have been thinking of you and now unexpected violin, posture, strange divine instrument. This presence makes thought of you leap toward me. You like to sit among the still rows of hushed human beings facing the platform, listening to those other human beings drawn together in the design of symphonic music—those servants—wearing their fabric of sound—solemn rapt faces. You were one—perhaps the stillest, sitting alone among the hushed listeners.

I feel as if I had never seen a violin before. It looks like a fabulous creature-phantom-fox spirit—wedded to the human-turned head and the left shoulder and the hands. As if something had been missing when man was created and now he has found his needed thing—his needed voice for uttering his strangest cry by his lonely spirit. I only know that yours is like a bird. It flutters like a bird.

Everyone here seems to be starving or else utterly insensitive. The starving ones are looking for something they will never find, which is absolute love. They go ravenously through the jungle like wild animals, howling in pain, homesick for something never to be found. The most Cleopatralike person I have ever seen, with much experience, is utterly disillusioned. She says to love and to be loved even for one hour in all one's life is almost a miracle, and one can't expect more. So I think maybe I have had my share, and now if you don't need me any more I intend to find something better than love. I'm going back to Castine and be a child of Nature (and perhaps marry a native) and live in the consciousness of trees and farmhouses and animals and the bay and the rivers, and the patient humble exercise of my talent.

I will also have about six bee-hives and raise English sheep dogs and learn about horticulture from Mrs. Butler. I will be peaceful and simple and live under God's most kind protection, and my patron saint will be Mrs. Olsen. Isn't this rather a good plan?

All is marvelously well with me. New York is being very kind to me, or perhaps more likely it is God who gives me through this city, through Phyllis, Jack Powys, such a fresh overwhelming sense of life. Whatever it is, I am happy in a kind of terrifying way. New York is a great challenge and thrilling to accept as a challenge. It seems to be a happiness that includes all my past happiness and yet surpasses it, because it accepts the loss of the past and the transitory nature of things. It is like the terrible and marvelous fact of returning spring—the dynamic upheaval in the earth.

This happiness includes you and the soft sound of the curtain rustling tonight in my room. It includes what passed between us and the reality that existed, the reality within the reality—the thing that words or misunderstanding or time can never touch or alter.

I can't sleep very well, but even that doesn't seem to matter, and I certainly look rather haggard, but even that I don't mind. It seems to me frightfully silly to want to look untouched by experience when one is not untouched.

I am not wasting much time in sleep in this marvelous cosmic city. I don't seem to need sleep and as I can't get it, that is lucky. Even when some kind person has given me a strong drink warranted to cure insomnia, it makes no difference, and about 1 A.M. I hear the deep thundering voices of the ocean liners calling out, "We are going now! We are going!" And I can almost smell the piers and see the huge boat blazing with lights.

Although I can't sleep in this marvelous cosmic city, I am having quite a wonderful time. I feel as if I had lived through several lifetimes of consciousness since I came here. But perhaps continual sleeplessness will make a wreck of me. It will be a glorious wreck anyway.

I don't know whether I am getting very wise or very silly, but the only comment I seem to be able to make about anything is,"All is well," or "So be it." I am getting so terribly humble toward existence, toward the mystery of each living creature and toward the continual weaving of episodes that make the pattern of each life, that I can't think I understand it enough to say, "She is so and so," or "He meant this or that," or "I was in love with him," or "He wasn't in love with me." There is no such thing as definite conclusion. Everything must be followed by a question mark. All I can do is act according to my deepest instinct, and be whatever I must be, crazy or ribald or sad or compassionate or loving or indifferent. That is all anybody can do. And as for analyzing one's self or anybody else, it is rather blind business. And I am sure any attitude of mind is bad which in its arrogance prevents one from feeling more and more all the time the sense of utter humility, and the sense of the great and terrible mystery which surrounds us.

It is only by following your deepest instinct that you can live a rich life and if you let your fear of consequence prevent you from following your deepest instinct, then your life will be safe, expedient and thin.

Oh, please don't be a cagey boy when it comes to anything really great. Throw yourself away, and then you will find out that you are really alive.

That is what I did in Castine, and I am not sorry.

[To CATHARINE HUNTINGTON]

May, 1929

SEVERAL items to tell you. Taro is going to Castine with us. He will take Lytton in his roadster. If my car is all right, you and I will go in that, otherwise boat, don't you think? I have written to Mrs. Olsen to get the house ready, and to the gardener to set out dahlia bulbs, plant morning glory seeds around the Thimble, and cut grass. I think Taro will stay for a while and paint—and be a help to us. He seems to like the idea. I had a very enchanting idiotic letter from Toshihiko yesterday in which he signed himself, "Your loving pig."

Well, it exhausts me so to write in items that I must stop and be more flowing. I am beginning to pant for Castine, and for leaning out of the window in the morning and wandering about out of doors in rippling pajamas and straw sandals I just got, and singing and shouting and being nourished and consoled by Ma Olsen. I shall write to Alva to bring the red bed downstairs and put it in the library for Lytton, where he can have his own fireplace, and go quite easily through the hall to the plumbing or call out for a bed-pan if he prefers that.

I hope he won't be shy about asking. He is an invalid, and Creighton would reproach me again for mentioning the facts of life, and say I ought instead to be making a sampler.

I expect to take the boat from here May 31st, and on reaching Boston go to your house and meet Lytton. I told Taro we would be in a hurry to start, but he says his car will need a few days' attention after the winter,

95

so perhaps it will be about the sixth or seventh we will go.
This is the time of lovely beginnings.

June 23, 1929

It is really all right. I think it is only a temporary
parting from Taro. Anyway, I feel so calm and unhurt, yet
lost in a dream. You must see him. I am quite sure he will
call you up, but he may have tried in vain during your
absence in New York. Please let him know you understand. I cling to his constancy and something deep and
slow like nature. But I can't bear to use any words. And,
oh, please, tell me if he is safe and alive.

What would I do if I didn't have you to write to? I
think that particular kind of horror, self-tormenting remorse, gets terribly large and eclipses everything else
when you're sick and alone. If you wait a little, it shrinks
to smaller size. I'm always having something like that,
and it seems like a boil: it grows so fast, and then a
climax, and then disappears.

It's so beautiful here today, I can hardly think of
leaving it. I am thankful the work is all done, and there is
nobody here to bother me or disturb the feeling. Seven
days of dripping fog and clouds. Today everything is
warm and sunny, birds, moving air, and such calmness
and this morning lying on the porch I read what is for me,
full of meaning: A thing I would love to send to Taro and
that is what you may despise, *The Woman of Andros.* If
you haven't read it, do read it!

I think it is like Taro and like my own illusion. It
moved me very much.

Another day—Sunday afternoon. Just came back from
a picnic on an island. Warren is at the von Saltzas'; house is

empty with wind blowing softly, red and white roses on the table in the same blue-green bowl. Mrs. Olsen made the bouquet, just like last year. They seem so living, as if they remembered, too, fresh and yet the same roses, wakeful and tender and pitying. I don't know why I think of one of Cummings' poems, a line about the moon. There is the moon—there is something faithful and mad.

Last night was so beautiful. I wanted to have courage enough to die. Death seemed the answer to such beauty and such memories, and yet everything flows on and becomes easy and soft again.

September 28, 1929

I ANSWER you instantly, very grateful for your letter. In the same mail, letter from Toshihiko, terribly strange, saying only that Taro had arrived in Japan on the 19th, then plunged into his own state of mind, not as connected with me or Taro, only painting, ambition, and all very low-spirited. But so curiously cold and impersonal, and going to France, but no mention of coming here on the way. I must leave here as soon as I can. I am getting too haunted and too conscious of waiting a word from Taro.

I didn't realize how much I longed to hear from Toshihiko about Taro instead of about himself, and a kind of generous interest in me. He sounds very lost and unhappy himself—poor one.

A new idea. How would you like to come up now, and go down with me first or middle of next week, just you and I, a sentimental farewell, a farewell perhaps to this era? I do wish you could. I shan't drive down alone, but leave the car here, if there is nobody to go with me. I'm feeling sad. I've been staying in bed the last two days, heart troubling me quite a lot, probably from this accumulated uneasiness of waiting and uncertainty. I don't feel like driving now; maybe next week and with you for companion, I might. If not, I would go down by train, which makes transportation more expensive for both of us, and probably not worth while to you, although it is so lovely here now and so still and full of memories, not sad, really, only rather wonderful and strange, and not over yet, for any of us.

October 15, 1929

OTHER people, millions of others, have had to endure these things, so really I think we can, too, and not tragically, not like E. Dickinson (whose poems ought to be suppressed), but lightly, turning easily—easily to some other quarter—not to expect too much, ever—not to make one's self hopelessly a slave. If one has been a slave, though, and got happiness out of it, then the moment it is over, take the banishment with the humble submissiveness of a slave, try to accept the latter dream as much as the earlier one. There is peace in this reality. The most beautiful thing is inevitability of events, and the most ugly thing is trying to resist inevitability. I do not struggle.

I'm getting myself used to the idea that Taro's love was a brief illusion of his, not lasting any more, and I find peace in submitting to this. It's the only way to live without horrible suffering. Don't agonize, don't let yourself be disintegrated by struggling and going in two directions. You can live without him, and if you aren't happy with him, it's better to do that.

You hate the word renunciation, and so do I. I don't mean that, but I mean acting in yourself, gracefully and strongly. Don't be obsessed with the idea that there is only one possibility. If you think so, there is only one. If you open your eyes and your whole being, there are endless possibilities for happiness.

I've been writing this to myself as much as to you.

[To Toshihiko]

I THINK there is something rather to be ashamed of in the egotism of love which encloses two people and shuts other people out. You know the letter I wrote you about you being at the bottom of a well and I looking down to watch you and you answered and said please keep on watching me! I'm thinking of that today, and although I could have said any day or any night ever since we left Castine that February—I'm still watching you and it would have been true, now I find I can't say it and I feel ashamed because it is the egotism of another love that shut the old one out.

[To Taro]

I HAVE a feeling I want to tell you about, this night.

I am on my porch. The house is all dark and still.

First, the crickets have begun to chirp. I don't know how many nights ago they began, but suddenly I was conscious of that sound, the little vibrating trill out of the grass. Now I hear it all the time (and hardly ever the frog any more).

I just went downstairs in the dark to get something, and I found the logs still burning in the fireplace. The light and shadows moving over the room and the ceiling gave me a feeling of ancient love of fire, and of primitive night and loneliness. I thought almost I remembered my earliest human ancestors and lying on the ground beside a crumbling protecting fire close to another being afraid of darkness and in love with fire, and also in love with darkness. It was quite a wonderful feeling, if only I could tell it.

August 16, 1929

I JUST was walking round the house, everything very still, nobody here, and a cold wind blowing. I went down to-ward the studio and I felt lonely for you. I hadn't been into the studio. I opened the door, and it seemed warm inside. It holds the heat of the day so long. There I saw the drawing of mine that you put up. And the very funny thing about that is that it looks like you. Did you notice that?

October 13, 1929

I HAVE just come to my sister's house in the country to live here two weeks, and take care of my two little nieces. There is a very nice Irish maid who does the cooking, and a funny high-school girl who dresses the children and un-dresses them and has patience enough to read them all the funny section in the Sunday papers. Or rather, not patience but enjoyment. I am grateful for that, because otherwise I would have to read every word of every paper of the comics, very painful and difficult work. As it is, I have quite an easy job, merely being here to settle such questions as how many pieces of candy each may have before dinner, untying their bibs after dinner, taking them in my car to school every day and bringing them home again, and letting them explore my purse, my box of jewelry, and simply by being here giving them the feeling that somebody is here who belongs to them and to whom they belong. It gives me a feeling of peace to find that I can do it peacefully.

After you went away I found you had left me with something that is more real to me all the time. It is a

101

feeling of calmness, which isn't just a copy of your calmness. It is my own calmness. It is beginning to cure my American restlessness. Even if I never see you again I will have it just the same.

Before, I had the idea of calmness and the idea of submitting to destiny, but now I'm beginning to have the thing itself. It is such a marvelous cure for my bad habits of feeling. I tell you this because I am grateful to you for it.

I haven't had a letter from you since you sailed from Vancouver. So I wonder if this means you are having some kind of a hard time, or you find you can't go on with the plan of our marriage. This silence of yours helps my calmness by making it absolutely necessary. If nothing has changed in you and I hear from you that you are ready for me to come, it will be a happy surprise. But now I am really peaceful, no matter what, not dependent on anything, happiness or unhappiness.

I can't send to you the love that has passionate longings. Maybe what I send you now is the core of the peach.

4 Patchin Place, New York

IT IS five o'clock in the afternoon. The air is very fresh and sweet on one's face, and there is the light feeling of spring. It is lovely! I bought four pieces of filet of flounder, and it seemed carrying the little cold package, as I went very merry along the street among all the other human beings hurrying along under the spring sky, as if there was a connection between the freshness and coolness of the air and the freshness and coolness of the fish, which I could almost think had just been taken out of the marvelous cold water of Castine Bay. Do you have that crazily happy feeling doing simple things? Do you sing? Shout out loud? I wonder if you do.

What has happened, Taro? Can't you write me one line and tell me? You see, I haven't had any letter from you since you were in Vancouver. Somehow I can't feel that it is because you have changed toward me, although, of course, that is easily possible, but I feel it is something troubling you very much, something about your father or your family which makes you feel that you can't invite me to Tokyo, or else your family are trying to make you marry a Japanese girl. Whatever it is, I feel terribly sad to feel that you are in trouble.

I'm sitting in my room in Patchin Place again. Your beautiful painting, "Thoughts without words," is on the wall. I have too many things to tell you about that painting, and a thousand other things.

I think that painting is really beautiful. You can't stop painting after doing anything like that, can you?

I put my pen down on the table, and I think it is useless to write a letter. If I could take this room, even the cracked fireplace included, and put it on a magic carpet, and carry it with myself to Japan, then you could knock on the door, and come in like spring.

[To Toshihiko]

April 24, 1930

I MIGHT be able to write you a letter tonight. Sometimes I could say quite a lot and sometimes nothing. Your letter just came, though, and that makes it easier, more like talking, because your letters are like talking. So now I've just had my dinner, and I'm lying on a sofa next to the fire.

Toshihiko, did Taro tell you nothing, nothing about the apple blossoms of last June? Somehow even to you I can scarcely speak a word of it, because, although it was

103

me it was not the K. B. that you know. But this much of the external part I can tell you, that he asked me to come to Japan and marry and live in his own little house in Tokyo. I was to go over soon after he went, after hearing from him about how things were. Then he wrote that he was married, saying, "I have begun life in two, and carry essence of life in one." At Christmas, he wrote, "It is a strange pleasure to let my mind wander over nearest object, the little white handkerchief, and far beyond the ocean—"

Dear Tosh, I did not try to make him love me. It was not my doing. It was utterly a surprise to me, and I said when it began, "Taro, you mustn't make me love you and then go away," as I knew then he had to go so soon. So he asked me to come, and I said I would. But in it I had always a sense of doom, and suffering and such uncertainty, because he was leaving so soon and going into such a different life.

The handkerchief was one I gave him the night he went away, when we went to the station together one hot night in Boston last July and he took the train to Montreal.

Please don't be cross to me when you write again, after reading this, or give me any cold explanations, only pity me a little as you can, because something like this happened to you. And I know these things happen to everybody and we do understand ourselves so much better for them, and can be happy and grateful at least for the very brief and mysterious gift, the joy for just as long as apple blossoms last. Although it is such pain to miss the one who is gone.

I wanted so much to live with him in Japan. Taro said I must come, even long ago, when I first began to know him in New York. He said I would like it so much there, and we read the Lafcadio Hearn book, and he began to teach me some Japanese. So having lost that dream of

going, I feel lost, and almost exile in my own country, as
if I really had the illusion, partly created for me by Taro,
that I would find in Japan a country more like me, or more
like what I want, than the U.S.A. I still long for it, or for
the illusion: it may not be what is really in existence.

But don't think of me as really sad. In some curious
way I am not, at the same time that I am. I'm getting to
be such an ancient and old person, and anyway, so used
to things that now I can bear them much better than I
used to and not be so babyishly desperate as sometimes
before; and whatever happens, its mysteriousness makes
it always wonderful. I mean whatever happens I like it,
even if it kills me. I will probably like dying when it
comes. I'm really happy, Toshihiko. When you have gone
through a certain door of your life, and gone into a certain room, even if you could stay in that room only a
short, short time, it's enough just to remember that. It's
enough to carry inside you all your life, and you aren't
looking for anything any more because you carry it always. It's part of you and nobody can take it away from
you. So then you can roam around the world, and laugh,
and see the flowers and buildings and other people's faces.

I wish you were nearer. How lovely it would be to see
you and talk together now that I am free of love's obsession. I could be just a contented old grandmother to you,
at least. It would be wonderful fun.

And I hope you aren't still feeling what you call "neurasthenic," which I think is a bad word for natural feelings.
Why should we have to call it such an insulting word, as
if the only healthy feeling is happiness or endless self-
confidence? You say you are afraid you are feeling rather
neurasthenic and you tell me not to mind. I think everybody in the world would feel *nonbili*, if only people would
all say, "of course" oftener when somebody feels crazy, or

105

just sad. If another person would say to you, "Of course you feel sad, or crazy, or whatever it is," you would feel all right, or much better anyway. I want to say just, "Of course," and have people say that to me; then everybody feels a great worry gone. That's all there is about me that you ever liked. It's simple enough, just saying, "Of course, how natural." I don't know anything else but that.

So, good-by and do write again, next time you sit down in the *closerie des lilas.* Such a nice name that is. Don't feel you must try to say just the right thing. Just write me about yourself or anything, anything you feel like saying to me. I imagine you quite clearly now, sitting on your Castine bench in front of your stove. Toshihiko!

May Day, 1930

THERE'S a cracking thunderstorm going on in New York City this minute, and goodness, what a crash then! I'm going to mark this thunderstorm, first one this year, by sending you a cable just as soon as it is safe to become involved in the electric machinery of the telephone. I like to make a combination of a great act of Nature with some act of my own. It's like a band of music that suddenly rouses you. Oh, it sounds grand rumbling all around this New York sky. And it reminds me so much of the first thunder last year, one day just like this last May, when sudden summer came, and something rather strange happened that afternoon.

I remember so vividly, Taro was sitting there. I had just been having a party, including a fortuneteller, and after they all went away, Taro and I were alone, and the thunderstorm came. I had such a funny feeling because the fortuneteller had told me some strange things, and now I know they were true. It has all happened, the year has

106

passed, completed now by this thunder. I don't go to fortunetellers any more.

This letter is really to say that I expect to go to Europe in about two or three weeks.

[To CATHARINE HUNTINGTON]

Castine, Saturday

TUESDAY Morning: Last night seemed endless. I couldn't sleep on account of this pain. I thought I had appendicitis or pleurisy or God knows what, and I couldn't get the doctor at all. Today he is so terribly busy he hasn't yet come. I'm in the great bed among the canopies. Barbara is playing the victrola downstairs and getting me little things to eat.

It's so long since I've had any kind of pain, I forgot what it is like—so uncomfortable and uneasy feeling. I said good-by to someone yesterday, thinking I was leaving this morning. Now perhaps I can put a codicil in my will. It's hot and glittering here—day after day so fair and warm, and more and more cases of typhoid because of the lack of rain. Jazz downstairs—flies buzzing in the window here. I was all in the mood to go and hurry to Paris. A letter from Toshihiko the other day, waiting, he says, for me to come. Anyway, I've done some more drawings, portraits, and if I'm stuck here longer perhaps I can do some more. So many interesting faces here that I might hope to do.

Philip and Beata left after swift packing and closing of shutters. Other friends left yesterday. I have had continual drawing parties the last few days.

Wed. Afternoon: Nothing serious only muscle strain, from too much drawing, but feeling poorly today and may postpone leaving for another day or two.

107

Patchin Place Still
June 7, 1930

I was so thankful to hear from you at last, and such a wonderful letter in spite of everything. Heavens, what did Hadley do to you! You mustn't go there again. Quite a while ago I wrote down some of Kitty's remarks to send you. I've lost it now, but it was something like this—very spontaneous and sudden.

"If you go back to Catharine Huntington's house, will she hug you? I like the curly hair on top of her head, don't you? She has short hair in the back. Are you glad she gave you all those dresses?" I said, "Yes." She said, "I'm not." I said, "Why?" "Well, I like *her* too, don't I?" very vehemently. "She wanted you to wear the dresses." Also, "I like her voice, don't you?" I'm sure I think the young are more discriminating than the old. Your aunt's remark about your hair had nothing in it except proof of sad lack of eyesight and perhaps an unconscious willful distortion to bring everybody to her period. One morning I looked at my own face in despair, in bright morning light, and I exclaimed to Kitty, "Oh, my face is so homely, don't you think so?" She said, "No, I wouldn't call it homely. I'd call it more sad than homely." The evening before she said, "Why do you look so sad?" This gave me a pang. She likes sad things. Tears came in her eyes listening to a record of "Deep River." She said, "I like slow, sad things, don't you? It makes you feel like crying."

I hope you'll write again very soon. I'm anxious to know how you are. It was pretty desperate, I should say, and I do hope it's better. Very rotten luck, but you mustn't let Hadley affect you. Whatever happens, please believe you can never lose your beauty or any bit of your quality. That was a terrible phrase you used, "degrading loss of beauty and youth." I must say I feel it in myself sometimes, but I

108

think it's only that one sinks sometimes and then rises again. It isn't anything permanent. There are days of oldness, and then one gets young again. It goes backward and forward, not in one direction. The stars, no doubt rhythmic like eclipse of the moon, coming and going, and recurrence is just as nice and fresh as ever. You surely have had that experience. I've seen it in you and others. It's all the condition of the spirit, I'm sure, not the body, now dull, now shining, ever renewing.

June 11, 1930

CREIGHTON gave me a long unflattering lecture on my qualities when he was in New York the other time, and evidently thought I was purely half-witted even to mourn over anything lost. He says to me I am a coarse creature and for such a person there's no excuse for moping or for missing anything. It was a good line and I think of it now and then. I'll begin to roam soon and make a specialty of my coarse nature.

Adieu, ma chère— It was praise, by the way, what J.C.P. said.

There passed quite an interval when I went up to the crazy hardware store, and the fat daughter was all dressed up with powder and rouge and earrings, and when I admired her looks, she giggled and said, "Oh, yes, I thought I'd put my earrings on tonight, I'm feeling foolish." It was quite a change because she usually looks like a sour drudge and very dirty. Then I stopped in at the pock-marked jeweler's to get my silver necklace, but he leaned over from the balcony where he works in a cubbyhole and said it wasn't finished yet. It's a South American lead ornament which I'm having made into a necklace, hoping to look beautiful for Easter. I wish I could give you a really sumptuous Easter present, such as the new biography of Queen Mary, so full of touching anecdotes and quoted remarks, such as saying to the Duke of York, when he failed at first to win Elizabeth Bowes-Lyon, "I've often observed that there is a great deal of truth in the old adage, 'Faint heart never won fair lady.'" The fact of this remark spread over England, and Queen Mary has been noted ever since as a very gifted matchmaker.

This is a chattering letter, and I will stop now to continue on the blue silk pajamas.

Goodnight—
and damn their souls to Hell.

It's all the better to curse, it makes one more noble—able to be noble, by silent cursing. I wish I could get very fat. I think it is impossible to be sad if you are thickly covered. I feel it immediately after eating dinner; a kind of jolly coarseness creeps in.

Saturday

MY POOR maid has not appeared since early in the week, so I had to drudge for a long time this morning in order to push back the oncoming tide of disintegration, the terrible force of destructiveness which seems to lie in a chaos of dirty dishes, unmade bed, dusty tables, etc. How nice it feels after this is all restored. Otherwise you feel like a victim of the tropics, like a movie, *White Cargo*, which I went to the other night at the 8th Street Cinema with this young Dan Curtis, friend of Mary's, who works at Macmillan's. The refrain of the movie was, "It's the damp rot—it gets everyone, it will get you," to the young man out from England who didn't even drink in the beginning and desperately fought off the alluring native girl only to yield in the end, drinking, stopping shaving, stopping taking a bath, etc., all on account of the Damp Rot! It seems to me there is a touch of the damp rot even in this climate.

110

Why not just go to the tropics and give in to it, once and for all.

There's a detective in Patchin Place this afternoon hunting for a rich girl from Brookline who ran away from home two weeks ago. I hope she manages to hide in the coal bin until the danger is over.

Sunday

FIVE P.M. Sunday and I have just come in from Dorothy's where I let myself in with a key and worked alone for four hours. This might be called one of those really terrible Sundays, when everyone is suddenly away. D. went to the country, leaving work for me to do, but I have the consolation of wearing your much-admired black sleeveless dress. Last night upstairs while I was drawing Mr. Powys, he interrupted his pose by turning and staring at me, and explained that he was admiring my beautiful arms and then embroidered the theme by saying I had the most beautiful arms he had ever seen, and that he was an epicure on arms and scarcely ever could admire. Again this morning he commanded me to get a sleeveless blouse, in fact never to wear sleeves again, wishing first to assure me, however, that the fashion is perfectly ladylike. Well, strange taste, it seems, but most welcome. So I'll be an exhibitionist of arms from now on. Lucy Goodwin burst in after the drawing episode and she made the same exclamation, about the dress, and we went out and she bought some gin, and stayed late, telling me about her life in Paris. She is terribly entertaining, so funny, really.

This morning the whole Goodwin party, including Mary, went home to Hartford, and I miss them. And now it is a really terrible Sunday afternoon, and my ivy hanging on the window sill resembles Emily Dickinson, terribly blighted and sere.

After reading so many authors' letters to Mencken I am

111

disgusted with the almost invariably rotten taste of the writers, the high-school facetious quality of their letters. They're not grown up. That special kind of literary facetiousness makes me so sick. Yet I almost hear the same tone in my own letters.

Pause— Fixing the tire, walking around the room, reading the Sunday *Times,* and finding advertisement of house to rent in Castine, $2000.00 for the season. This is the house on the road opposite the entrance to the von Saltzas'. Do you remember? Jade green blinds and innumerable awning parasols and settees? If this is worth $2000.00, way out of the summer colony, mine must be worth half as much. Mary has offered me $500.00 immediate payment. I am thinking it over. It's very small compared with others I know of. That little place opposite Philip's, Toshihiko used to say, looked like stage scenery for musical comedy set on Long Island. He expected a dancing chorus to appear out of the barn. Imagine $2000.00 for two months! It's ridiculous, of course.

Another pause—for making a little meal, then eating it, and now it is nine o'clock and the terrible Sunday afternoon is over and can't ever come back again, although there may be very perfect copies of it. But now it's raining outside, and lovely to hear and so cozy inside and it might be so much less charming and less alive. It might easily happen that one might look back on one's solitude as terribly precious because next to being with one particular person, or one particular friend, it's the best there is. Imagine the people one might have to live with!

[TO DR. IZETTE DE FOREST]

Castine, October 1, 1930

LATE cold Castinish autumn afternoon, hot fire burning, and I am lying on the floor to write to you.

Things Japanese

A week ago Susumu Hirota was here. He suddenly wrote to me and asked to come. We had the most *gay and delicious* time.

He is *like the sun,* so warm and gay—and Taro is *like the moon.* This happiness and pleasure has nothing to do with love. I'm keeping Taro alone in a silent part of myself, just as I *keep the sad part of myself locked up* there in a silent place alone, as somebody might keep the memory of a dead child closest of all during external joy. Hirota hasn't got this sense of tragedy, or if he has he is afraid of it. One pleasure of being with him was his pleasure in my drawing, and the effect he had on my drawing. We went off painting and drawing almost every day. I got the most perfect joy out of it. My hand seemed to be electrified, alive, and joyous—and he enjoyed and praised my drawing so much. "The beautiful line," he was always saying. It was a wonderful kind of alive feeling— perfect pleasure. He expressed his feelings so easily. "Isn't that pretty!" he would exclaim if he came in and saw the half-written sheet of a letter I was writing. "Oh, I like your cunning little writing!"

I just got up to get a cigarette and turn on the victrola. *"Ich küsse Ihre Hand, Madame!"* and I stopped and looked at my drawings and thought of sending them to you to look at if you wouldn't mind sending them back.

I forgot to say that Hirota asked me to postpone going to Paris. He wants to leave his job in Boston and live in Castine and try to become a painter, and he wants me to stay. He telephoned me last night from Boston, and I said I was going to Paris.

I wonder how your face looks while you are reading this, darling. Are you looking terribly, oh, marvelously, serious and compassionate with your wonderful sweet pitying brown eyes? You see, I haven't forgotten you—and how your face looked once or twice when I happened to

113

turn around and see you when you were listening to me. It is late evening now. I've written this before and after supper, and just now I've been out in the cold moonlit town, and playing parchesi on the floor of a boarding-house sitting room with some cunning children.

I hope you'll write to me. I was so pleased when you answered the other time. I'll be here until after October 12th and perhaps longer. A man wants to buy a piece of my land, which I don't need, and I am hoping to pay my debt to you.

Tomorrow is my birthday—Christ help me.

[To CATHARINE HUNTINGTON]

Castine, October 6, 1930

YES, in the evenin' of life—I had to laugh when you said that. Draw the curtains and light the lamp and be cozy, sitting hand in hand. It's very nice to think of, and probably it won't be anything like that. I like your description of something wilder at the end. It was beautiful.

It's Sunday noon, and I'm just interrupting myself to write this to you. It's freezing cold and a wild noisy wind. My, this is a windy northern peninsula. The trees are shaking and the corners of the house are screaming a high-pitched, muttering scream. My left leg and my right arm have been punctured, one with smallpox vaccine and the other with typhoid, in preparation for Europe and for protection against the local danger of typhoid, the water supply being very low, and one very serious case.

My goodness, the wind!! It's terrifying.

A half-witted pauper, male, who lives in a coal shed down on the wharf just passed the house, coming out of the graveyard carrying a geranium in a pot—stealing from the dead to decorate his own poor home. A half-witted girl from the same neighborhood is in the hospital, having just given birth to a bastard child whose father, an old man, left town when he found out that she was to become a mother. Mrs. M., Beata's insane neighbor at the top of the lane, is screaming and raving all the time lately because it happens that several babies have been born in her neighborhood, and she thinks her husband is the father of all of them. She is also jealous, as I told you, of all the attractive cows in the neighborhood. It's about 2:30 now, and I've opened the window and discovered to my surprise that the screaming wind is a soft, warm, voluptuous creature, not Arctic as I thought. I've been cutting and sewing so long, and my leg hurts and now I feel like crying, a little fit of lonesomeness and missing somebody, I'm not sure whom. Why is Sunday such an empty day, anywhere, city or country? My leg hurts. Oh, go ahead and cry. What the hell—

November 8, 1930

COLD gray morning in New York. It looks like snow. I am awake early, before anybody else, lying on Tony's bed, sending last letters. Exciting day yesterday, going to bank, and to Hamburg American office, and just by chance being reminded that I can't get on the boat without French consul's visa on passport. Consequently hasty visit to consul's office on Pier 59. All is well. Very happy time with Fergus and Gladys, arriving here yesterday A.M. just as they were stirring and marvelous evening last night. F. and G. and I at 21 Washington Square, Harry all alone, giving us cocktails and unbearably entrancing and desperately lonely, tragic sort of gaiety, singing all the nicest songs for us, and blinking as he pours another cocktail. The last evening at your house was terribly nice. You were so very sweet to me. Oh, do be happy and forever yourself—that's enough, and come to Paris with C. very soon.

115

5. *Paris*

[To Catharine Huntington]

22 novembre 1930

Camille met me on the tender that came out from Cherbourg to the *St. Louis,* and we drove to Paris. It was too dreamlike. I was absolutely dazed when we got to the place where they are living. She didn't have the key and she had to leave me on the landing—the hall outside the apartment—while she went down to the *Herald* office to get the key. I was lying on the floor on my fur coat, travelstrained, dazed, disheveled, with my luggage around me. The elevator came up, and out stepped Toshihiko. I should hardly have known him—so much older, thin and academic-looking. This was about 3 P.M. He stayed and we four had dinner together, and he stayed with me in the evening. There was a studio over their room which I had for a few days. It was so strange being with Toshihiko that first time. I couldn't even understand why I had ever loved him so much. I felt amazed at myself.

The second time I saw him, he seemed less strange. We had dinner and evening together. He examined all my clothes in the trunk and is crazy about the famous woolly dress trimmed with leather. He snatched up the brown wooden beads and said, "You still have these. My favorites." I showed him my drawings, and he just nearly died of surprise and admiration. I didn't expect that. He kept exclaiming, "Oh, I am tickled! You know, these are marvelous! They are really marvelous and no flattery." He said they make him feel ashamed of his own work, and he wants me to exhibit in the Paris Independent. He wants me to get a canvas and begin to paint. This second time I felt more natural with him. He didn't seem queer to me. We haven't really begun to talk. I haven't yet asked him about Taro, but he has spoken of him quite a lot and says he may come to Paris.

I am staying temporarily at this hotel, and I shall try with Toshihiko's help to find an atelier or some kind of little place to live in. Elliot and Camille are living in Montmartre, and that is miles away from where Toshihiko is, in Montparnasse. So he thought I should move over here. It troubled me having Camille do so much for me. She has taken me in the car every day, looking for a place, and it is a tremendous expedition to come to Montparnasse every day. So now I am here where I can look about myself in leisure and learn the neighborhood. Elliot scorns this quarter. But Toshihiko thinks it is the best thing for me at first, and besides, so much nearer for him. He is just in the midst of moving into a new atelier himself, buying furniture and directing painters and paperhangers, so I haven't yet been to his own place. He seemed to feel quite disturbed to be in the midst of confusion at the time of my arrival.

Camille and Elliot seem very happy together. She has been wonderfully kind to me, but it really distressed me to be staying with her and having her feel so much responsibility for me. Since last night I am alone staying in this very comfortable little place.

The voyage seemed endless, terribly boring—only Germans on the boat—quite rough seas—I was the only

117

ELLIOT PAUL

passenger not seasick. I slept for days. I can't find your letter to Camille, but I shall when I unpack my things.

She asked about you immediately and overjoyed at the possibility of your coming. She and I are both wearing your clothes—so we feel as if you were partly here. This is all, really—I arrived a day late, last Monday. We spent Monday night at Evrenz and arrived here Tuesday. This is Saturday—I can't sleep yet—very wakeful and excited and sometimes afraid I shall die of homesickness. Yet, I think not—especially with the new adventure of drawing and making such a grand success on Toshihiko with my drawings. Perhaps I shall be admitted among the artists of this quarter.

118

Sunday, November 24

TOSHIHIKO is very sweet to me—taking care of me very nicely, telephoning, coming to take me out, showing me how to buy stamps, where to go for this and that, buying bromide for me, and laughing, and telling me when I say I feel very provincial that I don't look "terribly funny at all," that I have a cosmopolitan air because my clothes are somber and rather shabby. We have been sitting for hours and hours, telling each other all the history of our past two and a half years, laughing and teasing each other. Now he brought me here for midday breakfast, and he left me here supplied with paper and ink while he has gone to buy furniture for his new atelier. I am beginning to enjoy it very much after some hours of disappointment thinking I should die of homesick loneliness. That is gone now, and I feel a new life is beginning for me. He continually sings "Blue Heaven" and other old songs of our Castine days. Nothing bothers me, nothing troubles me— everything is easy and *nonbili*. It suits me deliciously. He has been helping me to look for a place to live, although the hotel is very good for the present. He doesn't seem so lonely as his letters sounded. He has got rather hard-boiled, egotistical, and yet softening into inevitable solicitude and familiarity—and remembering everything of Castine. He asks about you and sends his best regards. Says how very charming you are, says "fiss" and "squass" and imitates you and remembers you eating supper at midnight in Chinatown after the play.

When I am not with him, I am still thinking of the past two and a half years and desperately wishing that I could make him feel the quality of each experience. It is so easy and natural to tell him everything and yet I am not satisfied, and I begin to feel the utter necessity of writing it ... and now perhaps the discrepancy between the need to

119

convey it, to give everything its precious true value, and the limitations of telling it to him will make me really write this history, supposedly for him but perhaps to satisfy myself. And I feel for the first time the irresistible desire to write something, and also my hand desires to draw. He is so enthusiastic about my drawing, he says I must become an artist, that I will be famous—not that I care for that—but perhaps to satisfy myself that is the happiness to come in Paris. I want him to understand what has been precious to me, what has caused tears, what has been misunderstood. I feel some burden gone here. It really is lovely, and I enjoy walking about alone. Maybe this is the first excitement, but let it be that. I am enjoying it anyway. I keep looking up to watch the people moving past—*old* ladies as gay as young ones—children—all kinds. I am glad I can let myself slide into this pleasure—let the knots untie themselves.

This is really *nonbili*. At first Toshihiko said I hadn't changed, but last night he said, "You have changed!" I don't know how...it took several times before I felt natural with him...before I could talk easily. Now it is all right.

I feel so happy and relieved. I don't know why. The stars, I suppose.

December 6, 1930

TODAY I had my hair cut at the ritziest place in Paris—Antoine. It is still rather long in the back, with curls, and brushed behind the ears. It's after midnight now, and I just came in, after having dinner with Elliot and Camille and the evening at the house of their friends, the Jons. And last night also I had dinner with them. The last few days have been strange. Toshihiko and I have almost quarreled. My old ancient feeling of love being gone, I see him in a different light, and he noticed the change and said he couldn't understand me as he used to be able to, without words, and he said I was inhibiting something, so at last I said I didn't like him any more, in fact almost hate him. He has grown more and more egotistical and selfish in his thought and theories, although in spite of himself he can be quite sweet when he forgets his theories. He is terribly mocking and ruthless, and he says he has no faith in anybody. It's really sad, and he doesn't seem to like me any more either. Now it's all changed, and perhaps I shall not see him any more. Nevertheless, it's terribly lonely not having that friendship which I had looked forward to.

Next day— I was desperately unhappy yesterday when I wrote the first of this letter. In fact, every day I accumulated a terrible disappointment in Toshihiko, and I thought it was I who affected him this way. But today I see that it is everybody, or rather it is some terrible irritation within himself or some agony he is trying to escape from. He has a friend—a Japanese girl artist, who was put into his care when he embarked from Japan, and they entered Paris together, and had adjoining studios until just now when he has moved away by himself. She seems to me a very sweet girl. I enjoy being with her, although we have only French for a common language and very little of that. Today he attacked her just as he has been attacking me, criticizing her mood, her attitude, most bitterly. I thought when I first met her, and we three went about together a little, how lucky he was to have such a companion, and I said, "How lucky you are to have Masako. You can't be so lonely." He exclaimed almost with contempt, "So lonely!" And began to tell me how she gets on his nerves and how they fight continually. He says he has no friends in Paris, only acquaintances. Something very strange and terrible is in him. Our meetings so far have been here and there, sitting in cafés or going to a movie *à trois*, or going to tea yesterday at the Dudleys'. He is moving into a new studio but is not yet settled. Today, thanks to Masako, a studio has been found for me—really marvelous luck—wonderful. In the courtyard of a hotel close by here, opposite the Coupole Café on the ground floor with large window, electricity, gas stove, coal stove for heat, and furnished by the hotel. It is really perfect for me, no stairs, and the hotel *femme de ménage* to clean it and bring breakfast. It is amazing luck because it is so very difficult to find a studio at any price; this price is $25.00 a month. I am too delighted, and when I am settled there, probably there will be more sense of leisure and calmness to see Toshihiko, and less nerves.

These are really bitter days as far as myself and Toshihiko are concerned. If it weren't for him, I think I would be enjoying Paris. I can't seem to forget his cruelty and egotism. He insists on waiting until his studio is completely settled before asking me to come there. Once, just by accident, we had dinner there. Masako cooking the *skiaki;* but one would have expected to disregard such formality and just go and sit there and talk. Even if it is not settled—what of it? Hirota said when I was going to buy Toshihiko some Lucky Strikes, "You don't need to bring him a present, just bringing yourself is enough. He won't be lonely any more." What a mistake! Hirota kept saying, "Tosh is a very selfish boy." And I never realized it before, although Philip and Beata always said so. Beata said a little while ago that Philip used to be very mad because T.Y. was selfish toward me. *Alors!* It's a new experience, and so it is worth having. A crazy fortuneteller said, "You will get your wish and you won't want it," and so here it is—quite true—I feel glad when a day passes without seeing him. He is terribly aware of things in his head—frighteningly perceptive, critical, brilliant—but the heart is cold. It is teaching me something, certainly.

Paris

Yesterday after he attacked Masako so severely, she came back with me to the hotel, so *fatiguée,* and lay on my bed. She said, *"Il est égoïste..."* And she said most of her friends in Paris—artists—are egoists, but he is *plus fort égoïste* of them all. She was quite soft and exhausted, although, as he says, she is *égoïste* also, very stubborn, masculine, unlike other Japanese women. I begin to think maybe the difference between occidentals and orientals is the curious quality of kindness, the "icy waters of forgiveness" that Douys speaks of in his book of culture—the Christian quality—never condemning utterly, saving the lost lamb—always giving another chance—something beyond self, beyond the brain.

Maybe this letter is crazy; in a month I shall understand it better.

December 16, 1930

PERHAPS slightly reeling—just after dinner with a carafe of white wine—I feel like writing to you—sitting in the lobby of the hotel where there are writing tables where people pass in and out—to tell you that the painfulness that I felt with Toshihiko is gone now—quite smoothed, and he would probably be amazed if he knew what I had felt. I have an idea that in most relationships between a man and a woman one is the contained and one is the container; and this balance, once having been determined, can't ever be changed. He once said I was to him an unsinkable ship—on which he was a passenger. The passenger being gone, the ship was not so steady or so unsinkable, but that was nothing for him to know or to bother about. Coming strange to France and undergoing the convalescence, almost the sickness of the change, I was very unsteady; and I think it irritated him, besides other troubles of his own. Now I have a feeling of balance. Last night when he came to take me out for the evening, it was all smooth and natural and familiar, for the first time. He notices a change in me, and very penetratingly said, "You had a territory that was all your own, and you had developed it and made it quite perfect, all contained within itself. But now, like a ruler invading another country, you have gone out of your own territory and captured another territory. You don't know yet exactly what to do with your new territory, and in the meantime your old territory suffers from your neglect and absence, and is not so perfect as it was."

I feel so much better and am beginning to enjoy being here—impatiently waiting for the studio which will not be vacant until Xmas. It is in the courtyard of Hôtel de Blois, rue Vavin, just opposite Café Coupole, center of Montparnasse. It is a very damp and unhealthy studio like a greenhouse, on the ground, in the courtyard, but very good, I think—one nice largish room with a big window in a slanting roof, where one will hear the Paris rain. And, like Patchin Place, unheated, except by coal fire which I take care of myself, as I prefer no radiators; and a mysterious and cozy little kitchen in the courtyard where they cook meals which they will send in if one desires. This place, when furnished with large-leaved green luxuriant plants and a cat, will be very nice, I think. A friend of Harry Harvey's who is in the American Hospital here with t.b. and a bad cold and just convalescent from pneumonia, has offered to make a purple wadded jacket for me to wear in the studio. She is Grace Thompson, the heroine of a long and amazing and tragic story, too, too much to try to tell; but she is a very nice girl with rough husky voice like Pauline Lord only not so languid, and I went all the way to Neuilly yesterday in autobuses and tramways to see her. Toshihiko installed me in the Alliance Française to take daily lessons in French, but I can hardly bear it and have cut it now for at least a week. The other

élèves are worse than the worst type of Radcliffe—dreary
New England schoolteachers with a sprinkling of baffled
and wondering Japanese and too much grammar and home-
work for me who never went to school. At a coiffeur's next
door to the hotel, a very modest and friendly little place,
the other day, a client sitting next to me, a middle-aged
French woman with a very kind, placid, and intelligent
face, took pity on me and offered to interpret for me to
the *coiffeuse.* I said I would like to find somebody who
would give me lessons in French, and she gave me the
address of a friend. This afternoon I called there, very
near by, and found a lovely person, about twenty years,
a girl, *très bien élevée,* very *reservante* and sweet, who will
give me lessons every day for 15 francs an hour. The apartment was the place of a friend, I felt—a very good modern
painting on the wall, so I am quite eager for my first
lesson tomorrow.

The other night I went to a great party at Elliot's and
Camille's apartment where there was an assembly of
American newspaper men and ladies—one couple being
the writer John Herman and his wife, who are friends
of J. C. Powys and Phyllis. They often spoke of his coming
to see them in Patchin Place and their admiration for his
work.

And now soon it will be Christmas. And I am not skillful enough yet to go shopping and find lovely little things
to send. I am sorry. Perhaps a little later I can. You will
be lighting your little church and putting a wreath on the
door, and moving about your house in candlelight, wearing a lovely dress.

December 18, 1930

I AM sitting in the shop next door, the coiffeur, smoking a
High Life cigarette—called Higlif by the French. The
coiffeur is giving me an *indéfrisable* permanent wave—

which seems foreign to my nature but seems to be inevitable in the cold humidity of France and the present length of my hair. It has to be *bouclé* in the back, and without the *indéfrisable* and in this cold dampness one has to go nearly every day to have it curled with irons. This is a cozy place—continual murmur of their mysterious language, and a little white cat named Blanchette who lies and sleeps in my lap.

I realized today is the eighteenth and Christmas much nearer than I realized. I am *désolée* because I can't take possession of my studio before then, and I don't know how to celebrate. I haven't heard anything about a Dudley party—Dorothy is expected, but not Caroline. I believe Katharine is too somehow *ennuyée* to bother about the trouble of a very fancy party. She seems to regard everything with skepticism and detachment.

Next day— Last night, having dinner with Toshihiko. I had this letter unsealed, unfinished in my pocket, and I asked if he had messages for you then. He said yes indeed and would have written something then, but there was no bit of paper. I said, "You aren't going to just send your regards, are you?" This is his usual way. Then he said, "What I would really like to say to Catharine is that I should like sometime to have a chance to talk to her intimately." So there's his message.

This morning I was *indisposée*. I have caught cold and sore throat, also discovered a bad blister on the back of my head where the coiffeur burned me.

December 20, 1930

WHAT shall I tell you? Paris is gray and damp and cold. Yet even now, in December, they keep the chairs and tables on the sidewalk in front of the cafés, partly closed in with glass screens and warmed with tall braziers. You can sit close to a brazier which holds a red coal fire and drink something and be quite comfy on the sidewalk about four or five or six o'clock and in the late evening too.

Oh, I am waiting so impatiently for my atelier. But it is not yet vacated. So I still am in a hotel bedroom. When I get in and spread your plaid tablecloth on a table and begin to draw, I shall feel better—just now I am so unsettled, unsatisfied. Toshihiko has been unsettled and disturbed, moving into a new atelier. It has been very difficult to get used to each other again—I feel a certain shyness or constraint after such a long time and he is changed and finds me changed. After we both get settled I think it will be better. He is very, very temperamental, nervous, irritable. He is used to my being the calm one but upon first arriving in a strange city I can't be so serene as in Castine. He said long ago I was an unsinkable ship, and he felt all right if he knew I was somewhere in the house. The other night he said, "You used to be like a harbor one could take refuge in in stormy weather." But since those days I have had stormy weather myself, and no human being can always be an unsinkable ship or a quiet harbor. But I do know how he feels and what he needs, so when I feel desperate or lonely it is better not to see him, so I walk alone in the rain and say to myself what I can remember of Santa Teresa's prayer that Henry once recited to me. "Let nothing disturb thee, nothing afright thee. All things pass," etc. I can't remember any more.

He took me to the Salon d'Automne where two of his pictures were hung, so after going through room after room of strange various paintings we came suddenly upon the lovely dark, dark dawn of Penobscot—with two ghostly horses standing on a hill. It was utterly Castine. He still keeps in his mind the images of those places and paints them in his Paris atelier. He was terribly surprised and delighted with my little Castine pictures, and I am so impatient to do some more. He thinks I can do something very good—he wants me to work very hard—but he is inconsistent! Another day he says, you ought not to do anything—you should be a container—an overlapping person. He is strange, marvelously perceiving, changeable, torturing, amusing, maddening, appealing. He has got a Japanese book he adores and after January 1st—after I am settled—he says we will begin to work on translation.

Do you miss me? I have thought of you so often. You understand so many things. I appreciate that more and more, and I am grateful, and I hope that you are quite peaceful now. I've dreamed several times that I couldn't stand Paris and homesickness and went back to Castine. I haven't got so much courage as you sometimes think. I am a baby—I often want to cry.

[TO DR. DE FOREST]

December 20, 1930

I HAVE written you several letters. One I burned for a reason too long to explain; one was returned and although I still have it, it is too stale to send. I'm writing this now to say that I am in Paris, and that I will write you a long letter soon. I was in New York only for one night and a few hours the next day. I wanted to see you, but yet I was afraid to because there was too much to put into one hour, and I felt it would be only agonizing to have that one short hour.

One day last summer Tony—the fifteen-year-old boy whom you met last winter at my brother's—was being told of some sadness that had happened to one of my generation. He said very sadly, "Too bad!" Then he said that he would never suffer like that—his motto is going to be Mad, not Sad.

That's how I find myself now, mad not sad—and I sud-

128

denly remember that I have had the same feeling before
—the refreshed strong feeling that *is* really elastic, and
the last days with you last spring when I began to feel
that elasticity come back to memory.

I never forget you.

[To CATHARINE HUNTINGTON]

December 26, 1930

You know, speaking of Paris, I've just discovered that the
queer shrill cry of Paris taxis is like seagulls. If you have
ever been on the Bangor boat you know how they follow
the boat down the river during the daylight after you
leave Bucksport and they float up and down with a curious
detachment yet predatory, following the smell of the
ship's cooking and continually crying, just the same note
as Paris taxis, which are also predatory and yet have
detachment as if knowing that, sad as it may seem, there
is a tragic universe where the taximeter isn't very important. American taxi voice is so childish, extrovert; just
one simple idea and no emotion. I'm listening to them
from the stillness of my attic.

Two days before Xmas I had sudden news that it would
be vacant the next day. It was frightfully dirty but it has
been fairly well scrubbed and swept for me, and I came
in yesterday, Christmas Day. This makes everything all
right. I mean I am all right now. It amuses me so to have
something to do, some material to work on. And Christ! to
get away from the hotel wallpaper! It was really making
me quite crazy.

Toshihiko and I went to a grand Christmas party *chez*
Dudley, beginning about 5 P.M. and continuing all night.
We left about 11:30, getting so sleepy, neither of us used
to large numbers of people lately. I met at last Waldo
Pierce, product of Bangor, Maine, old lumber family. He

is a painter, crazy as anything; very amusing to meet Bangor in Paris because he is really very Bangor and very Paris. Huge creature with large untidy black beard, half drunk and pouring out realistic story of his wife's recent accouchement and describing his Bangor parents and brother and sisters and their incapability of having children and how he made his legitimate a month ago.

I do love rather rough, tough creatures, certainly better than delicate refined ones.

Alors! This Bangor theme makes me feel homesick for my rough, tough friends in Castine—for Harold Babcock and Joe and Jake, and the steep snowy street jutting down to Wardwell's Market and into the bay. The boys and girls all out on the moonlight nights coasting all over the town. I feel my primitive American blood, and I could say worse things to the Parisians than free matches. I bet Waldo Pierce was a wild boy in Bangor when he was young.

December 30, 1930

It was Christmas Day or Christmas Night, rather, when I began to tell you that I have moved into my atelier. Also, that Toshihiko and I went to a lovely party at the Dudleys'. Dorothy had arrived with Jason a day or two before, from Switzerland. I am so glad to see her again. She came to my studio this afternoon, the first chance really to talk with her. She was entranced by my studio and wants one just like it. It is lovely, really, and I feel so much more myself in it—quite restored to tranquil feelings. One room, not too small and seeming larger because of very high sloping ceiling—high window—and bare high walls—coal stove with long thin stovepipe climbing up the wall—nice wide low bed in one corner—wide table—several chairs—new electric lamp on table—bouquet of calendulas and freesias in brown pitcher—wide dark chest of drawers with cover of velvet cloth which I had—sort of black and silvery brown velvet, and certain gold-topped bottles and boxes posed elegantly, a Jerusalem cherry tree sent for Xmas by Elliot and Camille—a not bad silly little sofa which I covered with brownish orange and white plaid cotton, a little bookcase hanging on wall over bed—primitive washing arrangements and cooking arrangements in one corner—soon to be beautifully *soigné*—copper pots, etc., scrubbed and hung in a row. Beautifully tranquil, I think. Dorothy wanted to find a room in this hotel—the studio is in the courtyard of the hotel, you see. She wants to find a place to write and asked me to do some work for her. It would have been convenient and so pleasant to be in the same place, but the French cannot conceive of removing an enormous double bed under any circumstances, and there was no room for writing tables in the rooms we looked at. It seemed to them most bizarre, and there is no vacant studio.

Alors, as I was sitting here by the stove I wanted to talk to you, but it is so hard to catch the floating thoughts and feelings about the queerness of seeing Toshihiko. I think perhaps we really like each other very much, and that is the reason why we are each so disappointed in the meeting, and so cross to each other. There is a kind of angry warfare at times. You see, the magic is gone that I used to feel, and the amorousness. I can't feel a trace of it in myself, and I suppose it angers me to have spent so much essence of life upon him. I mean it's the poor dog in me that feels this. I still have rushes of admiration and pleasure, the old feeling of responsibility and protecting, but even that goes down before the anger.

Last night he came and we had dinner together and went to a movie. He was crazily teasing me, saying such mean sadistic things—and so restless—so mocking—so fantastic, and once in a while interrupting himself saying,

131

"Something is dead in me. I am sick of myself—I can't love anything or anybody. Something is dead in me."

When he left last night I felt so tired of his teasing I thought I wouldn't see him any more. Then this morning just after breakfast, before I was dressed, he knocked on the door. It was incredible because he never gets up until afternoon. He had been up all night talking with a Japanese painter—a man he hadn't seen for a long time and met by chance just after he left me. This long conversation had somehow pacified him and made him much better, and he said at last he could sit still. He made a portrait of me and a lot of crazy little drawings, and went home to go to bed about three. I don't know what is wrong with him. He says something is. But I am so glad I have this nice place. Nothing can bother me so much, and everything is more natural here.

Anne and Dorothy are coming to dinner tomorrow night. I miss my lovely friend Madame Bergsma, my French teacher, whom I discovered by chance and whom I see every day when she is in Paris. She has gone to Holland for a little holiday. I have been in this atelier only four days, and it isn't quite settled. Yesterday Camille took me to the Flea Market, which was really marvelous, and I got a beautiful large mirror for twenty francs and a little table for the same.

Now—I tried to draw it for you. Now the victrola is giving "I know the moonlight—I know the starlight—I lay this body—down." I love this place. I am glad I came to Paris, although the first four weeks were hell. It is wonderful having Dorothy here. Everything is better now.

Next morning— Your letter!! The first letter to arrive at the new address. I was asleep. The *garçon* bringing breakfast—"*Vous avez une lettre!*" Imagine my pleasure to have a letter from you to read with my breakfast. Now, as you say, the linking of letters is established. And don't, don't stop! This is a wonderful one—you tell me so many things and it all sounds so nice, but freezing cold seems queer because it isn't so here. I suppose never in Paris. For instance, the four studios in this courtyard share a little cabinet which is just outside my door. Apparently out of doors the plumbing never freezes. It's very filthy—no toilet paper except pieces of newspaper. It is like Patchin Place, living here.

Reading your letter, I am surprised that I conveyed so much about Toshihiko. The last few times—especially the last—I recognized his sadistic teasing as being the way he acted in Castine, when he was desirous and resisted the feeling and took revenge upon it. It's terribly childish. I feel revengeful myself although sometimes all I feel is intense sadness—not from being hurt myself, but just from seeing him so perverse—so twisted—so tortured. I retain my maternal sense of his preciousness—of his being one I have cherished. I savagely resist the self-destruction of the being I gave life to. Yet, if you met him at a party at the Dudleys', for instance, you would see how elegant and charming is his shiny black head like a seal's, turned so attentively, and you wouldn't think there was anything wrong with him.

Yesterday he was drawing me and took off his coat. It was so hot. I was watching him as I posed and trying to amuse myself. I noticed the tucks somebody had carefully made in the sleeves of his shirt to make the sleeves short enough. I said it reminded me that I used to do that for him in Castine. I said, "Somebody did that very nicely— I remember how difficult it was." He said, "Do you know who did this? You did. This is the shirt that our haughty friend gave me." I remember the incident of the shirt being given in a manner that offended the oriental taste and pride and yet was taken as a joke.

Rain sounds delicious now on the skylight . . . I play

Creighton's "Water Boy," "You Jack of Diamonds, I know you of old, boy. You rob-a my pocket—yes, you rob-a my pocket—of a silver and a gold." This Jack of Diamonds. This oriental spoiled prince, as you call him—did rob my pocket of a silver and a gold—of precious things and I know him of old.

Pause— Have got up and me *baignée* and scrubbing a little the dirty walls, shelf, table in the little corner where the last tenant left a horrible mess. It makes me sick, but soon, with *garçon's* help, it will be all right. They treat me like a queen here—I suppose from slightly lavish tipping in the beginning. A *garçon* is here now—a little monkey—grinning at me—quite proud of helping *faire salon* out of the once filthy mess, and listening to my victrola—*Chanson de nègre*.

This letter seems to be black with coal dust. So are my hands—just as in Patchin Place, from taking care of a coal fire. But it is amusing to be victorious in such a place as this, to force it into being clean and good and graceful.

I have that feeling that something very nice happened to me today, and then I remember it was your letter—like a *très charmante* visitor to begin the day. Please continue. Your dancing party sounds very gay. So much love and best encouragement for everything grand and gay—dancing parties, drinking, and doing beautiful plays. I am so glad of that.

le janvier, 1931

I HAVE been staying away for four or five days while my dirty atelier has been washed. It was terribly dirty when I took it and I didn't know what to do about it. My refined charming Dutch lady sent a protégé of hers—penniless Spanish artist—to come to scrub. Such wild black eyes. He scrubbed so hard and had such wild eyes I had to move out and stay with Camille.

Paris

They joke a great deal about my wild Spaniard, but until today he has been *ouvrier,* working in white overalls. Just now he took them off, standing behind my trunk, and when he started to take off white trousers smilingly reassured me that he had on other *pantalons* underneath. "*Voyez!*" he said, showing how dressed he was. Then he asked to look at my drawings and then took me to a picture gallery.

I am eating a very hot sticky Welsh rarebit and *café crème.* I am beginning to like Paris very much. I had a strange disease—it lasted several days and only just now faded away, leaving me feeling very much better than before, like a grand accumulation of something and then cleansing—like Easter. It was the climax of acclimatizing, I think. Now I feel strong and pure and in very good spirits. I bought a lovely dress at a funny shop where they sell models worn by mannequins. It is black chiffon velvet with plaid lines, green and pale yellow—very simple cut with long sleeves—just to wear all the time. I *will* get the cape. Truly, I haven't been capable of shopping even for toothpaste. It has been so complicated getting myself settled and established and also being sick in bed twice. K. Dudley is so occupied and rather inaccessible for any kind of thing. But I will persist in it. Your letter sounds very gay!

26 janvier 1931

I just got your merry letter about all the gay parties. Camille and I have enjoyed the idea of your dancing party very much—the quadrilles and minuets among the candles, you and Philip bowing and curtsying in eighteenth-century court style. You keep telling me about the dancing party in every letter, and every time the floor is more waxen and slippery—more *disques*—more punch—more everything. I am jealous because we have no dancing

135

parties in Paris—at least not *chez moi,* and I wonder why I left Boston for this gray damp city and a cross Japanese. You express so much charming appreciation of my atelier, the drawing of it placed on your mantel, etc., and it seems ironical because your letter came just as I was lying in bed hating this place—having bronchitis and fever mounting, and no bell to call the *garçon* and necessity of stepping outdoors to the w.c. and no toilet paper, never any that—only the Japanese, Spanish, and French newspapers of the various occupants of the other ateliers, to which I flamboyantly add the Paris *New York Herald.* I am madly, flamboyantly, insolently American. I feel like Abraham Lincoln. I talk as nasally as possible. Well, the French doctor advised me to move in to the hotel for a few days, so I'm here now with a *sonnette* and *eau chaud courant* and *chauffage centralle* and a lot of bottles of medicine and tablets and mustard plasters. And in your letter you said so wisely always to wear—what did you call it?—eiderdown. It's so true. I did buy a woolly shirt, but only one, and on a mild day I took it off to wash it and for two or three days I didn't wear it, and so I got bronchitis. Before that I had another strange repulsive illness—my whole body and face covered with bright red spots and swollen. It was horrible. This lasted almost a week. It came, the doctor said, from eating shellfish. And now I think of America as a country where there is a most strange genius for comfort, where one can have a delicious poached egg on toast and doctors are sensible people instead of fantastic figures out of the Middle Ages curing everything with three methods—cupping glasses, mustard plaster, and a little pill of mashed potato.

Everything changes every day. Toshihiko is unbearable and then lovely. Last night he came and after a very merry evening of singing and playing victrola and drawing each other, suddenly he was very severe to me and

went off very coldly. I thought, Well, I won't see him again for a long time. This morning he appeared feeling so benign and humorous—wearing beret—and had breakfast with me—and sat and made two lovely drawings of me all the morning. He is in a very triumphant mood because he has begun to paint again after a spell of doldrums. Last night he was like a prince again, very aristocratic-looking and so intelligent—leaning over the victrola. He was making a victrola needle out of a match—so it would be very soft and the hotel wouldn't tell us to stop playing. He just had to hear Josephine Baker again and again singing, *"J'ai deux amours, mon pays et Paris,"* because he was learning the words. One thing about him that is really unique in this world is the honesty—it breaks all rules of politeness and kindness. But somehow when you get used to it—it makes the regular politeness taste terribly flat. He is like a bitter tonic—but then he is also so childishly merry sometimes.

Tonight I am *seule,* and I am beginning to think one needs a female companion in the absence of something else. I'm sick of living alone, and yet in Patchin Place it was what I wanted—probably on account of Dr. de Forest at that time. I read a book called *Marriage in India,* written in a stupid way and yet showing the inexorable tragedy of interracial marriage. Very interesting and especially to me—the autobiographical account of American girl married to an East Indian and at last, a failure.

Something makes the thought of Taro come back to me—very close again, and I find myself crying as I have not for so long.

But I can't think of Taro—it's too much—and I have learned not to. It's too much for every day—it's intolerable to think of that quality of his and the being he transformed me into for a little while. Even the clothes I wore then seem to possess magic when I see them and touch them now. That was my real spring. It's something to measure everything else by. I only hope he remembers once in a while, those hot evenings in New York and "the time of apple blossoms." I think I have put it at last where it belongs—in the past, not in the present or the future. That kind of feeling doesn't go with ordinary life. It can't perhaps—it is too much—and I am glad it stopped when it did. It is just as near as it ever was, and yet safe and can't be hurt, and it can't hurt me any more because I have left it now—complete and finished—with no more power to change or be reinterpreted. And for a lasting souvenir always fresh of that spring, there is the big painting hanging on the porch in Castine. How lovely it will be to go back and find it still over my bed.

I'm terribly sleepy now—I can't write very well. I stayed awake all night with a most irritating cough, which seemed to be splitting my appendix or something, and I remembered your warnings.

It is a curious irony that Toshihiko misses my letters so much. He says before I came he would open a letter of mine in the Dome and read it and be transported —out of what he calls this rotten reality—into another world. He says if I were in Castine and wrote that I was sick and taking citrate of magnesia, it would all have romantic glamour. He would imagine me lying on the floor by the fire, etc. But here when he sees me sick and sees the bottle of citrate of magnesia it doesn't have any glamour. The curse of the artist, and the art of writing letters, etc., as when you wrote the last time about the atmosphere I had given you in a letter describing this. I told him how funny that was. Just as I was hating all this, your letter came reflecting what I had written, and somewhere, somehow in this transit some transformation took place. We've been laughing at all this, laughing at ourselves—for these illusions and transformations. Do you remember the face-throwing game we used to play with Philip? One makes an awful face and then wipes it off with the hand and throws it at somebody else, who has to reproduce it, and then make another awful one and throw it at somebody else. Last week I felt very rotten and desolate, and Toshihiko was very excited and pleased and happy painting so much and so well. Then two or three days later he lost this felicity and sank again. He said it was like the face-throwing game. I felt better and he felt worse—had caught my face—and now is looking for somebody else to throw it at.

I can hear the rain on the window in the roof. These days are so short, it's hard to do anything—so little light and besides I wake up so late, since *la grippe,* rather tired —breakfast at one o'clock—then *sortir*—today to Bon Marché simply to buy tea tray and frying pan—took all the afternoon in that crazy *mêlée* of French department store. Large oblong *papier-mâché* tray—red with little gold stars —you know the kind. Yesterday T. D. asked for tea and I had to borrow teapot from restaurant next door, and had no tray except large block of watercolor paper and two cups, one large and one small, and sugar in paper bag. It takes so long to establish these little things. Next Sunday I must go to the Flea Market to find tea set.

I have been drawing—pencil portraits of Elliot, two of myself, Edith Farnsworth. Now I want to get some exotic fishes to draw. I have seen a shop, Aux Poissons Exotiques, but now I can't find it again. The names of shops—Aux Rêves des Mamans, full of babies' jackets and bibs; Aux Corsets Merveilleux. Too silly, I think.

I hate Paris most of the time. It seems like something dead—ashes—and smells always everywhere of the *lavabo.* It really is a kind of nightmare. Toshihiko thinks one should endure it—that there is some kind of necessity for enduring it. This is probably true for him, for his painting. He doesn't want to escape—or rather, he doesn't believe in escaping. He wants to get to the bottom of it. I think it is his attitude and desperateness which affect me so much. He takes everything so hard. When we are together it is as if we were both exiles, homesick for Castine. He is always fighting against his feelings, which makes them worse. There isn't any reason that I see why I should endure it. I'm not fighting to be a painter. And yet perhaps there is a reason. I shall know that it isn't easy to live in a foreign country, and I think of what it would have been if I had gone to Japan—where I would have been so much more alone. I miss so many people—you, particularly, and Ranie and Kitty and Ann, and the sense of familiar places. I realize now what it was for Toshihiko to be sent off to America so young to face not only a strange language and strange country, but everywhere to be shown the idea that he belonged to an inferior race—after being brought up as an aristocrat in an aristocratic country.

I keep thinking what a terrible climate to have a war in. Bad enough to get used to in peace, but with bombs in addition must have been terrible.

I seem to write most disconnectedly. Please don't mind. I am in bed in the room in the hotel which I took when I was sick. Tomorrow I think I'll leave it and sleep in atelier again. I feel comfortable and peaceful now—tomorrow I'm going to get up early and go out and buy dishes. I must establish a little domesticity. I think it will be better to be able to have people come for tea and supper. I do enjoy going shopping, or rather not shopping. I hate the department stores, but I love walking, and I can walk a long way nowadays and begin to know where things are.

141

14 février 1931

I FEEL like writing you a nice long cozy letter. It must be two o'clock in the afternoon. My atelier is really easy to look at now—very clean and with a beautiful rich red tapis on the floor, bought a week ago with Camille at the Flea Market. Just interrupted by Madame Balbainchki, with whom I had a semi-date to go to Flea Market this afternoon. She has just gone out to buy a little steak and milk to make lunch for me, and then I have to get myself together and proceed to Clignancourt (the Flea Market). I have been thinking often lately that I am getting to be more and more like Lottie. The thought haunts me as I see myself doing nearly all the things she used to do in the far-off days in Concord when Eleanor and I, two innocents, used to be quite annoyed at her habits. I stay awake all night and sleep all the morning; it's a habit that I have been trying to break. I don't know why it is I am more wide-awake and ambitious between twelve and four than any other time. Also I still smoke too much and eat rather irregularly. When I was first in Paris I began to feel like Lottie, and I dreamed one night that she was dead—which meant, I suppose, that I wished to be dead myself. But, there's a springlike feeling coming into me now, some kind of salvation, during the last two or three days, which comes from sudden dawning of the realization that the irritating, unsatisfying, pain-making intermittent presence of Toshihiko is the bottom of my trouble. And I've decided to be surgical, quick and neat use of the knife, and cut the connection. It's ridiculous how much I have let him bother me, and now that I've decided not to any more, the feeling of freedom is grand, like fresh air. Now I shall be able and free to enjoy Paris and other people.

Now I have come back from the cold Flea Market to

my warm fire, and I am lying on the floor on the red rug—
wine-color—with a glass of wine on the floor, cigarettes,
and your really too, too marvelous letter which I found
when I stepped out to go to the Flea Market, and read in
the Métro—and read over again in the Métro coming
back and read over again now lying on the wine-colored
rug. It's the best letter—it gave me more pleasure than
anything for a long time.

One can only laugh at life after seeing such things.
And one laughs better after using the knife, I am
sure. I haven't yet seen Toshihiko since deciding this. It
really is better to do this. I have only been really happy
with him perhaps twice—once when he asked me to mend
his overcoat and another time when he talked in a certain
way one evening. It's ridiculous. The sweet quality is
gone, or buried somewhere very deep, *et je n'aime pas.*
But why submit to any suffering? Why passively wait for
a few crumbs? *Allons!* Give it up! Be free—*Ça ne marche
pas.* When one has used the knife one is free, otherwise
there is a cloud over one and nothing else seems attractive.
I would advise the same for you.

I'm sure that's what Elliot thinks. I mean, either endure
or escape. And the escape gives wonderful relief from the
uneasiness and uncertainty and continual listening for
telephone or key in keyhole. Toshihiko knows that he has
lost something. He says, "Something is dead in me," but
he doesn't know how to find it again. It seems so simple—
like the hummingbird I am always referring to that got
caught in my Thimble and flew back and forth under the
ceiling for two hours while the door and windows were
open all the time. We are all like that, perhaps. We suffer
unnecessarily, willfully.

Encore: le jour prochain—dimanche 12:30 p.m.

I have been out, Métro to Chatelet to take a little birthday present to Camille, a little perfume bottle—Canton

china with silver top I bought yesterday at the Flea Market. At top of Métro stairs was a flower peddler with violets. I got a little bunch for one franc for Camille, and walked across Pont Neuf to Quai de l'Horloge. Concierge said, *"Ils sont sortis—tout de suite! tout de suite—il y a deux minutes!"* So I walked in the direction of the garage but could not find them, so came back here with my little presents and violets. And it's nice here. I am beginning to be happy and feel so free, getting rid of the burden of Toshihiko. I look quite nice today—the gray hat just came back from the Nettoyerie, and I have on the black and green plaid velvet dress—*et je suis heureuse.*

17 février 1931

It's the next morning, and stenographer is correcting letter, numbering pages and putting in envelope. This letter dictated to me by Toshihiko will probably make you laugh. It was written between midnight and 1 A.M. Toshihiko lying on my sofa, and I lying on the floor. This is the way the evening ended when I told him I didn't want to see him any more.

DICTATED BY T.Y.

Dear C-Catharine.

How are you? I am not so good. Tonight I came to see K-Katharine at her own studio because she wrote me a letter that *je ne te recevrai plus,* but she wasn't either dead or cuddling with any Parisian gigolo, and I found that was only another form or style you might say of her urgency of my paying her duly homage that I have been obliged to overlook on account of my getting busy for sending off my cousin—couple who have been here as a military attaché to the Embassy of Imperial Japan.

As nothing really happened to Katharine except few

activities, *nostalgique, hystérique* strictly personal to the feminine gender, after talking about Hirota, from whom we both received letters, then having gone to supper at a small restaurant about five doors from the Coupole, of which proprietor whose face is angelically beaming with great deal of rollo (rollo made synthetically with cognac) whom I take Katharine, Katharine has found rather agreeable because his looks rather agitates her monotonous gray day life of Paris in spite of Montparnasse, of course I found rather a bore to see Katharine's red rug which she thinks it's wonderful bargain at the Flea Market and see her lying down like a antiquated odalisque, so I amuse myself dreaming of you C-Catharine, of the Beacon Hill. Incidentally, in Paris it happens to be hailing slightly. The sound of this against Katharine's obliterated skylight of studio makes a sound as though you might have been eating rather fragile crackers in a corner of your Pinckney room of what-you-may-call-it style, but Catharinely attractive.

This reminds me of the time when you sat in the kitchen of Katharine's Castine house, your back against one of the two windows that gave a view to the yard beside the table upon which white and red checkered tablecloth was spread. Katharine was standing with cigarette in one hand somewhere between you and stove, and I don't remember that was after our drive to Penobscot or else just late morning around eleven o'clock which we felt rather timid for asking Mrs. Olsen to toss her belly * to make another breakfast for the late wakers. At any rate, the sun was shining sweetly upon the yard and the rays slanting in the window and made tablecloth look rather fuzzy. Well, I ought to be able to figure it out if it was afternoon or

* This is a Japanese expression T.Y. says when speaking of a fat person making an effort—"wrinkle one's belly to do so and so."—K.B.

morning if I manipulate angle of the kitchen, but it is not essential to what I want to say to this. The thing I really want to say is you then made funny noise with your front teeth when you were eating. I think it was Melba toast of which one is *incroyable* that such a fat woman as Mrs. Olsen could produce. Either Katharine or I said, "You eat like rabbit," and you smiled shyly and yet gladly, not offended by the saying of either of us, then you did some more of the same thing as though a delightful secret of one's habit was found so amusing to the audience. This might happen rather often to a vaudeville artist very genuinely, but they only spoil it with trying to make it better or unsubtle. I can never forget that because you yourself didn't knew your delightful habit, and we felt all of the three found some little flower in an unexpected spot of woods, but this does not apply that every woman should eat like a rabbit. It needs funny knot upon the special coiffure, it needs rather sallow face, large eyes a bit wetty, in a way intellectual, not I mean in its extreme sense of mathematical intellectualism, but something like pre-Raphaelitic, and a certain kind of naïveté as though white cloud slowly moving around the high tower of the Arthurian tale. (I just asked Katharine whether my stenographer understands this metaphor or not, then she proudly said, tossing her blondy curls, "Yes.")

I think I received your letter sometime last year. Thank you very much. I wanted to answer—never could. My life seems to me rather cockeyed. Just don't know what-the-hell-I-am-doing. In a way I think I am doing fairly well: like the average young painter of mediocre category passed Salon d'Automne, exhibit in the Independent Show, etc. But somewhat I daresay I feel cockeyed, very egotistical (this Katharine claims very much) self-centered, and frightfully *nostalgique* to somewhere I cannot tell to myself. It might be somewhere in the seventh heaven, but *I ain't got no ladder. That* sounds rather boring, degenerating, but I am it.

I look around every corner of Katharine's studio, but I don't find any of my thought hanging there, and I am well consummated my desire to write you tonight. The stove has consummated some coals and going beautifully now. I ought to be going beautifully now with the thought that I have written you such a long letter.

The hail stopped. Your image has gone. I shall be going home, but I don't like to think of the dark corner where *sales types* hang around to hold me up for money I really can't spare. In spite of my increasing my age, I am adding to my feeling more things I am scared of in this life. I am not afraid of ghosts, spirits, like that, but the most I am afraid of and scared of is the human being, especially the species that have long curly hair that chirps like a bird and smiles like a butterfly.

You see, even well-regulated trolley car of a great city such as Paris or New York derails sometimes without bit of alcohol, so please just consider that such an insignificant person as Mr. Yamaguchi could be derailed for a mere incident not accident.

I am living 32 bis rue de Cotentin, Paris (15e). If you also happen to be derailed in the course of your time, please write me, just as a report that will be all right. If I keep on dictating Katharine like this, I shall be, and probably Katharine will be so cockeyedly derailed that our cars won't go again. I am really tired. I suppose Katharine must be. As an epilogue, I sincerely would like to show my gratitude to Miss Katharine Butler of Castine, commonly known as Hocus pocus Kitty in Montparnasse for her untiring endeavor to produce much anticipated letter. Without her help I could never have done it. In showing this unworthy gratitude of mine (I am balled up) I want to thank her for her kindness.

Toshihiko

21 février 1931

10 P.M. Anne has been here twice in the last two days— one evening for drawing—we had a young Russian gentleman as model. Anne and I decided to make masks for ourselves and go out in the street wearing them, as it was Mardi gras. We made beautiful ones but the young Russian was too dignified to wear his, which I made—a bluebeard —for him and he ordered Anne and me to take ours off as we stood on a curbstone on Blvd. Montparnasse. I with long smiling white doll's face, beautiful red smile, and green eyebrows; and Anne with long, thin, ghostly face with rippling white beard. A. and I were crushed and disappointed. Yesterday afternoon Camille brought a young Frenchman to tea to meet Anne, as he is protégé needing young friends. So I have passed two days presenting young men to Anne, which Dorothy is delighted with—the evening before these events Anne took me to Russian ballet.

I have gone to bed earlier than usual, hoping to sleep, but now wakeful. I turned on the light, ate an apple, lighted a cigarette, and found pen and paper.

Elliot keeps saying very extravagant things about my talent for drawing and urges me to paint. I have bought paints but not tried them yet. He looks at every new drawing and says only two or three people in the world, including Picasso, can draw as well as I, and that if I work and learn to paint I could be world-famous. I suspect him of being drunk, but he says it drunk or sober, and if I laugh he says rather crossly that he knows good draw-

148

ing when he sees it. But in spite of the fact that I have made a number of portraits in pencil, and believe really that I am improving, I have only done it halfheartedly. Toshihiko's disturbing presence has been like a paralysis on me. When he is coming in and out in all his varying moods, my instinct is always to be what I always was with him—a listener, a consoler, simply a woman; and this mood is utterly contrary to creative mood. If I am an artist, I am neither a man nor a woman. It is intense, impersonal, and nonhuman. It kills the impulse to go out toward him or any other man, I think.

But today Camille played a trick on me. She took me to the Louvre—the first time, and I felt irresistibly a power rising in me which says "to hell with T.Y.; put all this devotion and patience and faithfulness and adaptability and love into painting." All the things one longs to have understood by another human being, which never are—the grand, tender, amorous, fierce feelings—put them into designs. Let one's hand become electric and amorous and very proud.

The joy I felt in the Louvre made me so sure that good painting—healthy painting or other works of art—come from superabundant consciousness and delight in existence. Not as an escape from hated life—as Toshihiko seems to think. It's only when I've been made unhappy by someone else that I have needed any escape. By myself I enjoy living, whereas Toshihiko despises it, finds no freshness, no simple pleasure, always trying to find some way of getting a kick out of something, having exhausted simple things, seeking grotesque things—so he says.

Unless I do this active creative thing, I am subject only to the wild despair which we both know so well, being hurt, injured, disappointed, vulnerable. As soon as you pick up your own self, your own tools, then you are armed, and strong, and happy, and active instead of passive. You lose the very soft subjugated quality which is part of your flesh, your aura of yielding. But if you have experienced this terribly fully and know it in your blood—perhaps the hour has come for expressing it and so leaving it—saying good-by to all that—have a fling—a kind of cosmic fling of cosmic joy. It's terrible to be a female artist who has never known *l'amour,* not knowing what it is you are substituting art for. But if you have known—*voilà* your strength and your triumphs.

What makes the world go round? Nothing but love. And it is certainly love that makes one paint, or makes me paint. It's a childish joy of love. According to Toshihiko it is competition, and escape from "rotten reality." It is with him nostalgia—I think, very neurasthenic, and very limited—unliberated. I feel like giving him a surprise. And yet with me it's ambition—it's not the pursuing devil that I used to feel a long time ago, in writing—that I *must* fulfill the expectation with which I was surrounded. The expectations of one's family because of one's alleged talents. I don't care what anybody expects. I would almost rather live perfectly idle, unknown. It is only this uprising of queer joy and sense of power in my hand—a grand pleasure within reach. I really want to do quite bold things.

You can see from this letter that I am in better health. Your letter was so sweet that came this morning about my being sick. I think I'm past that now ... getting up ... eating another apple, turning on victrola ... Carl Sandburg ... straight up to heaven and straight right back—all night long. When I'm gone, gone, gone, when I'm gone to come no more, Children, I know you're going to miss me when I'm gone! Maybe this letter is a little crazy. It's all from going to the Louvre. C. took me quite casually—then while we were there, I felt so much and I told her she had done something fatal. She said, "I meant it to be."

150

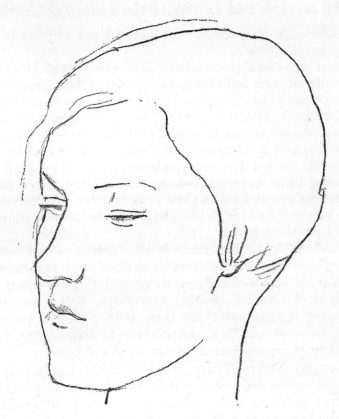

CAMILLE PAUL

Now I'm all waked up! It's disappointing I have had so much trouble about sleeping—never able to sleep until morning and half the daylight wasted. C. is coming to pose for me tomorrow—probably just as I'll be waking up. She is so good to me—adorable. She has at last got a maid to come on Monday, and from then on she says she must try to write some articles to send to U.S. to the *New York Times*, and wants me to go around with her making illus-

151

trations—collecting scenes and material out of Paris life. Wonderful idea—

Next day—Sunday—*très beau jour!* I've begun! Making drawing of two full-blown yellow tulips and dropping leaves—*que je suis heureuse!* Just resting now—Josephine Baker singing idiotic song victrola—more coal on the fire—*tout le monde chante ce matin, j'ai dit au garçon,* and he said, "*Ah oui! C'est parce qu'il fait beau aujourdhui—tout le monde est gai.* He wants to pose for me. He is such a cunning little Auvergnois—from town of Roquefort. My neighbors are singing as they work in opposite studios—two young Spaniards in one and old Frenchman in other, and I am singing, too.

Sunday Night— Just came in after sitting in café with Camille, and lighted two candles in front of the two drawings I did today—the dying tulips and this afternoon a portrait of Camille—gloating over them. *Très heureuse!* Drawing is more satisfying than writing ever was—perhaps because wordless and dealing in form—using the hand to caress—an intense caress of the object.

Tuesday Night— Today, laughing at the lovely fun, I bought apples and tulips, put three red tulips in pitcher, opened paintbox, and made a very funny painting—like a baby learning to walk. But really I couldn't help laughing and giggling while I was doing it—like an orgasm—really too delicious.

Yesterday Toshihiko came in and a strange conversation developed in which he told me that he has been thinking ever since I came to Paris that I am in the same state over him as I was in Castine, and after I told him I was not, and really tried to persuade him, it was as if this queer burden were lifted off both of us and for the first time there was real *nonbili* and intimacy and gaiety between us. I have felt like laughing ever since with joy.

It was natural for him to think so, I never explained how deep an effect Dr. de Forest had on me, and how utterly cured I am of being capable of masochistic love again. The thing that has irritated me so long and hurt me so has been that I thought we could feel so free and happy without my ridiculous obstinate desire, and somehow it was still not free and I didn't know why.

I misinterpret myself whenever I suffer over anything. That sounds rather false to you, probably, as if I were deserting the ship that we are all floating in. But, really, I do begin to think that we can step out of the door like the hummingbird. It's open all the time. Why cling to something that isn't good? Of course, like any animal, there is an anguish and a cry, but there is a terribly stormy strong force of healing if you only let it work. We seem to resist the vitality of healing—we really wish to suffer.

I dreamed last night arrived back in Castine and driving my old car, which I found there. The always marvelous feeling of driving around the town for the first time, and breathing in the air, and then I felt the gasoline tank getting empty and got out to look at the gauge in the back and found the whole back of the car changed, and recognized the beautiful old mahogany stern of an old ship had been substituted, as I supposed, by the Dennetts. There was old scroll writing on it—dates, etc., and "Raina, the ship that will never sail again." What does that mean, I wonder!

[TO DR. DE FOREST]

March 6, 1931

PARIS *minuit*, very still in the courtyard of the Hôtel de Blois, only the very muffled roar of the Métro underneath, and somebody, *un peintre Espagnol*, shaking the ashes out of his stove in the studio opposite. I am in bed, the fire in the stove burning nicely, window open, red tapis from the Flea Market spread richly on the floor, on the walls all my little Castine drawings in pale frames. I am smoking a cigarette, very cheap Maryland James, and putting the ashes very tenderly into the little blue China slipper from —now I can't think where it was from, Shanghai or where —which Hirota gave me last spring, a pair of them.

I have been sick quite a lot in this terrible Paris winter climate, and one doctor said I was threatened with tuberculosis. That was about three months ago, and I haven't dared to go back and see him, although I have a really bad cough which doesn't seem to be the kind of vomiting cough of not liking something. Still, I really can't believe that I have got tuberculosis, because it doesn't seem to be my kind of a thing to have. I don't feel at all related to it, although his theory was that the fact that I once had it in the spine makes me specially susceptible, an idea I never heard before.

One reason why I am telling you of having been sick is because I wish to send you the money. In spite of it I am confidingly writing you a letter, still feeling a claim upon you, besides many, many times wishing to come back to you and lie on the sofa day after day and tell you all the things that have accumulated since then—much too much to write on these small pieces of pink paper. Many things about last summer, about Maine, to which I often long to return, liking it in a way better than anywhere else, feeling safe and knowing that whatever craziness I may have or whatever fluctuations, it will always contain me, the most peaceful feeling of all.

Long pause here, meditating, Castine-loving pause. I feel like taking the next boat. Perhaps partly because this afternoon I was at Waldo Pierce's, and he and I talked about Bangor and Orland and Penobscot Bay, each knowing the same language of those places, and he showed me some pictures in a scrapbook of those places.

Now I am staring at a lovely little *pâtisserie* which is on a plate near by, and it begins to look rather succulent. And coincidentally it begins to seem hopeless to write you any more.

In my desperate moments I always think of you. There have been some desperate ones in Paris—*comme l'enfer.*

Listen, I think the Japanese spell is broken. I feel quite indifferent to my Japanese, as if the cycle is finished. I can't forget or cease treasuring those poignant experiences, but the poignance is not active now, only a memory.

[To CATHARINE HUNTINGTON]

dimanche soir
8 mars 1931

I'VE been painting nearly every day—canvases getting bigger and bigger. I do it in the most ignorant way. I feel it is a great joke while I am doing it, but Elliot admires the result and says anybody ought to be killed who teaches me anything. He says I paint like Henri Rousseau, which I know is a great compliment. But really I don't know what I am doing, and I am absolutely blind as to whether it is any good or not. Only it is fun—it is really a wonderful feeling, the electricity between the hand and the object— that's all, and so absorbing hours pass unnoticed. But the result doesn't really interest me. I can't see anything in it, and I can't see why anybody wants pictures. It seems just a one-sided pleasure, only for the one who does it. I know I never used to like looking at paintings. I remember long ago going to exhibitions with you, and I felt as if something were missing in me. I couldn't feel them at all. Pleasure of making them seems entirely different—although maybe after making them I might see exhibitions differently. Paintings that I like I think I only like for personal reasons, or some personal quality. Elliot tells me to do everything life-size. Today still life, life-size half-apple, seeds showing—two tulips in pitchers, and a bunch of paint brushes in cup.

I had supper tonight for four francs! Went to the kitchen door of the restaurant, a little cubicle in the courtyard—the maids and *patronne* are so very nice, great friends—and got macaroni au gratin and lettuce. While the maid was fixing the lettuce we could see through the square hole going into the passage in the dark, very narrow little dark place, the arms and shoulders turning round and round of the cunning little *patronne* dancing with her husband, the husband a big tall, gay charming creature singing the dance music in a low voice. They had scarcely room to turn, and it was a dark passage—just a little corner. They stopped, and we could hear the wife gasping for breath, rather a fat little one, and the husband said in the most charming, adoring, humorous voice, "*Ah, ma pauvre vieille!*" The first night I was here I was standing at the kitchen door, and he leaped through and said, "*Bon soir, ma petite dame,*" to me. I've told you, I suppose, that when I have dinner *chez moi* with a guest, the maid comes running through the courtyard with the different courses, very sweet one, sings in the morning, just like Lurana's voice.

Just staring around the room at my pictures. The little Castine drawings are all framed, in frames of natural wood, light, without any trace of varnish or stain, like a Japanese box. Anne's idea and very successful. Also, a larger pencil drawing of the corner of this studio which is most depressing, old cracked washbowl, old dirty gas stove—pipes—meter, and little table and rickety towel-rack. This is framed in same light wood. I was just imagin-

ing packing all these things to go to America. Painting at
this rate, finishing a picture every other day, it is appalling
to think of the vast number that will accumulate—and I
suppose I will be too attached to them to throw them
away.

When I see my paintbox lying around now getting
splashed with paint, it seems terribly funny for me to be
the owner. I have always been the friend of owners of
paintboxes, and often held them carefully while the owner
drove, and never been an owner. It's very pretty—lovely
satiny wood on the outside.

In the mood of painting still lifes—such continual, almost insane infatuation for all objects, obsessed with every
shape and texture, and realize how endlessly the world
is filled with endless variety of objects—sea life, plant life,
ink bottles, stoves, and animals in zoos, plumbing, clothes,
musical instruments, beds, pillows—*c'est formidable!* This
word seems to solve everything in France.

March 13, 1931

SOMETIMES everything seems to come together in one spot.
I mean, past, present, future—no, not future, but past and
present. I just came across some pieces of unfinished
letters I wrote last year to you and to Taro, and to Toshihiko, and time folds back and it is all like different scenes
painted on a fan suddenly unfolded. Also, rather funny,
after writing you the other day about last Easter I just
found something I wrote, while we were lying on the
grass, a little memoir of that moment—saying you and
Elsie and I were lying in the sun and Frederick was comb-
ing and brushing Dorée. I am always so grateful for
having written down a little scene, and then after it is
forgotten it comes to the surface and is alive again.

157

Yesterday afternoon Elliot sent for me to make an illustration for his Sunday article, a drawing of one of the statues on the outside of the treasury building, so Camille brought her Ford and we sat there for a couple of hours attracting a crowd while I nearly broke my neck looking up high at the statue and sitting half out of the car. The drawing pleased Elliot very much and will appear day after tomorrow. He says we can do a lot more things like that—I can do illustrations for his articles.

Now I am in a rage with the *lavabo,* which is entirely broken, and the good patient little *garçon* is struggling with it. The patron should buy a new one, but will not—which puts me in a rage, because I have improved the atelier already very much, and he does nothing for me, an amiable but slow and stupid man who never does anything, only comes and stares helplessly and politely, wearing always gray spats, and then disappears.

After all, this is more amusing than Boston or New York. Now that I am used to it I'm getting rather fond of the crazy Dôme and feeling at home knowing the waiters and seeing the same people sitting around—getting a smile now and then. But I'm rather unresponsive to strangers.

All the time, ever since I came, this Paris consciousness seems like a queer dream, really not my kind, not really pleasant except at times, and I often feel as if I would wake up in the faraway pearls and sapphires of Castine dawn, and I'd see the apple blossoms again, and that would be· the only real thing I have ever known. If you should keep these Paris letters, and I should look at them later, it would probably explain to me what I don't know now—what kind of a period this is, and what is the matter, as fundamentally something seems to be. I think of last summer—the radiance of Castine, the wonderful peacefulness of the desirous elms—the slow rhythm of that, and the lightheartedness time—and all that does seem such a lovely innocent time.

[TO DR. DE FOREST]

April 18, 1931

YES, they are selling mimosa on the street, women with shawls on, crying in shrill voices, "*J'ai de petits enfants,*" also violets and little purple pansies. Nevertheless the women need their black knitted shawls. It's cold and gray still, after a few days of lovely spring when the awnings were rolled back and the braziers carried away and all of Paris was like a huge flower suddenly opening its petals. But now "rough winds do shake the darling buds of May."

There are too many things to tell you. I am still in Paris, and uncertain whether to stay through the summer or go back to America. A rather uncommunicative French doctor is treating me for some sort of vague suspicion of tuberculosis. And I feel as if I could write a lovely book about winter in Paris, especially in the damp sunless studios of Montparnasse where one hears choruses of people coughing their lungs out and sees the pale faces on the venereally diseased. I have been paying this winter for all my sins of cruelty, selfishness, and egoism; and I have learned just how it feels to be on the other side of these unlovely characteristics. It seems as if I am fated to play all roles at one time or another.

I know how your eyes will look while you read this letter, and I am grateful that your eyes exist in this world. It's lovely to think of them, and I can't make any excuses for giving them that look again. I can't believe that psychoanalysis will empty the world of the kind of happenings and bewildered half-wits, like me, which find in a few rare eyes that rare look. It's worth the suffering.

Do you want me to come back?

The Journals and Letters of the Little Locksmith

[To Catharine Huntington]

21 avril 1931

Your last letter, written on Easter Day when you were suffering, just breaks my heart. I suppose the mood has passed now, and I oughtn't to remind you, but I am afraid it's a mood that is always in the next room and the door not shut even when it doesn't really possess you. I recognize it as one of my own familiars too, even in different circumstances; but I find it is so easily driven away, changed like Alice in Wonderland into nothing but a pack of cards, by some very simple diversion. With me the tension is relieved just by quite simple interchange with some nice friend. What seems to be tragic doesn't really need a sublime cure, as one might suppose. At least in my case, a mood that seems to be tragic can be quite ridiculously charmed away by playing dominoes with somebody, as if one could fool a tiger by giving it an ice-cream cone. So I cherish these little games—anything that alters solitude, too much of which is certainly poisonous. I used to like it and enjoy it in Patchin Place, but not now. Or, to speak again of the tricks of disarming the tiger, just now it would amuse me to tell you that the stove is roaring and there is rain on the roof, and I can hear my Spanish neighbor singing. This isn't very successful as a charming picture, but to go into it further, to play with it and cajole it, takes away for a while anyway the feeling I might be having of curses and despair. It's all a trick, like distracting a baby's attention. Subtle tricks are notoriously more successful than raging storms of feeling.

At the present moment my visit to Germany and afterwards to Elliot has stopped me from working, but I hope to begin something soon. Camille came back from Spain two nights ago, and today I brought my things and my self back to my own place. She had a very thrilling time

in Spain, but I wasn't a terribly successful substitute for
Elliot. It was grand for several days, and then he disappeared and got cockeyed, as he says, and everything
went to pieces. He was lovely to me, though. We wandered around together to exhibitions and cafés and Lux-
embourg Gardens until the cockeyed episode began, and
then I had to amuse myself. I was very glad to have
Camille back again. In spite of the slack times—the
stretches of solitude—or, no, not stretches but the lack of
continual intimacy of one other, which one is always
nervously conscious of in spite of other very nice connections—this terrific fundamental lack is always with me,
but apart from that there have been many interesting
things and encounters. It would make a nice book—to describe this winter in Paris, Toshihiko, Grace, her beau
named Ivan, so tall and huge with such large, curious,
sleepy eyes—also Madame Balbainschky and her son
Percy, John Weld and his wife, and my *garçon* and my
neighbors and the sounds and sights all around. It rather
pleases me now to think of writing this; I'm beginning to
want to do something after three years of not even wanting to. I'm grateful for this terrible winter in Paris. I've
learned a few little things, I think. Toshihiko is so much
like me in egoism, selfishness, and cruelty—qualities which,
when we were together, we called something else, the
necessary elimination by the artist of certain human obli-
gations. But this year, not being part of him as I was
before, I have begun experiencing the boomerang. I have
been the passive participant of these qualities. I can't
blame him or myself—only I can enjoy a certain enlightenment of realizing what it feels like to be treated as I have
sometimes treated others. The truth is by nature he is
good and generous, but somehow he isn't flexible or on
a very large scale, and he can't do one thing without

eliminating every other thing. He can't skim over many things.

Short interval of going to the Dôme from 4:30 to 6:00 in very happy mood—hungrily eating cheese and brioches and coffee, and feeling almost saintly peacefulness and pleasure. And when one feels happy and content and rather like a flower opening its petals, it's funny how waiters have friendly smiling eyes, who, other days, are blank or cold.

In spite of everything I shall miss Paris after I am back in America. I'm sure of it.

6. *Interlude in the Haute Savoie*

[TO DR. DE FOREST]

In the Alps
15 or 16 mai 1931

IF YOU remember *The Magic Mountain*, you will know what this is like, only instead of a grand sanatorium it is a cheap little three-story hotel, with bare unpainted floors and stairways, coarse lace curtains in windows, little balconies that shake and threaten to fall off, a filthy-smelling cabinet with toilet which never flushes, a café in one side of the hotel where workmen who are working on a new sanatorium come and eat and drink and dance and sing and play cards all night—just like the chorus in an opera, really —as they gesticulate and sing and lift their glasses. In the little dining room apart from the café are three tables, and I find myself in a very jolly atmosphere—also *très sympathique,* in a way. They are very attentive and nice to me, very informal running in and out of my bedroom, bringing bouquets of Alpine flowers and looking at my drawings and making rendezvous for their own portraits. Next to me sits a young French boy born in America, his father in New York in silk business making frequent trips to Japan, a pretty French girl, very young with both lungs gassed; a blond Jew who runs a store connected with the

163

Grand Hôtel de Mont Blanc; a young French woman, ex-trained nurse; a very handsome French boy who works in the Grand Hôtel part of each day; Monsieur Georges, a Russian ex-officer in White Army, once living in New York and before the revolution stationed in Canada at the head of some sort of Allied testing ground for high explosives. All of them have tuberculosis. I don't know what I am doing here except that it's near the sanatorium where Grace is, and I thought it would be nice to have a dose of sun and air. It is lovely to see pear trees in blossom and forget-me-nots and lilies-of-the-valley growing wild in the grass and Alpine sun.

MY STORY—Grace would tell it another way, Jacques certainly still another way. And Marcel would probably never tell it at all.

It was a lovely graceful May morning when I came there the first time. I took the night train from Paris. At first I couldn't sleep because I was so excited to be taking a journey. And when I woke in the morning and pushed up the curtain and saw plowed earth and trees in blossom, I knew suddenly how terribly unhappy I had become during the winter in Paris. Something, not only on account of Toshihiko, like a heavy stone suddenly melted in me, and when I looked out the train window I felt as if I had been dead a long time and had just opened my eyes and just begun to breathe. The train stopped at Bellegarde about six o'clock long enough to step down on the platform and take coffee and rolls from the little wagon there. And I knew again that I loved earth and garden and spring. It was wonderful to stand out there and smell blossoming trees and actually feel sunshine. I can't tell you how wonderful that morning was—as if just one little door had opened and all of the spring was there. I forgot to say that I had Lady with me, the little wire-haired terrier that

belonged to Irene. I never had a dog of my own, and I
had had Lady with me for two days before I left Paris;
and, although she had mange and her skin was quite bare
in spots, I was proud of her. She had such an elegant
little dancing step, and she knew just how to behave on
the train—sitting up very pleased and proud on the white
linen-covered seat of our luxurious couchette. *"Vous avez
votre petit guardien, Madame,"* the conductor said when
he stopped at the door of the compartment in the evening.
He smiled and the porter smiled, and she was allowed to
travel without any complaining from anybody.

The train stopped at Le Fayet, and we got off and went
out in front of the station to find the bus they had told
me about. It was lovely in front of the station, trees in
blossom and sunlight. The bus was standing there under
one of the big flowering trees. I told the bus driver I
wanted to stop at the Hôtel du Tourisme. He didn't seem
to know the place, and a fat smiling woman standing near
said, "Oh, yes, you pass right by the door now." It seems
they were rebuilding part of the regular road, and the
new detour passed the door of the hotel. They heaved my
trunk up on top of the bus, and I climbed in through the
door at the end, and Lady and I sat down on one of the
puffy brown leather seats, and a few other passengers got
in, and we started.

Then I rode for the first time up that wild swinging
mountain route that I knew so well afterward, walking
in my cloth sandal espadrilles or riding late at night in
Crottet's old Renault when we had been down in the
plain at the Café de l'Aérodrome. On that Sunday morning it was my first wide-eyed staring as the plain
dropped and we swung around the edge of the route as if
from the sky and I saw dusty feet walking, everybody,
workmen or visitors, carrying a cane. Whenever I noticed
anybody, it was always the human body climbing slowly

165

up the mountain prodding the ground with the cane, or else descending, swinging downward fast and light. And I was so happy to breathe that lazy sweetness of morning air. It was a world of steepness, people trained to it submissively by long habit of scrambling up or sliding down.

I hadn't seen mountains from the train or even from Le Fayet station because it was so enclosed by the trees and a wall. But as the bus climbed I stared with a most funny joy at the first peak I saw. Then the next minute we would swing round and up, and other mountains were facing me. Soon they were too high and too near, and they frightened me. I didn't like to look at the high ones. I liked the grass and the fields and the plowed gardens, and I tried not to look up too high. They were too frightening. The second gear kept grinding on and on. I was almost lying back horizontal in the seat as we climbed and climbed. We stopped at Passy beside the Hôtel Vallet and the Mairie. Then on and on, higher and higher. I got excited and nervous, and I was afraid the driver would miss my stop. It is such a bewildered, scared feeling to go for the first time to a place and not know where to call out to the driver to stop. But the other passengers knew all about it and said they would tell him. And in another minute I was stepping out of the bus with Lady pulling the leash, and the driver tumbled my trunk down beside the door, and the bus went on, and I was standing by the little high, narrow, rickety hotel beside the dusty road there where the bus had dropped me and the motion stopped.

The hotel was cream plaster with its name painted on the outside in tall red letters, and rickety painted balconies running round the second and third stories. The door into the narrow entrance was open, and it became all suddenly a lazy feeling of Sunday morning in spring, and through the little passageway there was the current of fragrant sunny air all with smell of wild flowers. Two or three workmen lounging in the sun and a dirty handsome girl with fluffy blonde hair, daughter of the patron, met me just inside the door. Phine, they called her, for Josephine, and she always looked at me with a rather lazy curious stare. She knew too much—a deep husky voice—powerful, not more than eighteen. She said they were expecting me, and Mr. Goudina would be back soon, and he had engaged a room for me. He had gone up to the sanatorium to see Irene.

We stood for a moment in the passage, and just then he came hurrying in from the dusty road looking for me with a kind of nervous politeness because he had been a second late. He was quite an elegant Russian, speaking English, and very polite to me—about fifty years old. "And here is Lady!" And he thanked me very politely for taking the trouble to bring Lady down from Paris for his daughter.

He took me upstairs and showed me my room. It was a slipshod little hotel, and the guests took care of themselves and each other, so it was Mr. Goudina who seemed to be my host. Phine didn't bother. Then he took me to show me his room, which he was quite proud of because it was on the corner at the back of the hotel where the view was. We stepped out of his room onto the rickety balcony, and there one would almost faint with wonder to see the vast plain below and on the left. I really didn't like to look because there was Mont Blanc, too vast, too high, and too white. There were three little doors opening onto the balcony from the three rooms on the back. There was hardly space for two people to stand, it was so narrow, and it was rather cluttered with a chaise longue in front of each door, and rugs and pillows. Mr. Goudina had an old torn screen, and the occupants at the other end had a piece of faded awning, so they could separate themselves for the *cure de silence.*

167

A young boy stepped toward us from the other end, and Mr. Goudina introduced him as Duran. Duran was about twenty-one, and he had a nice smile. He wore a blue shirt and shorts, and his knees were bare. He had an Alpine look. He talked fast. He was a French boy born in New York and brought back to France when he was ten years old. He wanted to show me everything and explain everything. He spoke American with a nice French charm. He asked me about my journey and then began to point out the different mountains to me, naming each peak, and I couldn't possibly remember. He traced the whole horizon with his finger. He and Mr. Goudina explained to me how they had thought the middle room between them would have been nice for me, but a sick girl had written at the same time to engage a room, and as she was sick and would stay several months it was being reserved for her. I was only expecting to stay two weeks, and I wasn't sick, so I had been given the only other vacant room, not a very nice one, overlooking the road and without a balcony. I was rather disappointed because I liked the idea of having a balcony even if it was so narrow and rickety. Duran took me inside to see his room and showed me a hand-woven scarf and said, "We are going to make some of these scarves to sell." And he showed me his photographs. He said, "We do developing and printing, and we sell these photographs." He told me about the big snowstorm they had had in the winter and showed me a picture he had taken of a snow scene.

He looked like a perfectly healthy boy, and I felt troubled somehow to see what a narrow life he was having and how little he seemed to realize that it was narrow. He said, "Miss Thompson looks very well. She is looking forward to seeing you." Mr. Goudina said there was one of the guests in the hotel, M. Boupart, who had a taxi, and I could engage him to take me up to the sanatorium at 4 o'clock after the *cure de silence.*

Then the lunch gong sounded, and they took me down to the dining room. It was a little narrow room, with three dirty table-clothed tables with scarcely room to walk between, yellow painted woodwork, and a door open onto the balcony and the hot Alpine sun. On the walls were three bad little watercolor pictures done by some former guest—the sort of feeble watercolors. Mr. Goudina introduced me to the others—Mlle Mercier, M. Dutri, M. Boupart, M. Baneau, and the coiffeur, whose name I never could remember. Duran and Mr. Goudina on each side of me talked with me in English, and once in a while in the midst of the loud and incessant conversation in French somebody would look at me and try to make a phrase in English.

I remember on that first day especially M. Baneau, who sat alone at a little table—a tall dignified man with red beard and narrow shoulders. He watched and listened and smiled, but talked very little. The others made a joke about his just having had his beard cut, and they said to him that he had made himself very beautiful. I wondered how tremendously bearded he had been before. It was a long thick curly one, parted in the middle. I was rather shocked by their treating such a dignified person so facetiously, and they did it, I could see, a little cautiously; but he responded with a benevolent smile, and he even blushed a little. I often noticed afterward that M. Baneau blushed easily. M. Dutri was the boldest one—a very bold boy, handsome and Jewish-looking. It was Dutri who always used to tip back in his chair against the wall and roar for Simone, the waitress, when she was busy serving in the workmen's dining room or down in the kitchen underneath. Suddenly if there was a pause in the meal, "Simone," Dutri would bellow, and Boupart would stamp his feet; and then if Simone didn't come the coiffeur too would shout, "Simone!" and somebody would bang a glass on the table. They never seemed to get tired of this amusement, and they were rather glad when Simone was slow so that they could roar and bang for her.

But all this was not so exaggerated the first day. I think they were a little quiet because a stranger was there. When lunch was over Duran told me about the *cure de silence,* how each person went to his room and rested from two to four, and nobody was supposed to speak. Mr. Goudina talked for me with M. Boupart and engaged him to be ready with his taxi at four o'clock to take me up to Praz Coutant to see Grace and to take Lady to see Irene. So Lady and I went up to my room on the third floor and took the *cure,* but I was busy opening my trunk and finding all the little things I had brought down from Paris for Grace—the little packs of cards, and darning thread she had asked for, and the little bedside reading lamp.

I can always remember the rough wooden stairs going up to my room. It was such a cheap, bare hotel, bare as a barn. I used to pass the workmen on the half-dark stairs going up and down to their rooms on the top floor. Nobody spoke to them or paid any attention to them. It was almost as if they didn't really exist—just shadows in their white dusty clothes. They used to climb up slowly at night as if they were terribly tired, and they would glance diffidently at me, or two would be talking together in low voices as they climbed. I noticed their cloth sandals with laces tied around the ankles. As I passed the little window on the landing I could see the roof of Sancelleuros—the new sanatorium among the trees—and higher up in the forest a little glimpse of Praz Coutant and the crazy bare peak that thrust into the blue sky above Praz Coutant.

When I remember going that first time up to Praz Coutant, winding up the serpentine loops of that steep road through the forest, I remember all the later times in the big bus with slippery seats, and I remember the last time of all when I went alone on foot on a Sunday morning to meet Marcel and go into the forest and sit with him there. *"Une jolie cascade!"* He pointed up at it as we entered the forest.

I had no idea where to find Grace. There was nobody in sight when we drove into the long driveway between the low buildings of the sanatorium. That bent sharp peak of gray stone seemed very near, and you could see two or three long white waterfalls pouring down the side of it. Boupart left me at the main entrance, and inside a severe lady in the office directed me into a parlor to wait. There was nobody there, and I stepped out of the long open window onto the balcony, holding Lady's leash. And I was standing there smoking a cigarette when a door at the far end of the room opened and Grace came in. She had on knickerbockers and a gray flannel shirt. She gave one wild excited look around and then saw me, and she rushed toward me and grabbed me in her arms and kissed me and hugged me. She was terribly excited. She is rather tall, and she has a sort of typical American girl's figure —lanky and graceful. I was excited myself also. She has short red-gold hair, very shiny and flat and soft, nicely waved in ripples around her forehead—penciled eyebrows and rouged lips. She has a Ziegfeld Follies look always, but quite unconscious and tomboyish about her clothes, or she was then, at least. She was terribly excited, asking me hundreds of questions and worrying right off about Lady and what the Sisters would say. She didn't like Lady at first. It shows how nervous she was then that she didn't like Lady. She just looked at her with disgust, as if her being there was an awful nuisance. She said, "Irene is outside. We'll have to go and see her right off. Anybody would think you were her friend and you came to see her

171

instead of me. She's crazy to see her damned dog. We'll have to go and talk to her now—that kid makes me sick the way she talks about you, as if she knew you. She could hardly wait for you to come. Imagine!" She said the sanatorium was like a prison and the Sisters were bitches. She was very nervous and jumpy about the Sisters. She always seemed to feel as if she was going to get caught doing something—and I got the feeling right off myself.

We met Irene in another little parlor. I began right off, even though I didn't know what any of the rules were, to sneak around with them as if we were all in boarding school.

There were several buildings. There was the main building on one side by the driveway, and on the other side was the little chapel and several chalets for girls. The nuns' chalets and main building were nearer the main road. Grace took me over to her chalet. We had to climb a steep little path and go around to the back door under the trees on the edge of a little forest. It was rocky and steep. Visitors weren't supposed to go into the chalets, but she took me just the same, trusting to luck that we wouldn't meet a nun or be watched from the windows of the main building.

Irene's hair was almost exactly the same color as Grace's —red-gold, and thick and curly. She was about twenty. She had a dumb pretty little face and a very pretty smile, but the cure had made her enormously fat. Irene was waiting for us in another little parlor. She flung out her arms to Lady, and Lady recognized her and danced and trembled. There was a great hubbub between them in the little room. Then Irene stood up, breathless and rosy, and thanked me for bringing her. She had a childish, wheedling, petulant voice and a childish way of talking. She had been a professional dancer in a cabaret in Paris when she suddenly broke down with t.b. a few months before. She

172

was married, and her name was Madame Dudon. Married to a rotten Frenchman, Grace told me. She spoke English very easily, and she was always talking about wanting to go back to America, where she had lived during part of her childhood. She felt very superior to the French girls in the sanatorium because they hated America, and she liked to impress them and infuriate them by telling them about the elevators and subways of New York.

"They are so provincial, so ignorant, they don't know anything, and they are so jealous," she said.

We talked for a while, and then the bell rang at 5 o'clock for the next *cure,* and Irene had to go upstairs to her room in the main building, and Grace said she would take me over to her chalet. I had to take Lady with me. Irene said good-by to Lady. She spoke French and Russian to her. Lady was supposed not to understand English.

Then Grace took me over to the chalet. She couldn't bear to let me go back to the hotel, and she wanted me to stay until 7 o'clock when the bell would ring for supper. That was the end of the last *cure* for the day and then she could come out of her room again and walk back to the main building with me and see me off. But she was very nervous on account of Lady, for fear one of the nuns would hear her barking in the room. I tried to make Lady lie on the bed and keep still. "If the Sister comes in, just cover yourself and the dog up with this blanket and maybe she won't see you."

She cursed every time Lady stirred or made a sound.

"You don't have to bring that damned dog every time you come up here, do you?" she said. "I won't have it in my room. It makes me too nervous. You can leave it with Mr. Goudina. Let him bring it when he comes up to see Irene. You've done enough, bringing it down from Paris. I know these Russians. You've got to be careful. They'll let you do everything if you don't look out. They're so

173

sorry for themselves, they are always taking advantage of everybody that is decent." She told me to be sure to make Mr. Goudina keep Lady in his room at night. She said if I let her sleep in my room the first night, I would have to have her all the time. She told me to be sure and tell him how much I had paid for Lady's ticket and to ask him to pay me. He had already paid me. He had been very punctilious about it that very afternoon, and it was sixty francs which was a good deal to him, I was afraid.

I was getting nervous about finding my way back to the hotel. The telephone office was always closed Sunday afternoon, and there was no way of getting a taxi. I had stayed over the last bus. Grace began to be nervous too. But she couldn't be seen coming out of her chalet until the bell rang at seven and neither could I. She told me it only took a few minutes to walk down to the hotel by the short cuts. She herself had never been out of the grounds of the sanatorium since the day she arrived, so she didn't know the way herself, but Mr. Goudina always walked down after calling on Irene, and he had told about his quick way of going by the short cuts. I was afraid, myself, of leaving the main road. Suddenly there was a mountain chill in the air and the sun was going down. Grace said I must wear her old polo coat and take her cane. The bell rang and we went out. "I'm worried about you. I ought not to have let you stay so late," she said. She had to say good-by to me at the main entrance, and I started down the broad winding route alone, with her heavy coat over my shoulders and the cane clattering on the little stones.

It's a lonesome sound on a steep road with nobody in sight and the vast mountains behind and in front of you. I was really frightened. I remembered the stories of people lost in the Alps. I hurried down the road, and my heart beat too fast with a panic of the huge mountains. The light seemed to be going very fast, and I was glad when

174

I met two or three workmen on the road, but the road turned so quickly that they disappeared in a moment and I was alone again. I stopped and thought I had almost better go back to the sanatorium and try to spend the night there, but it was a very steep climb to go back, so I went on again. At the next curve underneath some trees I saw a young workman stepping on the route from a footpath. I spoke to him and asked him how to go to Assy.

"*Je suis étrangère*," I said. "*Je ne suis pas habituée. Je ne connais pas la route. Est-ce que c'est loin?*"

I asked him if he had time to accompany me the rest of the way, and I said I would gladly pay him to guide me.

He looked at me rather gravely and softly and said he was *pressé* and he couldn't go all the way down. "*C'est assez loin à peu près, Mlle—une heure à pied.*" "It is rather far," he said. "It will take an hour on foot." But he took my arm and led me down the very rocky steep footpath through the trees until we reached the route again, having cut off a big loop. He stopped there and I thanked him and he wouldn't take any money. We stood there for a moment at the opening of the forest, in the cold gorgeous twilight. He stood quite close to me for a moment, looking at me, unsmiling yet silent and close as if he were going to kiss me. He was very young and had a solitary hushed face which I think the mountains sometimes give to one who is sensitive to them. He pointed to the lights just a little way below and said there was a hotel there where somebody had a taxi, and he said I could get the taxi to take me the rest of the way down. I hadn't remembered any little village between the hotel and the sanatorium, but he said it was a village of only three or four houses.

I said, "*Bon soir, Monsieur, et merci mille fois.*" "*Ce n'est rien, Mademoiselle. Bon soir, Mademoiselle,*" he said

in a soft grave voice, and he climbed back again, disappearing through the trees.

After that I was not afraid, and in about five minutes I reached the little inn. The door on the road was shut, and I couldn't open it. I went down to the side and the back. The back of the hotel was much lower than the front, on the steep hillside. I found a door there and a boy and girl standing outside. I half recognized the curly-

176

haired Phine, and I thought she must be a friend or relative of these people, but it's a little funny to see her again in another hotel, I thought. I was afraid I was going to be hours late for supper at my hotel. So I spoke badly and hurriedly, asking if there was somebody there with a taxi. I said I met a young man on the road who told me to ask here for a taxi. I want to go to Assy, I said, to the Hôtel du Tourisme. The girl seemed terribly stupid. She kept staring at me as if she didn't understand, and I kept repeating clumsily the same thing.

"*Mais vous êtes déja arrivée!*" she said. "*C'est Assy ici. C'est l'hôtel du Tourisme ici.*" She took me round to the front door and into the passageway, and I saw everybody sitting in the dining room.

"*Voilà M. Goudina!*" she said. "*Vous êtes arrivée!*" She laughed quite a rich laugh and went back downstairs.

Everybody exclaimed and shouted as Lady and I came into the dining room, and I had to tell how stupid I had been, and how I had misunderstood the young man or he had misunderstood me, thinking I meant Passy instead of Assy. Duran said they had all been wondering what had happened to me when the bus came down without me, and they were really beginning to be worried and to think what to do. I had to try to tell my story in French also because Dutri, the young man opposite me, asked me questions smilingly and insisted on my trying to explain to him. And Mlle Mercier, the thin little nurse with shrewd eyes close together, watched me and made polite comments. The little dining room seemed cozy and sheltering, though the electric light was very bright and the voices very noisy after being out alone on the dark mountainside. M. Baneau, the tall red-bearded man who sat alone, listened and smiled.

There was an old broken chair in the corner next to Mr. Goudina. He called for a special plate, and he asked for the scraps from everybody's plate and made Lady sit on the chair and eat her supper. He was very particular about her manners, and she was obedient and good. After supper I told him I would like to have Lady sleep in my room. I went against Grace's advice because I was really so attached to my little guardian, and I knew I would be lonesome without her. Duran went down to the kitchen and asked for a wooden box for her to sleep in. He put her in it, laughing as the box turned out to be rather small and she tried her best to fold her legs up neatly and get in. He carried her up to my room in the box, giggling because she looked so funny.

"M. Dutri asked me if I play bridge," I said to Duran as we were going up. "But I don't, unfortunately." There isn't anything to do in the evening.

"Vous jouez au bridge, Mademoiselle?" Dutri had asked me at supper and I said regretfully, "No." In the evening there was nothing to do, not like a boarding school. They gathered in each others' room and played bridge or developed films. Duran stopped for a moment in my room and arranged the box for Lady and then asked to look at my drawings. He talked about Paris galleries and said my drawings were like Foujita, the Japanese. He was excited when he thought about Paris.

"It's a year and a half since I have been in Paris," he said, "but I am going this month. I have got my ticket to the Exposition Coloniale, and I can stay in Paris for ten days. I stay with my grandmother in the rue Verneuil. If you are back in Paris then, let us meet at the Dôme and have *café crème* together."

He turned over my drawings again. They pleased him.

"Your line is very delicate," he said, "like the Japanese. Well, I have to go now. I promised Mr. Goudina I would help him develop some films. I hope you sleep well. Do you like your room? It's too bad you haven't got a balcony.

178

Well, good night. Do you come downstairs for breakfast or do you take it in your room?"

"Oh, I take it in my room," I said. "And I wonder what about letting Lady out in the morning?"

He said he or Mr. Goudina would come and take her out for me.

He went and I shut the door, and then I leaned out of my open window. I heard M. Baneau walk down the hall and go into his room next to mine. He turned on his light, and it shone out on his little balcony. Down below I could see the dark shapes of the little pear trees, and the edge of the road as it turned at the corner of the hotel. I could hear the workmen singing in their café dining room down underneath me on the ground floor and the café light shining out on the ground and touching the edge of the pear tree. I felt lonely and excited, and I wondered why I was there. I thought about Grace, and I wondered how soon I would speak to her about Alec. I was glad I was there, leaning out of the window. The exciting air of the mountains made me happy and expectant, yet terribly lonely. It seemed to me even so a thousand times better than Paris.

I turned around to look at Lady. She was watching me, her head on one side. I decided to put her in her box for the night. She tried to get in, but the box was certainly too small.

"*Couche, couche-toi,* Lady!" I said, but she kept barking in protest. The wall was terribly thin between my room and M. Baneau's, and I was afraid of disturbing him because there seemed to be such a sacred rule of quiet there. I could hear every turn and rustle he made. Lady couldn't seem to be comfortable in the box, so I spread my old coat on the foot of the bed and put her there.

"*Couche, couche là,* Lady," I whispered and she trembled with pleasure, cozy and deep in the fur coat.

179

Then I undressed and I lay in bed with Lady's hot weight, submissive and motionless, next to my feet. The air and the stillness of the mountains of spring filled the room. It seemed terribly exciting and wonderful to be there.

In the morning a little old woman brought my breakfast as I was sitting up in bed. She was Mme Thérèse, an Italian woman with a little wrinkled laughing face. She stopped to talk with me, and she spoke in very queer French, comic and terribly hard for me to understand, but I remember how she insisted on explaining that her brother had died in America, in Brazil, and another brother worked in Detroit. She was more friendly and gay with me than Phine or Simone. She made me feel more at home that morning as she lingered in my doorway, smiling with little sharp black eyes. Then it was wonderful, that morning, the first daybreak in a new place, a spring morning in the mountains. Leaning out of my window I felt the sweet tender sunlight, and I saw a workman strolling in the yard, and he wore red cloth sandals. I dressed at noon and went down the stairs. Mr. Goudina had come early to my door and taken Lady. I went out into the yard and sat on a bench beside the little arbor, where the valley dropped steep below, and I could see the plain and the mountains and Mont Blanc. It was so delicious sitting in the sun, to feel the sun in the strange place—delicate cool air. Sleepily I sat there looking at the untidy yard and kitchen entrance—and the jutting balconies overhead where shawls and ragtag awnings and umbrellas protruded. Lady saw me and barked from Mr. Goudina's balcony, and in a minute she came darting out the door below and rushed to me, kissing and jumping. It was nearly lunchtime, nobody was about—but presently M. Baneau appeared, the tall dignified man with a red beard. He came toward me, pacing across the yard in a most dignified courteous manner.

Interlude in the Haute Savoie

"*Bon jour, Mademoiselle*," he said. "You are not afraid of the sun?"

I was surprised. I had never heard of being afraid of the sun, except in the tropics. He explained that the Alpine sun is very dangerous to people ill with tuberculosis—that it causes hemorrhages and fever. I told him I was very surprised to hear that, and also that I was not ill. He said he had noticed that I spoke French very well. He said he had heard me talking with Mme Thérèse. He laughed about her Italian accent. He said he had noticed the day before in the dining room that it was very difficult for me when more than one person was talking, also that they spoke too fast for me. He spoke very slowly and clearly for me. I asked him to sit down, but he said he feared the sun, he couldn't stay more than a moment. He had very attentive, smiling, sympathetic eyes. He warned me again, for myself, not to stay in the sun. Nobody in the tuberculosis country will believe that one is not ill—or likely to become so. I was sorry to have him go back in the house. He seemed to me, among the strangers, the one sensitive noticing person. And I remember other moments during those few weeks of friendship with M. Baneau, how in the beginning I felt very lonely and envious of the other young occupants of the hotel, who always met in each other's rooms after the *cures* and in the evening, and I almost always went to my room, and M. Baneau went to his room. I felt that he was lonely like me and rather separate from the others.

There was no parlor, no meeting place, in the hotel, and after dinner everybody sat a long time in the dining room but in such uncomfortable little hard chairs—yet always talking, discussing, joking, arguing as French people do —exciting themselves over so little, carrying an argument bitterly to an end. Soon after I came M. Goudina had a hemorrhage and mounting temperature, and he stayed in

181

bed all the time. He was very neurasthenic, very egotistical and unhappy. The others, all of us, visited his room after tea, after dinner, for a little while, and the young nurses were good and attentive to him—and I myself wrote letters for him in English, and did errands for him—but things were quite different in the dining room without him.

I sat with Lady under my chair beside M. Baneau, and we often had quite amusing conversations. Always he helped me with French and used to appear to be delighted with my talk. Duran soon left for Paris for his holiday and his visit to the Exposition and his grandmother. Before he left, his girl friend, the Armenian whose mother worked in an embroidery shop in Paris, arrived. She had once been very ill in the sanatorium, and she had got better and tried to live in Paris again, but she got sick and came while I was there. I remember her little plump figure, tight in black satin, and her extremely unsympathetic eyes and her peremptory banging on the table and calling, with the others, for Simone. Mlle Nini, she was called, for Niniphar, which means water lily. She was quite a savage, and she possessed young Duran. She had the room beyond M. Baneau, with a balcony, and for several days after the evening of her arrival, she didn't appear and I could hear her coughing badly in the night. Duran, with his bags, waited in the road outside the inn door for the bus leaving for Paris. He wore a white sweater and a beret, and on top of his beret were pinned a forget-me-not and a lily-of-the-valley. I watched him from my window overhead. Boupart and his girl friend were standing on the front balcony to see him off. But he kept stepping around to one side to wave to Nini invisible on her balcony.

When Duran said good-by to me, he prophesied that I would still be there when he came back again, but I was doubtful. I only came for two or three weeks, and I

182

thought I would go back to Paris and maybe back to
America. But he said somehow very positively that he
knew I would not be able to leave the mountains so soon.
He himself was almost well, and he took long walks. He
used to wear shorts and go climbing and exploring. One
day at lunch he said he had just picked four hundred and
thirty-six gentians. He was taking them to give to friends
in Paris and, childish as he was, he counted as he picked.
But he insisted on giving me some of them, and I remember on my table the bouquet in a little glass—the amazing blinding blue of Duran's gentians. And the fields
around Praz Coutant were full of them. One day Grace
and I walked out in the hot field and picked them, and
we lay out there in the grass behind some trees hidden
from the nuns and Dr. Davey and talked about her plans.
She got more and more reckless about the nuns, however,
because she had made up her mind to leave the sanatorium.

After Duran left and Mr. Goudina was still in bed, there
was nobody in the dining room of my hotel who spoke
English, and I was somehow quite cherished and taken
care of by M. Baneau. On visiting days I made my trip
to the sanatorium in the wild bus and carried a lunch in
a newspaper and ate hidden in Grace's room while she
and Irene ate in the big dining room, and always sneaked
a little bottle of wine back to me. Her plans were developing with her kind of fever, resourceful and clever she was,
thinking of all sorts of possibilities. She had no more
money. Indeed, she couldn't stay any longer in the sanatorium, and she discussed her problem with Dr. Davey.
She thought she could go to some larger tuberculosis place
such as Davos and get a job as companion or secretary
and so stay in the necessary climate and support herself.
Dr. Davey was always attracted by her and promised to
help her with introductions to medical friends. He said

she was well enough to do it. Her last money from America would arrive July 1, and she decided to keep it as reserve and leave the sanatorium on that date. She had no clothes, she couldn't appear as she was, hunting for a job, and she wanted to stay with me in Assy for a few weeks and sew and make over her clothes and get herself ready—and write letters.

I had noticed another little hotel, up the road a little way from mine and standing higher, above terraces. There were striped umbrellas and tables on the terrace, and it looked much cooler and pleasanter than ours. Besides, there was no vacant room in the Hôtel du Tourisme, and mine was much too small for two. So I went to the Hôtel Morand one afternoon, and the maid who answered my knock showed me into the little corridor, and Mme Morand came out of the kitchen to speak to me. She said she had a vacant double room, but she and her husband were planning to rebuild the house sometime during the summer, and she couldn't take any permanent guests. I said that would be all right for us, and the maid showed me the room. It was high and cool and shady, with two long windows, and one window opened on a quite wide balcony overlooking the terrace and trees. The room was furnished with one wide iron bed, and a dry bouquet of mistletoe pinned on the wall over it, and large wardrobe and writing table and washstand with two bowls and two tall pitchers. The walls and floor were shabby but quite clean. Next door, in the corridor, was the cabinet—in rather bad condition, of course. Mme Morand had a lovely gentleness and quiet—a madonna, she was—and I felt drawn to her and I took the room, very happy indeed to find it. I was pleased also with the large, cool, empty dining room, with tables not too near together—marvelously peaceful in comparison with the overcrowded noisy little hole I had been in. I was really happy. I felt as if

184

something very pleasant was about to begin. I was so glad to leave the Hôtel du Tourisme where there was no escape from the blazing afternoon sun, no space, no trees, and my room so narrow and small, but I was very glad indeed to stop going up to the sanatorium to see Grace.

I had spoken to M. Baneau of my plans. He had heard all about Grace from me and M. Goudina, and he was very friendly about offering introductions to people he knew. That evening I told him I had engaged a room at the Hôtel Morand. It was after dinner. We had got up from the table and the others had left. We were standing in the deserted dining room. I remember his look, he said, "Have you made definite arrangements to leave us? I hoped you might decide to stay here!" And there was a look of real pain and embarrassment in his face. I was very much touched by that moment. I said of course it wasn't far away, only a few steps, and that we would meet often, just the same.

Before I left the Hôtel du Tourisme, the pear trees blossomed under my window. I used to lean out of my window the first thing every morning and look down at them, and almost I thought then that I must go back to Castine. The blossoms could not help making me think of Taro and the dream life of the apple blossoms, his apple blossoms always. Ever after his letter, the pear blossoms of France were not mine, and I felt terribly drawn to my own country, a faithfulness to return home before my own trees had bloomed and dropped their petals. Only once in a whole long year this tenderness, this marvel, would come, and I felt somehow I must go.

One night coming alone upstairs and into my room I felt a startling loneliness—loneliness that strikes you like a flash of lightning or an explosion and everything seems to stop, your heart stops. The more I felt the kindness and friendliness of M. Baneau and Duran and the others, the conventional kindness of nice people, the more I felt like crying and shouting to them all to go to hell. I could yell at them like Alice in a burst of defiance, "You are nothing but a pack of cards." There was the deep undercurrent not touched, not known, that moment when the feeling of loneliness exploded in me and everything was still—a clairvoyance telling me at that moment that there was somebody precious and close to me whom I had not yet seen. I felt something preparing yet still hidden. There is no such loneliness as one can feel among "nice" people. I felt silent kinship with those dusty, silent shapes of tired workmen going up the stairs to their big attic overhead. Their humbleness and silence and weariness were sweeter to me than the talkative smart people. "There is somebody under this roof, somebody I haven't yet seen."

That particular night the workmen were celebrating some fête down in the café. I leaned out of my window. The light fell on the tops of the pear trees, and it was warm. The men were playing in the yard, running out in the road, laughing and singing. Then one of them, light and quick, climbed up in the pear tree. I wanted to laugh and play with them instead of being with the refined people. So I was nowhere, just separate, looking out of a dark room, not seen by anybody, listening and joining in with the workmen in my feeling because they were more natural and more free than the bourgeois. But when I met a crowd of them coming along the road together I always felt rather afraid of their staring eyes, and I didn't like meeting them, and when I went to buy cigarettes in the café I always felt shy and discreet and never looked at them.

I forgot all this, though, in my pleasure in the thought of being with Grace in the Hôtel Morand. And I remember the glaring hot afternoon sun when I met her there. She came down in the bus from Praz Coutant with all her bags, but the bus, always erratic, didn't pass by Hôtel Morand that afternoon, and she was let out at the corner above, beside the old mill, carrying one of her bags. She was wearing her only dress, a black fagoted silk dress Katherine Dudley had given her, and a dreadful black velvet turban. I was worried when I saw her coming on foot, her face red from heat and exertion. I had been waiting for the bus to arrive at the Hôtel Morand. We explained to Ida, the waitress, that all her other bags were waiting beside the road by the mill, so Ida went and got them for us. So then we established ourselves in that great cool shabby room together. Grace unpacked her alcohol stove and a bottle of alcohol and a big yellow tin of Ovaltine, and she arranged everything on the shelves very quickly and cleverly and showed me how she was dividing the closet in half and the shelves in half and the washstand in half. She was awfully quick and energetic and jokingly bossy, and I was very lazy and slow.

Mr. Goudina, being still sick in bed, couldn't possibly take care of Lady, so I had brought her along. She trotted out on the balcony, and we went out and found our neighbor, the occupant of the next room, sitting in his chaise longue, and he looked at Lady with contempt and asked me rudely what was the matter with her because her back was bare in spots. He said she was horribly ugly—a very unpleasant dog. I called her away and told him she was on the contrary a very good dog. This neighbor was a coiffeur, with a fat white face and leering insulting eyes. There was war between us from that moment.

We found a nice screen in the room which we immediately fastened on the balcony to make complete privacy at our end. We put on thin dresses, and Grace put on her eyebrows and her mascara and attached her electric curling iron to the chandelier and waved her hair. I had still a little perfume—Sand Adieu. We went down to sit on the terrace under the balcony. There was a long narrow bench against the wall which I liked, leaning against the plaster wall, and a tin table with an umbrella over it, and a weather-beaten armchair. We were so happy to be there. Grace was wild with excitement to be out of the sanatorium. She couldn't believe that she was really free. She wanted to order an *apéritif*, and so we went and called Ida, the funny Italian maid, who was thin and frizzle-haired and wore thick eyeglasses and stared comically at us.

Grace said, "Let's have a Pernod."

I had never had Pernod, and I didn't know what it was. "It's good. It tastes like licorice," she said. "*Deux Pernods*," she said. Ida stared and grinned always when one gave an order, but she came back bringing the green bottle labeled *Pernod fils* and the bottle of water. She poured out a third of a glass of Pernod for each and filled the glasses with water, turning the liquid to cloudy yellow. We carried always packages of Maryland James cigarettes and little boxes of *allumettes*. Grace carried her knitting—a white sweater that Mrs. Dudley had ordered. Mrs. Dudley had sent the wool from Paris and was going to pay her for making it. The terrace dropped away into a vacant lot between us and the main road, thick with long grass and trees and bushes. We could see the white figures of the *ouvriers* walking along the road, coming down from Sancelleuros to their supper. Some of them went on to Hôtel du Tourisme, and some of them turned up the lane to come to Chez Morand.

Along the edge of the terrace was a flower bed and rosebushes just in bloom. We were on the side of the terrace reserved for the superior guests, and there were none in the hotel except ourselves and the coiffeur and another young man who was ill. In front was the entrance to the café, and there the workmen gathered and sat at tables outside. We felt amazingly grand and luxurious sitting there by ourselves that afternoon, myself glad to get out of my cramped room and the loneliness, and Grace joyous to escape from the bells and the nuns and the horrible dullness of the sanatorium.

She talked always, all the time. She was planning and scheming for her future, and I listened, always fascinated by her talk, always amusing and crazy and clever and making a spell over me, planning also for me, thinking of me a great deal. She wanted me to come with her to Davos. She said she couldn't stand going alone any more to strange places. She wanted a girl friend, she said, and she thought that I had been too lonely. She thought I had been foolish to let the thought of Alec bother me. She dismissed him as too stupid for anything. And I had finished thinking of Alec. She knew him much better than I, and it was only one evening when he had seemed lovable to me and I had imagined I had discovered something rare in him. But that was a mistake. I know. He had only been experimenting and exploiting me. There was nothing real in it. It was marvelously consoling to have her to talk to —more freely than one could talk to most people. She was utterly cynical above love. She only wanted to find a man who could support her. She had reason to fear poverty more than anything, and the one thing to think of was protection, she thought. She thought I was very sentimental and innocent.

"You need sex," she said. "It's just like anything else. If I feel like going swimming, I go. Sex is the same."

Still I kept my own feeling separate from her ideas, although I felt her power and I liked being with her. I was glad to follow and learn her way of living.

Such daring and gaiety stimulated me. We went in to dinner, and how we laughed and talked! Nobody could understand us, and it was amusing to talk freely. The dining room was almost empty and silent—the coiffeur alone at one small table and the very fragile young man always coughing alone at another, and ourselves at our table in one corner.

Nothing ever tasted so good as our first dinner there. Mme Morand's good rich soup, then cold meat, then kidneys in Sauce Madsine, then delicious fresh green beans, then fruit and cheese and crackers. We ordered a bottle of red wine and we poured it lavishly. The white tablecloths were clean and crisp, unlike the spotted and dirty cloth in the Hôtel du Tourisme, the tables neatly set and the silver polished, yet the tariff was only five francs more by the day.

After dinner we went to the kitchen door and asked for food for Lady. Mme Morand looked at us with her watchful, patient brown like a dog's eyes, her beautiful calmness mixed with a kind of French caution and reserve. She said she had noticed Lady's skin disease, and for that reason she would give us an old tin plate for her and always use the same one. One can't be too careful of any infection, she said. This seemed to me a perfect luxury of intelligence and *gentillesse* after the slovenly *de villes*. Her tall bearded husband, older than she, was always moving awkwardly about in the crowded busy kitchen; and their little child, a flowerlike blond boy, Jean Claude, was always close to his mother.

We carried Lady's hot supper upstairs. We decided always to leave her in our room during mealtimes and never let her get the bad habits of being noticed and fed by guests in the dining room. And after the coiffeur's insults we wished to guard her very carefully. After she finished, we put on her leash and took her downstairs to walk about a little in the dusk. We could hear accordion music in the café, and it made us feel gay and excited. So we walked around on the front terrace where we could see into the café without being seen ourselves. The coiffeur

and the sick boy were lounging in the chairs on our side
of the terrace, and all the workmen had gone into the café.
They had finished their dinner. The other maid, young
and pretty Simone, was serving drinks to them, and,
tipping back against the wall at the far end, a young man
with a cap over one eye was playing the accordion.

"Let's go in," said Grace.

"Let's not," I said. "We can't go in there. That's one
thing Elliot always says—that a woman can't go into a
bistro alone in France."

"That's silly," she said. "Don't be prim. What of it anyway? Just a few workmen. I want to hear the music and
have a liqueur."

"Oh, no, really!" I said. "Have the liqueur out here."

"You make me sick. You used to be more like me. I'll
get you over that. Come on. I'm going in. Don't forget
I've been in the san for five months, and I'm going to
have some fun now. You need me, really, to have a good
time."

I admired her naturalness, and I followed her in. We
sat at a table near the door and Lady underneath. The
men murmured, "*Bon soir, Mesdames,*" and we said, "*Bon
soir, Messieurs.*" Simone came, smiling attentively, and she
didn't seem shocked. Grace ordered two Cointreaux and
lifted up her knitting.

"Did you bring the cards?" she said.

"Yes," I said. I took them out of my pocket. "Do you
want to play canfield or tell fortunes?"

"No, let's have another Pernod," she said, "instead of
Cointreau."

She called Simone back again and changed the order,
blushing and laughing confidingly to Simone, and then
said to me, "You know, the French think it's awful to drink
Pernod after dinner. It's an *apéritif*, but what do we care
what they think? That girl is nice anyway. She didn't high-

191

hat us. Oh, I love this music. Aren't you glad we came in? Say you're glad. This is fun."

"Yes, it is fun." And it was. It was just what I had wanted in the other hotel, yet it was not related to the secret feeling I had leaning out of my window in the dark. I didn't feel the undercurrent near me then. I had forgotten that. And I was grateful to Grace for her freedom and easiness. I did feel happy, smiling to myself and feeling the gay music of the accordion.

"I've got to dance in a minute, Kitty. How I love to dance!" said Grace. She shimmied a little, her eyes on her knitting, and then she looked up and smiled at the musician. I looked at him too, trying to show appreciation in a refined way.

"Tell him how good his music is," she said. She was very shy about speaking French. The girls in the sanatorium had laughed at her too much.

"*C'est très jolie, la musique,*" I said. "*Nous aimons beaucoup la musique.*"

The boy playing didn't pay much attention to us. He had a sulky face. But the other men glanced at us and smiled. Still, I must say I felt rather uneasy. I didn't know how they were taking us, and I hoped they would be *gentil.* They were rather subdued. I suppose they were quietly wondering what to make of us. We didn't realize at the time what a sensation it made simply for us to go into the *bistro* and drink Pernod. The sulky boy with his cap over his eye, who we afterward learned was the husband of the little waitress, got tired of playing and shut up his accordion and slouched out, saying, "*Bon soir, Messieurs,*" but not speaking to us.

I don't remember just how we began to talk that evening, but it was easy and natural. Grace always talked to everybody. It began, I think, with Paros—a young Greek who was sitting at one of the tables. He knew a few words

192

of English, and he said them to me. Grace was fascinated by him from the first. He was quite beautiful—rather small and mysterious and charming. He knew he was beautiful, with his rather small head and truly Greek nose. His faded working blouse was unbuttoned at the neck. It was easier for me to understand what they said and to answer in French than it was for Grace, so I was interpreter. The other men began to talk after Paros began, and I remember how very *gentil* they all were, how they talked about different languages, and two or three of them were interested in Esperanto and really believed it would come some day to be the universal language.

Pretty soon we were like old friends, all laughing and talking together. Grace was throwing glances at Paros, and he was responding, but always with a certain unfathomableness—a reserve—a rather cynical reserve. He told us his name.

"*Je m'appelle* Paros Melis," he said. "Melis—*ça veut dire miel. Je suis comme le miel. Et vous, Mademoiselle, vous vous appelez Grace,*" he said. She laughed a great deal. She was getting so excited, so obviously that I was rather shocked.

He was an interesting young man really. He told us about his journey from Greece to France, and how he had lived in France several years and had an ambition to go to America. He said he was an electrician and was working at Sancelleuros like most of the others.

When we went upstairs to bed we were both quite pleased and excited about our new acquaintances. But there was a transom open over our door and over the door opposite ours, which was occupied by workmen. They were not all segregated in the attic as they were *chez de ville.* We had a bright electric light hanging from the ceiling, and Grace was undressing. As I went out to go to the cabinet, I saw a man's arm through the opposite

193

open transom, as if somebody had climbed up to look into our room through our transom. We knew who it was; we had noticed him going down the hall—a big dark man with heavy eyebrows. We had both noticed him and disliked him downstairs.

This didn't stop me from going into the *bistro*. We just paid no attention to the ones who were not *gentil*. So every evening after dinner, when it grew cool, first we went up to the room and gave Lady her dinner, then put her on the leash and took our coats, and Grace's knitting, and our cards or dominoes in our pockets and took Lady for a little walk and then went into the *bistro* and took our liqueurs.

When we were alone together, we were always talking, or Grace was talking, and during the day we were very busy. It was so very nice in the morning to wake up in that big cool room with the window open on the balcony. For weeks and weeks in the early summer the weather was fine. On those lovely fragrant mornings we were waked by Ida knocking on the door. She brought a nice big tray and put it on the bed, and it was always a delicious breakfast—the most perfect crisp rolls, fresh butter, coffee, and Mme Morand's wonderful big fresh eggs. Then after breakfast Grace would tell our fortunes, sitting up in bed with the cards spread out on her wooden invalid's bed table that she had carried around ever since she was in New Mexico. How seriously we used to consider what the cards told us—a large sum of money, a journey, a dark man, a great deal of love. And the wish card. It is funny to think now how frightened and eager we were over it, really believing because our wishes were so strong—always hard-boiled wishes for Grace—money, success, and a rich husband. For me, sentimental wishes always. She used to do it with real authority. I couldn't help believing. I believed almost everything about anything she said. She

194

spoke about every subject in the world with a kind of knowledge and authority. She told me I was too senti-mental about love, like an inexperienced person. She was always advising me to get over it. I was very lazy then, and she was very energetic. She used to jump out of bed and dress and carry our tall pitchers back and forth to the faucet in the cabinet. She dressed and began to work.

She was trying to make over her old clothes, but it was rather hopeless. She tried to make a black satin skirt out of an old dress, and I tried to help her, but it turned out very badly. Then she made over a black coat, took some black pleated satin ruffles off a dress and put them in the sleeves of the coat. This was not bad—in fact, quite sur-prisingly successful. She used to ask me to help her some-times, but I was so tired I couldn't feel like doing much. Then when on days she was tired I used to feel strong. We always complemented each other—always opposite. One did what the other didn't do. She was worried about me, though, because I was so languid. She thought perhaps I had t.b., and at first she made me take my temperature every day. We got a couple of reclining chairs, very cheap ones, and put them on the balcony. We slept every after-noon after lunch. Grace had promised herself that she would keep the schedule of the sanatorium for herself, and I used to worry about her when she didn't. But it was only the afternoon rest that she faithfully took, and when she got very excited about her sewing she didn't always take it, and in the evening we sometimes sat up late.

The second night that we sat in the *bistro* we saw the little boy who looked like a daguerreotype. He was a *munisié*. He was about eighteen, but he looked very babyish. He had a little smooth head with polished black hair, and he wore spectacles. He had watched us very gravely the first night, then Paros introduced him to us, and he was very polite and offered us a drink. We didn't like to take it, but his feelings would have been hurt if we hadn't. He was trying to be a man of the world. Paros kept glancing at him and at us, amused by him. He sat with us a long time but said almost nothing. The accordion player didn't play that night. He only played once or twice a week. Grace wanted it. She said she must dance. The little boy George said, "Tomorrow night there will be a dance, and you must come to the café. The musician will be here and you will dance." When Grace would laugh and move about, George would watch her adoringly. The next day I happened to meet Paros on the terrace. He said, "Don't be angry, your friend mustn't be angry, but the baby is in love with Mees Grace. It is very amusing. He is going to write her a letter. It is just for us to be amused. She mustn't be angry at the letter. You are both coming to the dance tonight?" I said, "Yes."

There was a big, coarse, buxom woman in a white nurse's uniform who used to be in the *bistro* sometimes. Her husband was a workman, and she, I suppose, was a nurse or attendant at Sancelleuros. They lived in our hotel. Paros said she knew a little English, and George had asked her to write a letter for him. When I went upstairs I told Grace about her admirer. She was quite excited. It seemed to make her blush a little to have such a naïve, serious little boy in love with her. We both hoped the men wouldn't laugh at him. We decided to tell Paros that we wouldn't like it at all if he were made fun of. So when we went into the *bistro* that night, George was sitting there, and the buxom woman was sitting near him. Evidently the letter had just been finished, and from her smile it was evident she had done it only to make a joke of him, not through sympathy. We sat down in our corner, of course pretending we knew nothing about the letter. The accordion player was sitting in his place. By twos and threes men came in, taking off caps or berets and saying,

Bon soir, Messieurs, Mesdames." They weren't dressed up, just wearing their working clothes, except for George, who had on a dark suit. George was too shy to come near us, but Grace smiled at him, and he smiled very naturally. Paros came and sat down at our table and whispered about him, laughing, "*Ne soyez pas fâchée,*" he said. "*Il est fou.*" He said that all during the day at work at Sancelleuros George had talked of nothing but Grace.

"He has written the letter," Paros said. "He is going to ask Mees Grace to dance, and while dancing he is going to slip it into her hand. What a joke. Oh, we will laugh!"

I urged him not to laugh at him.

"He won't know," he said. "He is a baby. He is foolish. He has never been away from home before. He has always spent all his time with his mother in the church—such a good little boy. This is his first love. A good chance for us to have a little fun."

The music began. There was really scarcely room to dance in the narrow little room. They moved out a few of the tables, and we stayed in our corner. The master of ceremonies was the man whose arm I had seen in the transom. He was a big creature with a brutal cynical face, always watching from under straight heavy brows. He used to stare at Grace, but he always spoke to us with exaggerated politeness. Paros asked Grace to dance, and they danced alone, the others watching. Paros was extraordinarily light and graceful, and he loved dancing. Grace had on that night a dark-green silk knitted dress that clung to her. Her hair was very red-gold under the bright electric light, and she looked very happy and alive, smiling with pleasure as she danced. She glanced and smiled at me. George watched her through his spectacles, leaning forward, childish and round-shouldered. When she came back to her chair the men applauded, then the master of ceremonies asked her to dance with him. Mme Morand came and stood in the doorway. Her beautiful calm face showed great respect and admiration for Grace's dancing. In the beginning we certainly had the respect of Mme Morand, just as if there were nothing at all strange about our going into the *bistro* and talking with the men. She had a rare, kind, uncritical face. Simone watched too, admiring and sweet. There was more clapping, and the men began to shout for "Jazz Americain!" and "Le Black Bottom." It seems that Paros, who was really a dancer, knew the Black Bottom, and he asked Grace to dance it with him. The men shouted and begged for it. But Grace was sitting at our table again, and she was excited and blushing but said she couldn't. The master of ceremonies came and most respectfully asked if she wouldn't do an exhibition dance for them of the Black Bottom. She was quite embarrassed and she said, "Not yet. Perhaps later." She wasn't used to dancing on account of her illness, and that first night she got quite out of breath. So she rested and had a Pernod, and the buxom woman danced, and Simone danced.

George was watching Grace, and we invited him to come and sit with us. He came and sat next to her. He couldn't seem to talk, but he kept turning his head to smile at her, and it was a most naïvely confident, possessive smile. We were wondering where the letter was. He was sitting close to her and could have given it to her. But she said to me in English that he hadn't given it to her yet.

"When he does, I won't let anybody see it, and I won't read it until we go upstairs," she said. After she had rested and the music began again, of course George asked her to dance, and she got up with him. She was too tall for him, and he couldn't really dance. They kept having to stop and begin over again. She had to help him and guide him as if he were a child. The men were all enjoying

198

it. But George was so entranced he wasn't embarrassed. Unsmilingly he kept moving awkwardly around the floor with her, not even knowing that he was dancing so badly. It was painful to watch them, and at last she gave it up, and they came back to sit down.

Now, sitting close to her, his smile was even more possessive, as if it never entered his head that there was any doubt that she was to be his. She gave him a warm beaming smile now and then, not to encourage him, surely, but not really aware of how deluded he was.

"I've got the letter," she said. "I put it down the front of my dress. I'll read it when we go upstairs."

She asked for a drink for all of us. He looked at me too, in kind of an affectionate grateful way, as if being her close friend gave me a very special value.

The buxom woman in white danced too. Her husband was a tall genial man, rather lanky, always wearing a beret. He liked to bob around and dance comically. After he had danced with his wife, he came and asked Grace to dance. He was agreeable and humorous. She liked him. She danced again with Paros, and he was the one she liked the best. He was a perfect partner for her. It was very pretty to watch them. I liked Paros too. When he wasn't dancing with Grace he came and sat at our table. George would smile at him too, as if Paros on account of closeness to Grace, had a certain value, like me, because it was evident that Grace liked him; and besides, he understood a little of our native language.

I think Grace really wanted to have every dance with Paros. She was getting more and more infatuated with him. But, although he flirted with her, there was his mysterious reserve behind it always, keeping himself separate. He was never excited. He didn't believe in anything. He would sit down at the table and sigh and shake his head and say, *"Ah, oui!"* as if that settled everything, as if he

199

had experienced everything and found everything empty. Grace laughed and mimicked him, heaving a great sigh and exclaiming, *"Ah, oui!"* and smiled at him with wild provocativeness. *"C'est joli!"* Grace would say for any enthusiasm.

George asked Grace to dance again, and she begged him to excuse her, saying she was tired. Then somebody called again for the Black Bottom, and she beckoned to Paros to dance with her, and they were on the floor again. He needed a little discouragement. He was too obsessed.

I was beginning to be afraid for her. It seemed just unbelievable that she had only been two or three days out of the sanatorium. The music was kind of imitation jazz, and all her old New York crazy gaiety was coming into her. I had never seen her like that before. She began to shimmy, and her eyes were shiny, her cheeks burning. She began to shake all over to the jazz and shout in Harlem style. Her gaiety was marvelous. The men applauded again, almost licking their lips over her. When she fell into her chair again, the master of ceremonies approached her and said her dancing was admirable, and asked if she would at last do them the honor of giving an exhibition solo dance of the Black Bottom. I began to hate him, feeling under his straight-browed mask of flattery only a desire to exploit her. She had a certain naïveté when she was happy and excited, and she didn't seem to notice this, or else all her life she had been exploited and she took it for granted. I watched her, so uneasy, hoping she wouldn't do it. I was afraid for her. She was too excited and breaking all the rules for her health.

"You mustn't do it," I said crossly. "It's almost eleven o'clock. We must go to bed."

"Oh, shut up, Kitty," she said.

It was just as if I were Alec. All he had labored with her to make her take care of herself, smoke less and drink less; and whenever, she had told me, anybody tried to stop her then she just *had* to do the thing. The men stood back, and Mme Morand and Simone. She did the exhibition for them.

Then it was time for the café to close, eleven o'clock. Madame Morand came forward and thanked us both for coming to the dance, and told Grace how beautifully she danced. I felt then as if everything was better. Mme Morand was so *gentille,* so gravely admiring.

We went up to our room, and she put her hand inside her dress and took out the letter. She read it sitting on the edge of the bed, with a tender smile. She appreciated so many things that were pitiable—children, animals, and men and anyone in trouble.

"I'll keep this all my life," she said. "He's a sweet kid. Christ, isn't he serious! I'll have to have a talk with him tomorrow. He wants me to go to walk with him, and I'll try to explain to him then 'Lac Vert.'"

The only sentence I can remember in the letter is, "I know I am young still, but my heart is full of love for you." It was written in very quaint hand on a little sheet of ruled paper.

We heard footsteps under the window. We looked out, and someone was standing down there in the dark.

"It's that kid," she whispered, coming away from the window. "Poor kid, he got pretty excited when he was dancing with me. I could feel him against me. Probably the first time he ever got excited. But the kid that gets me is that Paros. I am nuts about him. He's got charm—that Greek kid. *Ah, oui!* Something is going to happen before we get out of this place. Kitty, it's too bad we haven't got single rooms. This is going to be rather hard to manage, both of us in one room. It's funny, all the time I was in the sanatorium, I never gave a thought to sex. I'm not a very passionate person. It's only once in a while I get nuts about somebody, but even then I'm not very sexy. I like to have a good time. You need fun too, Kitty, more than anybody, I know. You liked it tonight, didn't you? Paros likes you, but— He really does. Besides, you can talk to him. I feel so dumb not being able to speak this crazy language."

We lay in bed a long time talking.

The next day we had two callers. Duran came before lunch. It was nice to see him again after his absence in Paris. He had such a nice eagerness, talking breathlessly and laughing, and he was nice to us, *bon camarade.* His childhood in America seemed to make him feel kinship with us. He seemed to be natural and boyishly friendly with everybody, like an eight-year-old boy, showing his kodak pictures and eagerly asking how we were getting along *chez* Morand, looking around the room and stepping out on the balcony. I remembered how he had seemed *chez de ville,* and how one night at dinner he held his own in argument against all the others—something about public schools in France and different methods of education. They all grew so passionate in arguments in that dining room. It was nice to see how everybody in France finds joy in exercising his mind, like a game, like tennis. The young girls, dumb-looking enough, used to enter into discussion as hotly as the men. Duran, the time he was against them all, seemed quite touchingly brave to me. He was much the youngest, but stubborn, and they hammered and hammered at him; and when Dutri finally got up to leave the room, he seemed insulting toward him as though he were disgusted with Duran and thought that he was almost imbecile and had not the right to hold an opinion.

I remember Mlle Lucienne Mercier at those dinners in her tight-waisted childish dresses, her hollow-chested submissive little figure, and page's cloud of hair parted in the middle standing out from her pale, stubborn, delicate face. She used to say less than the others, but when she talked she was very quick and eager and serious, and often turning her head to glance at M. Baneau for approval and support. She and M. Baneau both lived in Versailles, which gave them a kinship, and I think he liked her. Evidently she had wit too, and would tell a story gracefully, yet always rushing through it a little like an embarrassed child, excited, witty, and shy; and then, her face suddenly grave and closed, she kept something precious in herself, guarded and shy. She was evidently falling in love fast with Dutri. She was always watching him and catching his wishes and serving him almost like an oriental wife. When she arrived there, soon after I did, to spend her holiday, her sister, who was or had been sick, took her into the clique that she belonged to *chez de ville*. Their set was like a secret society in a boarding school. They used to gather in Dutri's room and have tea or coffee and play bridge. All the time that I was there, Dutri's girl friend was sick in bed. Her room was next to me, but she used to hold a sort of court in his room, and the day they first asked me to tea, she was propped up on pillows in his bed. She had a very kind, intelligent face, and a curious nasal voice that I liked. I felt more at home with her than with most of them. She was the only one of them who spoke any English, and she spoke rather well with an English accent. But of course there was always a busy conversation going on in French among them, and she really had no time to speak English for me.

During that time while she was sick in bed, she got news that her brother was very ill with pneumonia in Fontainebleau. She was very fond of him, evidently, and she was anxious about him, and before she was really able to travel she got up and went to Paris to see him. While she was in bed, Lucienne used to be in her room a great deal, very gentle and quiet, waiting on her and waiting on Dutri, making the tea while I was there. She wore cotton dresses cut like a child's of checkered gingham with tight waist and full skirt—or sometimes a scarlet sweater, and once a sweater she made herself in several shades of red wool, very exciting and becoming. She was an individual in dress, unlike most of the French girls.

All the girls carried knitting with them into the dining room and everywhere. They were all making what they called "Pullovairs." In the evening there were almost always extra people in the dining room because Georgette Mercier's boy friend would come from the Grand Hôtel du Mont Blanc. He was a blond Jew, attractive and genial and well-dressed. Dutri and he were partners in the little gift shop of the Grand Hôtel. He used to come to the afternoon tea parties in Dutri's room and sit on the end of the bed. This young man knew a man at the Grand Hôtel du Mont Blanc who had had a speak-easy in New York, and he was constantly referring to him and really felt proud of his inside knowledge of a speak-easy. He used to like to have an audience and make them open their eyes. It was almost as bizarre to me as when they talked about "gangstairs Jacques Diamond, and Capone." Their idea of American life being like the wildest movie and the end of their conversation always, *"C'est formidable!"*

The other extra people at night were Boupart's girl friend, who was a *téléphoniste* from Sancelleuros. She used to walk in at the end of dinner, wearing a sort of light evening cloak and no hat, a pale and dramatic face, like an actress, and a moving husky sort of voice and a breathless manner of talking. Her eyes shone in the sudden bright light. One always felt the air of the evening around her as she came in after walking down from Sancelleuros after dark. She didn't know she was like that, though. She never thought of herself at all or knew she had an interesting quality. She had never compared herself with Boupart. He was a crude, coarse fellow, and she was so uncritical she didn't even know it. Also, toward the end of dinner the pink and white *manicuriste* from the Grand Hôtel du Mont Blanc used to come in and lean over and kiss the coiffeur and sit down cuddling close to him. He used to feel restored inside when she arrived. He sat alone, not at all included in the secret society, and quite ignored except when they made dates for an *ondulation* or *shamponier*, so when she came dotingly in and made such a fuss over him like a kitten he used to look around, very pleased and smiling foolishly. When she wasn't there, even the slightest encouragement, which he rarely got, seemed to please him, and he was always ready to send flirtatious glances across the room.

Duran also was not included in the *haut monde* of the Hôtel du Tourisme. Once in Dutri's room, when they all were gathered, I heard them speaking of him, and I understood just a little they said, contemptuously, *"Ce garçon n'est pas moral."* I think at that time Mlle was planning to go to Paris to see her sick brother, and everyone felt it was dangerous for her to travel alone so soon after her hemorrhage. Duran was going to the Colonial Exposition on Friday, and the doctor said Mademoiselle must not get up before Saturday. She had asked Duran to wait over a day and accompany her, and he had refused. They said he was capricious and egotistical and had no humanity.

But all this is not very important, however. I began to tell of Duran coming to call on Grace and me, but idle things come into my memory—snatches of conversation, glimpses of the little *Tourisme* dining room, many fragments, and I want to tell them all because they all interest me. Mr. Goudina talked to me about Duran one day. He also was annoyed with him for his ungraciousness toward the sick girl, but I always thought there must be some reason back of it, not mere selfishness. They had certainly not been very nice to Duran. Mr. Goudina said, "I talk to him like a father. I tell him he mustn't do such stupid things. He says stupid things, and he cannot keep friends. He has not any tact. I tell him, and if he would do as I say, he would get along better."

But I liked him, I thought he was nicer than the others, more honest, and of better family, and for that reason had no real place for himself there. So he became devoted to the rather elegant Mr. Goudina, like a son, rushing away from the table to see him when he was sick and spending the evenings with him while they developed films together, and they could hear the victrola and talk and laughter in Dutri's room overhead. Mr. Goudina was rather military and exacting and gave Duran a certain discipline that Duran seemed to prefer to the frivolous society of his contemporaries. When Nina came back they were both like Mr. Goudina's children, but after a time they got out of hand, and he complained about them to Grace and me. "Duran is not good," he said. "He and Nina do nothing but make foolishness all the time now. They are not sensible any more. They have lost their heads. It is awful." They used to go off on excursions together high up in the mountains to the tiny chalets where the peasants keep their cows in summer, and they would camp there for a week at a time. Mr. Goudina was bereaved and angry.

Again I am getting far ahead of my story, at the moment when Grace and I were still in good standing at the Hôtel Morand, but really making a transition because we were becoming entranced with the interior of the *bistro,* and we told Duran laughingly how we had gone to the dance the night before and Grace told him about George and his love letter. She told it as a great joke, and

206

Duran was quite amused. We told of going into the *bistro* as if we were princesses who had condescended only to amuse ourselves. We didn't imagine then how serious it was going to be.

After Duran left, Grace said, "Of course he will run and tell Mr. Goudina that we have been talking with the workmen, and Mr. Goudina will tell Irene, and the next time I go up to the sanatorium she will be at me about it. They'll make a fine story out of it. Irene is a little snob, and so is her father. There was a man who worked around the sanatorium and he had a beautiful body. I told the girls he was beautiful, and they were such fools they were shocked. Irene would never even speak to a workman. She's the silliest kid I ever saw, such silly ideas. Well, when is your boy friend coming, dearie? I'll fix the room up grand for him."

She meant M. Baneau. We had invited him to come to tea. He had helped me to write a letter in French when I was at the Hôtel du Tourisme. I wrote to Paris to an art shop to order a little folding easel. I wanted to try painting out of doors there. The package never arrived, and M. Baneau had become very solicitous about it and said he would help me with another letter. Besides, I wanted him to see the Hôtel Morand. The dining room seemed to me much more dignified and calm and suitable to him than the dirty Tourisme, and I thought he might change. He was always complaining of the heat and lack of shade there. I used to think about him quite a lot those days. I knew he liked me, and he had been very *gentil*, and he reminded me of my father. Once when Grace was telling my fortune, my wish was to have a little love affair with him, and the cards said No. Grace thought he was nice, but too formal for her. She thought he was my kind but not her kind. She was humorously indulgent to me about him, and she got the tea ready and tidied the room

207

and picked wild flowers and told me what to wear, and I went to Bobolink's to buy some sweet biscuits.

He arrived very promptly just after four o'clock, after the *cure de silence*. We sat around the table having tea, and I felt quite shy and couldn't talk very much. He was charming to Grace. It was hard for her to talk French with him, but she tried her best, laughing at herself quite charmingly, and he seemed to like her. He asked about American sanatoriums, and she tried to describe the life in Santa Fe. He began to ask something I didn't understand very well, about the difference between France and America in the way of sexual freedom. It was funny how in a conversation of this kind Grace often caught the drift of things quicker than I did, by instinct or guessing, without knowing the vocabulary, and somehow she made herself understood. Even now I can't tell whether he said there was more or less freedom of the sexes in the French sanatoriums than in the American ones—certainly not more at Praz Coutant. She talked about Santa Fe and of how freely the men and women mingled on the grounds and in the cabins and in the lounging rooms, and she said that in spite of this freedom there was no immorality. I couldn't believe there was none, but this was what she said. She compared it with Praz Coutant, where the nuns and Dr. Davey keep such rigid discipline, and where the men and women only see each other from opposite sides of the chapel and by the most frantic intrigue manage to exchange notes and make rendezvous, and when they are caught are always expelled immediately; and of how the food at Praz Coutant all tastes horribly of some kind of strong anti-aphrodisiac. She talked about the nuns' neurasthenic horror of sex, and she told him the story of how one evening when she was undressing a Sister knocked at her door and came in. Grace happened to be just getting into her pajamas, and her breasts were uncovered. The nun exclaimed with horror and turned her face away and seized the top of the pajama and pushed it at Grace and told her to cover herself. M. Baneau listened, very amused, and agreed with us that the nuns have terribly distorted and unhealthy minds. I was rather surprised at him for entering on this subject with so much interest with us, and I wondered what he was thinking.

After we finished tea, Grace said she must go on with her sewing, and suggested that M. Baneau and I sit on the balcony. She did this in order to eliminate herself, like a good girl friend. We sat out there, and he dictated the sentences for a letter. We always had a joke about *"Acceptez, Monsieur, mes salutations très distinguées."* He had once told me that he knew an American during the war, working with him in the Y.M.C.A., and he never forgot how that American laughed at the formal closing of French letters and said that in America one said, simply, "Sincerely yours." M. Baneau explained to the others at Hôtel du Tourisme once, speaking of this, that to him this seemed typical of the difference between French and Americans. He spoke admiringly of the American gift for simplifying things and said it was a mistake for French people to take it as rudeness. So when he helped me write, I used to make the most elaborate fancy French endings and call it garniture. He seemed to enjoy this. He liked terribly any sort of playing and exaggeration. Things amused him that most people would never notice at all.

When we finished the letter, I told him how much Grace and I enjoyed the Hôtel Morand, and I said we had been into the *bistro* and had made friends with some of the workmen. I tried to explain to him how delightful and strange it seemed to Americans to find in all classes in France a certain intellectual eagerness and a kind of inborn taste. He said yes, it was true, and he said among the workmen there were many who were not just arrived.

I don't remember the word in French, but meaning that they had tradition and family culture. I remember feeling quite relieved that he seemed sympathetic with our mingling. But all the time it was taken as a condescension. We tried unconsciously to make it seem so—silly hypocrites. After he left, formally thanking us, I felt rather excited—foolishly sentimental. It was the first time Grace had really seen him and talked with him. I asked her very childishly if she thought he liked me, and she said yes. She was sure he did. "I noticed especially," she said, "and I can tell. He watched you all the time," she said, "and whenever you said anything amusing, he looked just delighted."

"Did he watch me really?" I said. "Do you really mean you think he likes me especially?"

"Of course he does. His eyes just shine when he looks at you. He wouldn't ever like me. I'm too crude for him, and I could never use him—he's too stiff. But you're his kind. You'll have to encourage him a little, that's all. He's so formal, but don't be so shy, Kitty. You don't talk enough. *If* you really want him, there's no reason why you shouldn't. He's interested in you, I know. Maybe he will move over here." I knew she didn't understand my feeling about him. She is direct and realistic.

"How about asking him to come to dinner with Mr. Goudina?" I said.

Mr. Goudina had got better and was up and around again. I had always noticed a round lump on one side of his face, and now the doctor had decided that it was this, a growth of the past few months, which caused his temperature, not his lungs. So his worry was relieved and like a true neurasthenic, his complaining, self-pitying, groaning voice was discarded, and he was natural again. The doctor operated on the lump, and he was wearing a white bandage round his head and looked ridiculous, like a

210

comic picture of a man with a toothache. He was quite
interested to see our hotel. His mind occupied itself always
with the smallest gossiping details, and he was an authority on everything in the infinitesimal neighborhood of
Assy—inns, boardinghouses, chalets, and *maisons meu-
bleés*. He had never dined at Morand, so we invited him
to come the next evening. I wanted to invite him because
he had been kind to me—in a perfunctory way, but still
kind and scrupulous about my comfort. I thought it would
be nice to invite M. Baneau to come with him, making a
party of four. We were so proud of Mme Morand's cooking, we wanted them to try it. And I felt it would be
graceful to repay M. Baneau for his kindness to me, which
had been so much more real and imaginative than Mr.
Goudina's.

I sent a little note to M. Baneau, inviting him. Grace
had already invited Mr. Goudina, and he had accepted.
We told Mme Morand that we expected two guests, and
our table was set for four. Nobody at the Tourisme ever
has a dinner engagement, so it seemed safe enough to
expect them both. We were sitting on the front terrace
when we began to expect them. Paros was sitting with us,
and one or two other workmen were at a table near by,
and we were all talking. We had thought that Mr. Goudina's delicate sense of propriety would be outraged by
the presence of the workmen, but we felt by now that
they were our friends, especially Paros, and we didn't
want to let them think we treated them any differently
because we were having an elegant guest. I felt uncomfortable. I didn't want to affront Mr. Goudina, and I didn't
want to high-hat the workmen.

"I don't care what he thinks," said Grace. "These men
have been awfully *gentil* to us. They're more intelligent
than old Goudina. We like them, and so let's be honest
about it and let him think what he wants to. When he

comes we'll take him around to the other side of the terrace and have an *apéritif*, but first we'll just sit here and introduce him to these men. What the hell."

The men were showing us snapshots they had taken. One of the men there was a dark little sailor with black beetling brows and a simple nice face. He told us he had been caught in a submarine. The submarine got out of order and wouldn't rise. They thought for several hours they were lost, and they were then rescued. This was his great story. He seemed to be thinking about it all the time. He liked to have us ask about it every time we met him after that. He was still always wide-eyed about it—not excited, but dull as if he were walking in his sleep; not wild or frightened any more, but always remembering it. The men wanted Grace to take pictures of them with her camera. They asked her if she ever walked past Sancelleuros, and asked her very respectfully and with childish eagerness if she wouldn't stop at Sancelleuros and take pictures of them at their work if she ever walked past there.

"All French people are like that," she said to me. "Just like children. They adore to have their pictures taken."

Presently Mr. Goudina's bandaged head appeared round the corner of the terrace, and he walked over to us, glancing rather coldly at the workmen. Grace introduced them to him—Paros, George, the sailor, and one or two I don't remember. One of the men had just ordered drinks for us, and we told Mr. Goudina in English, asking him to sit down with us. And the man who was treating us respectfully ordered another for Mr. Goudina, so he had to join us as we were. Grace picked up the snapshots and showed them to him. And I told him the sailor had been caught in a submarine. Mr. Goudina was quite amiable in a condescending way, and the sailor told his story again. But Paros, who had been joking and talking with Grace, acted as if he didn't know us at all as soon as Mr. Goudina arrived. It hurt me to see people so distorted by an ingrown sense of class distinction. Paros, being the most intelligent and sensitive, seemed to feel it the most. But there was kind of a chill on all of them in Mr. Goudina's presence. They weren't natural any more. And pretty soon they were all left out of the conversation and talked themselves in a subdued way, and we were still finishing the drinks they had given us. Mr. Goudina talked with us in English, and with his usual self-absorption gave us all the details about the operation on his face. I didn't like this at all, and I said, "Shall we show Mr. Goudina our room before it gets dark?" He said he would like to see it, so we said *bon soir* to the men and went upstairs. Paros scarcely glanced at us as we passed him. Mr. Goudina said on the way up, "Mr. Baneau tells me you have a wonderful room."

"Where is he?" said Grace. "Is he coming tonight?"

"He asked me to say that he regrets very much he is not able to come. He sent a little note to you with an explanation."

He took a little white envelope out of his pocket and gave it to me. It was addressed in very exquisite handwriting to both of us. I opened it in our room and read a formal note written in the third person, simply regretting that he was unable to come and begging us to accept his most distinguished salutations.

"What is it? Is he sick?" I said.

"Oh, Mr. Baneau is a very formal man," said Mr. Goudina impatiently. "He is not accustomed to things, and he takes everything too seriously. He was very much disturbed by your invitation. He came to me and talked it over with me, and said he didn't know what to do. He said to me, 'I have only known those young ladies during a few weeks, and I cannot accept their invitation after such a short acquaintance. What do I really know about

213

them?' he said. He was very embarrassed. A Frenchman of his class is very narrow-minded," said Mr. Goudina. "He is a very pleasant man, and intelligent, but narrow-minded. There is nothing you can explain to him."

Getting the typical old rebuff handed out by the elaborate European to the rough-diamond American. And I thought that for M. Baneau to make me feel that I had been crude and forward was a rudeness he should have avoided even at the cost of breaking his finicky little social rules and coming to dinner. I laugh to think of how funny I was, exaggerating this incident—boiling like an old Yankee in the presence of royalty. And I was really hurt. And I lost all my tenderness toward him then. That narrowness pinched me. I thought to be able to respond to an ingenuous friendly act in the manner in which it is done is the true gracefulness. But what did he think? I felt lavish and free, and unappreciated. I felt contempt for the shocking pettiness that counts the price of one dinner more or less and sees an invitation from this angle.

So there I was, a typical rebuffed, flamboyant American, boasting of generosity, simplicity, not very good, not very *gentille*. But then, it does exist, this difference.

I didn't say anything to Mr. Goudina, but really I was hurt and troubled the whole evening. We had a good dinner, which Mr. Goudina enjoyed. Also he enjoyed the large quiet dining room and said how much he was irritated by the bad manners at Tourisme—Boupart and Dutri banging and yelling and the slovenly maid that waited on table. That evening we talked about going to Chamonix and asked him about getting there. Grace had reached a point in her struggle with her pathetic old clothes which made us feel that we must go to a place where there were shops, and she would spend her little bit of hoarded money on one chic costume as her most important investment before starting out to seek her fortune in Davos or else-

214

where. Mr. Goudina told us that Bobolink had a very nice
touring car, and that he took people on trips for less than
Boupart. He advised us to go and ask him about it.

So when Mr. Goudina went home, we walked home
with him, taking Lady with us on the leash down the
dark little road to the Hôtel du Tourisme, only a few
steps. Mr. Goudina had to take his temperature and go
to bed at nine o'clock, so he said good night to us and
thanked us very politely for the dinner.

The light was still burning in Bobolink's shop. We
opened the door which tinkled a bell and found Mrs.
Bobolink knitting behind the counter. She always smiled
at us roguishly and seemed pleased with us. She was a
fat little bunchy woman, short as a child, with a black
frizzy bang on her forehead, with black eyebrows and a
very fuzzy soft double chin. She wore cotton dresses with
ruffles on the sleeves and a white crisp apron and many
little dangling bracelets and rings and a little gold watch
on a chain hanging into her bosom. She had soft, handsome gray eyes and thick black lashes. She was a coquet-
tish little dumpling, a little honey-bunch to her husband,
keeping always her charm over him in spite of age. We
always felt at home in the Bobolinks' shop. She used to
sit and look at us quite dotingly, and indulgently smile
at us playfully and admire our clothes, and she used to
shake her finger and say we mustn't smoke so many cigarettes. She would go to the big candy jars and give us
each a little piece of hard candy wrapped in butterfly
paper or flower paper or bird paper. I used to like the
framboises wrapped in butterfly paper. When you think
of a cigarette, take one of these instead, she said. It is
better for the cough.

There was an armchair and a wooden box to sit on.
Mme Bobolink used to insist on standing when we were
there and make us take the two seats. Sometimes the bell

would tinkle and a customer come in, a workman or a guest from Sancelleuros—never anybody from the Hôtel du Tourisme except M. Goudina or M. Baneau, because the others were too grand with their shopping trips to St. Gervais and Salauches and Dutri's gift shop at the Grand Hôtel du Mont Blanc. Sometimes the dentist's husband came in for a moment in the day. The sanatorium dentist was a pretty young French girl from Paris whose husband was a very beautiful romantic-looking young man, a tall Frenchman, son of a famous Paris doctor. He wore soft, elegant tweed clothes walking in the rain and mist, like a country gentleman slow and gentle and beautiful. They were madly in love with each other, and they lived in a peasant cottage hidden down a muddy lane behind the Hôtel du Tourisme.

When we spoke to Madame about the car and our trip to Chamonix, she called M. Bobolink, and he came running down the stairs from their apartment. He was a comic person, very thin and wiry and tall, with roguish black bead eyes near together and always gesticulating and whispering some joke, and then leaning back triumphantly to watch you appreciate it and laugh. Then he would laugh like a mischievous boy. We had a great consultation about the trip to Chamonix. He told us he would take us the next day for sixty francs, much less than Boupart, and Madame watched him as he talked and nodded confidentially at us, telling us to wear our warm clothes because Chamonix is beside the glacier, and there is a chill in the air.

"C'est beau, Chamonix!" she said, nodding her head slowly and her soft mouth almost whispering the words, gazing on us indulgently. *"Il faut partir de bonne heure pour faire tous vos achats et pour aller chez la couturière, ça prend du temps, oui, ça prend du temps. Mais, on peut rester toute la journée si vous partez tout de suite après*

le petit déjeuner. Oui, de bonne heure. Ah, oui, vous verrez toutes sortes de belles choses, ça fait une des plus belles courses. Bien sûr. C'est mieux qu'ici!" she said, roguishly deprecating their little shop with her glance. *"Plus de choix! Mais oui!"*

It was like a conspiracy, Mme Bobolink nodding, and M. Bobolink nodding at us and whispering, and so it was arranged.

We will go home and go to bed, *tout de suite,* we said, and be ready in the morning at ten o'clock. Will it be a fine day tomorrow?

"Ah, oui! C'est très clair ce soir, il fera beau demain, bien sur, il fera beau! Pas besoin de capote!"

7. *Dans Notre Péniche*

[To Catharine Huntington]

Pension Morand
Assy, Haute Savoie

Dearest Catharine—
I HAVE been living always in Haute Savoie since I wrote you the last time. A lovely *histoire*—oh, so charming!—began, and I can't leave here yet. Grace is with me, and we have just taken a lovely plaster house on the side of the mountain, and it's very lighthearted and lovely and amusing, and don't tell anyone! We have quite entirely escaped from the Magic Mountain, or at least the *malades* and their balconies. We have thrown in our lot with the *ouvriers*. The evenings we have spent lying in the grass on the mountainsides overlooking the deep plain and hearing the sound of the cascades, and boys singing to us the *chansons des montagnes* and laughing, laughing, laughing, and my pet boy has a big black dog Kiki, who lies on one side of me and barks if any sound of footsteps is heard, and the boy sits up and listens so still and says in such a charming soft voice, *"Couche, Kiki! Couche là!* All the past has fallen off me, and I feel nothing but this enclosed magic place—even the sound

of torrents and the lilies-of-the-valley and forget-me-nots and everything in French.

France is really delicious—now, in the country—not Paris, at least not for me; I feel myself now so completely escaped from the low spirits of the winter, the poison of Paris, that I wish you too could move and escape. It's possible—so easy, after all! From this distance I can know how down I was in Paris, how really poisoned and locked up—Toshihiko's bad aura—very, very bad for me—always such a feeling of effort. Now in Haute Savoie no effort except the stumbling, and so amusing and after all quite successful French—learned in the dark. Except for such lessons, I feel as if I had forgotten even how to read and write. Nothing left of habits except laughing and jokes and, yes, a sense of *tristesse* and poverty and tender sympathy.

The day after tomorrow I think we move to our house, which I think is in a little *hameau* called Maffray—and the house I think is called Maison de l'Echaix.

After I had been in Assy three weeks, Grace moved out of the sanatorium and I left Hôtel du Tourisme and we came to the Hôtel Morand together—much more pleasant rooms, etc., and here our amusing life began. It began with the music of the accordion in the *bistro*. This ex-Follies girl whose natural habitat is a speak-easy or night club felt it the most natural thing in the world to walk into the *bistro,* where a "nice" French woman would never go. The men were charming to us, however, and after a few evenings of dominoes, fortunetelling, and dancing our reputations spread, and our two came up from the other hotel to see the two Americans, and I happened to be drawing in the *bistro* a portrait of a young Greek workman with a lovely face, and the other workmen were all looking at my other portraits, and our two began to talk to us then. I remember my first conversation was our

219

speaking of the difference between saying that one is *contente* or *heureuse*.

July 3, 1931

Now we have moved into our house, a peasant's house. The front door of the house enters the kitchen, with white plaster walls, dark oiled woodwork, and cabinets for dishes. Marcel and Jacques are with us. Marcel is a Savoyard and Jacques is from Lyon. We have dinner in the kitchen, with plenty of red wine and just lovely fun. Marcel is very small and has a great deal of light in his eyes, very shining and excited and quite acrobatic and funny. He suddenly lifts me up and shoots me over his head as in a circus.

The night before last I had got very tired and hot going to the nearest town to buy provisions, and dinner was very late, and in the meantime I had had a lot of wine. During dinner I got very strange. I could hear what they said, and I could look at them, but all the life went out of me and I felt almost unconscious. Grace said she never saw anything in her life like the way my darling *ouvrier* was to me then—such tenderness—and I can remember myself the marvelous look of his face, carrying me to the bed and leaning over me, and then later taking me back to the table and feeding me as if I were a baby. He is very poor, and he has been working in the new sanatorium and then going down to his father's house in the little town in the valley and working all night sometimes, serving drinks in a dance hall, getting paler and paler.

He explained to me last night that he has a sister thirteen years old who is *très intelligente,* and he is trying to get enough money to send her to an academy.

I don't know what is happening, really. The stars are strange enough, but there is such beauty here, in this land

and in him and in all our way of living, all four so harmonious. It doesn't seem queer, just cut off completely from other times and places.

I'm sitting on a bench on the little terrace in front of the house. There are heavy pink roses, and the little dog that I brought down from Paris is sitting on the step. At night I have also Marcel's Kiki, big black mountain dog. She jumps on the bed and kisses me.

Two or three days later: I have such a need for a diary with everything changing every day, and this is my diary. The day after I wrote the first of this letter was Fourth of July. The day before the Fourth Marcel had gone to Chamonix to look for a job because the big sanatorium is practically finished and the men are leaving. He told me he would try to come that evening, but dinnertime came and Jacques arrived as usual, but not Marcel. After dinner, Jacques and Grace and I were sitting on the terrace. It was very warm and heavy and moonlight, and I felt sad being alone. We all went to bed early.

I'm now sitting at a neat kitchen table, waiting for the vegetables to cook. I have everything ready, as they say, and have only to wait a little. On the wall beside me is pasted a big map of Haute Savoie. Around it on the white plaster wall I painted a decoration of flowers and the words of a song that our *ouvriers* taught us, and I painted a red heart on the map where Passy is...

> *Dans notre péniche*
> *Sous le pont de St. Cloud*
> *On n'est pas riche*
> *Mais on s'en foue—*

We call our little peasant house our *péniche* [barge]. I'm cooking this dinner tonight for Jacques and myself —we are alone. Grace has gone south to search for a job for a few days, and my boy is away working now in Chamonix—unfortunately—on the dangerous *téléferique*. You may like to know that those two are very intelligent and quite Red, and the first night my boy entered this peasant's kitchen he spat at the cross which hangs on the door, not unpleasantly, though, very laughingly and charmingly. He is almost the most lovely person I have ever looked at or know the spirit of, and I shall be sad to leave him. My acquaintance with him is so much a passing dream.

I can hardly remember my first days in Assy, just above here, when I stayed at the Hôtel du Tourisme and looked out and saw the peach blossoms and felt that I was coming home very soon. In that hotel, besides the sick *pensionnaires*, there were workmen living on the top floors and eating in another dining room. I used to have a very funny feeling that somewhere in that mysterious top floor there was somebody connected with me, and yet I never noticed any workman. I used to pass them on the stairs— they were terribly dirty and tired-looking and sometimes I used to hear them singing in their dining room. I used to be sitting in the refined dining room with the ladies and gentlemen and have a terrible nostalgia for the other dining room. Just a few weeks after that I found Marcel in the *bistro* of the other hotel, and it was quite odd to walk with him past the sleeping Hôtel du Tourisme when he was taking me home after we had been on a mountainside, and I thought of the sleeping ladies and gentlemen, not one so charming or so intelligent or so funny as my *ouvrier*.

I haven't any plan yet about coming home. This is the kind of life when you forget about making plans. But suddenly probably there will be a day of autumn weather and it will seem suddenly that the dream is ended, and I will pack my trunk and rush to Castine.

Dans Notre Péniche

13 août 1931

Now it is evening. We ate very well and have been sitting a long time on the terrace, talking a great deal about our lives, and now Jacques is opposite me writing his first letter to Grace, asking me now and then for English words. Now he has stopped to make a nice little tea of herbs for us to drink—*verveine*. They love so much their herb teas—*tilleul*—(lime leaves, I think). The *ouvriers* drink these things very sweetly and quietly in the evenings —they are shocked and saddened if we drink wine or Pernod.

I have such a pretty little sweater on—very soft and light—kind of pale greenish with flecks of blue and orange. I bought it in Chamonix, and it is a marvelous place for everything knitted, and I thought of you when I saw those most entrancing sweaters—but at the moment I have no money. If you wish me to do a commission for you, I should feel very sympathetic toward a Chamonix sweater.

Now I must tell my fortune. I have learned to do this with cards, and it is very useful.

15 septembre 1931

THERE you are, just as lively as ever and more so and driving all alone (that is just grand), and for putting cock feathers on the new kind of hats! It is very alluring to me to think of it, and coming home as you say in the autumn weather. But I don't know—I don't know. I long to see everybody. Especially I can't let my mother wait for me too long. I know I must go soon. Tonight, just now, I arrived in Paris, coming from Lyon, where I just spent four or five days. You wrote in your letter of the things I had told you, and it sounded very charming, but I didn't tell you any of the sad part.

My boy has a terribly hard life, and it has been getting worse lately, and there is nothing I can do, it seems, and he is very much hindered from coming to our house. I have hardly seen him lately at all. But the last time he came he begged me to take him with me to America, or anywhere, away from his home. We talked of getting an old car and driving around France, and that is now in the air. He is so appealing—he touches me terribly. "*Veux-tu m'amener avec toi en Amérique?*" Of course I said yes, but I don't believe it would be possible or good for him. I may never see him again, and we haven't even said good-by. The thing that worries me the most is this devilish t.b. that seems to get all the young French, and I am terribly afraid for him lately—always working long, long hours in all kinds of weather and not well taken care of and with a great deal of *souci* for his family—his bad father and unhappy mother whom he adores.

I have been in our house for more than a month—or rather with Jacques. Grace went off to the Midi and to hunt for a job, and Jacques and I stayed in Passy. At last I couldn't stand being alone so much—every day all day until dinnertime—and I suddenly decided to go and hunt for an old car and be more free. Living on the side of a mountain, with no communication possible, is too much, and too costly. When I have that necessity, like a seagull who has been sitting too long on a rock—there is nothing to do but descend on foot to the nearest village and telephone for a car, which always costs fifty francs. We have another *ouvrier* friend—very lively and good—called Martin, who told me to come to Lyon and he would help me get a car. So I went to Lyon, intending also to go on to Paris for a few days, and I met my *ouvrier* in Lyon. He came around to my hotel, and we went rushing out to a *bistro,* and it seems he is coming to Paris tomorrow, so we have a rendezvous for Thursday to go to the market

of second-hand cars and get a car and drive back together
tous les deux, he says to Lyon and then to Passy. This one
is very sweet and gay. But I am getting so deep into this
life with French *ouvriers* that I find I can't even tell you
about it. I can't make it real to you. We are all Commu-
nists now, I tell you. They are so excited, intelligent, and
so wonderfully sympathetic. I had such a nice letter from
Jacques this morning, and he forwarded your letter and
others. I have told him about you and your struggle for
Sacco and Vanzetti, and he asks me to present him to you
if he comes to America, as he hopes to do. He is really a
Communist—a member of the Party.

I have had a very nice time with him. I have been
taking care of him and he of me. He sings, which is
very nice. Some nights we sit in the kitchen late, and he
sings me all the French songs he can remember, sad war
songs and songs of the *chagrin d'amour,* and I like it very
much. And sometimes he sings a very sad song about the
lover who won't come back until *le temps des cerises.*
They are so affectionate, so free with caresses. He
always kisses me the minute he comes in the house and
leaves a little note for me on the kitchen table before he
goes out in the morning, before I am awake. They are sympathetic. As soon as I get out of bed I run out in the
kitchen to read his note, and then I have courage to drag
in the wood and build the fire these freezing cold mornings.

Hôtel de la Mairie, Cannes

IN EVERY letter you congratulate me on the little poem of
Haute Savoie—I mean my so-called happiness—so I must
hurry to tell you that it is all twisted now, and a situation
has developed rather like an octopus—into a tangle of deception. If I told you the story it would sound like the kind
of thing written or told by the patients in insane asylums

who have nothing to do but imagine fantastic evil plots. And as far as I can see nobody in the combination except my good *ouvrier* and I have been really dumb and ingenuous, and we have been effectively separated, or at least so it seems.

Since the beginning of the summer Grace, this strange, intelligent, amusing, plausible, but somehow not quite reliable friend—not intentionally unreliable but with something inherently distorted in the quite brilliant head—she, from the beginning of the summer, has evolved a plan to take Jacques to America to find a fine job for him, using the influence of many—as I think now—imaginary friends. And the eager ambitious Jacques has been completely impregnated with this dream. She had no money, nor he either, but she had a sort of wild conviction that if she went off to seek her fortune on the Riviera she would find it. And of course, looking so very Ziegfeld Follies, she is always surrounded by men, and she understands them very well and might easily find someone to help her out. She left Passy about two months ago and went to Monte Carlo. She made a great stir and scandal by her tremendous drinking and general misbehavior, and was noticed and seized and rescued by an English painter. During the past two months the Englishman has killed the idea of Jacques and has left his own rich wife, and the rich wife—a person with a terrible British conception of playing the game, being noble and grand and generous —has arranged to support both Grace and her husband for the rest of their lives.

In the meantime Jacques and I were faithfully waiting in Passy, and I believed very much in Grace's sort of crazy heroism—which was sincere at the time—which led her to think she could by her wits gain enough money to take J. to America. Letters stopped suddenly, and J. became *intransigeant*—furious and suspicious, and I with my foolish idea of patience and always believing in a person I have been fond of, kept persuading him to believe in her....

At any rate, it seems quite evident now that Jacques got the idea quite early that the less money I might spend in helping Marcel, the more there would be to help him and Grace. He knew that I had paid bills for Grace in the summer—in fact that I was paying everything for our life in Passy—and he could easily imagine that if she failed to raise any money for their project that I, whom he imagines to be very rich, would be the one who would save the situation. It is quite obvious now that my lovely little *histoire* with my charming one was at least partly destroyed by the interest of Jacques. In the meantime Jacques and I were alone in the house, and Marcel mysteriously never came. Oh, well, I can't go on with this story. Anyway, there has been the greatest mystery and complication.

Paris, 18 octobre 1931

COLD, dark, wintery afternoon that could be nothing else but Sunday, and it is unbearable to be on the street, and I rush into the hotel and up to my present large fine gloomy but luxurious room, full of trunks and bags and everything I possess on this side of the Atlantic all being assembled for the voyage home.

The past few weeks have been the craziest of my life, and at its most crazy this life was suddenly interrupted and put in its place by a cable from Warren telling me Mother is ill and suggesting that I come back soon. I forgot everything else and began to arrange a passage. I was in Cannes at the time, and was just rushing from Cannes when I had another cable from Mother herself telling me not to hurry because she was better. This quieted my fear, which of course at such distance was immediately tormenting me with the worst possibilities, and it has given me time to collect myself a little. I also was obliged to go back to Passy, happy for the necessity of collecting a trunk I had left there because it gave me an unexpected chance to take leave of Marcel. There we sat on the steep bank beside a *jolie* cascade in the forest, and bitterly comparing notes we uncovered the most melodramatic plot outside of a Conrad novel, by which we had been deceived and separated. *"Nous sommes les sacrifices,"* he said bitterly. The little sweet one with his shiny eyes. Then later in the day I saw Jacques again and had the first great battle of my life.

When I get home I think I shall be like the Ancient Mariner, always looking for somebody who will hear and believe this story. I feel quite crazy and bruised by it all, and arriving in Paris just fell into bed and slept for several days. Toshihiko was nicer than he has ever been, understanding very well, and pleased with me because at last he thinks I am "beginning to understand life a little better." But I feel so terribly tired, so terribly shocked. I may have learned a little, but I feel as if the experience has destroyed me.

I am terribly glad to know that Castine is not deserted this winter, that Philip and Beata are there and also Edith Farnsworth and some people called Greenbie. I know I shall have a longing to go there when I get back, and I might not have the courage to go if they weren't there. Toshihiko is still dreaming of Castine and painting pictures of his dreams of long dark hills and coves. He says he must go back there to live at last.

4 novembre 1931

Just waiting here ten minutes for the Hamburg-American Line office to open next door. And what a comfort and joy to find a last letter from you this morning in the

Dans Notre Péniche

Bankers' Trust Company! That was certainly very smart and clever and sweet of you, and *much* appreciated, as I had given up looking for any more letters, having sent out such a definite impression that I am leaving, and I am—day after tomorrow on the same ship that brought your letter. The *New York*, due in New York Friday the thirteenth. My first encounter with a Friday the thirteenth within this year was certainly a curse and has followed me ever since like a curse, and I am hoping this coming Friday the thirteenth will maybe annul and finish the other.

Last days in Paris! What a kaleidoscope! Just now sitting on *terrasse* of Café de la Madelaine in the sun with a balmy wind ruffling me, as I sat lapping up your letter. What a wonderful day today! When the *garçon* brought my breakfast he said it is wonderfully warm today. *"C'est le vent du Midi qui souffle!"* So I jumped out of bed and took the bus to the Opéra, and found six thousand three hundred and thirteen francs waiting for me at the Bankers' Trust Company, by cable, relieving a great uneasiness for fear it wouldn't come in time for me to pay my debts and catch the boat. Then your letter, too, and now so near my anticipation for seeing you and passing long winter evenings unfolding the tales of adventures of the year.

I am thinking quite a lot of going to Castine later if I can. I got a lovely Castine costume at the Salon Lafayette yesterday, long trousers and tunic of midnight blue gabardine, like riding habits—*doublé,* zippered, very nicely tailored.

Well, I have to go to see the fat Germans now and get my ticket. After that, my last rendezvous with the doctor.

I have to stop now—very quickly. *A bientôt!!!* Whatever has happened may sound rather terrific, but I myself am in the best mood—the more slings and arrows of outrageous fortune, it seems, the more alive I am. Really

229

getting to be a fighter, too. Toshihiko is very much pleased with me now, most abnormally complimentary, and he seems to enjoy the effect of my adventures on me. He thinks a great change of some sort has been produced, something which pleases him very much.

Alors—good-by to all that, and good morning America— (as Robert Graves and Carl Sandburg say). So impatient now!!

8. *Mr. and Mrs. Muffet*

[To Dr. de Forest]

80 Myrtle Street
Boston, April 7, 1932

IT IS spring in Boston. Last year it was spring in Haute Savoie. The year before that it was spring in Patchin Place. Such egotism! Perhaps it was spring in other places, too—possibly. But all I know is now in this tiny spot the whistles are blowing for 12 o'clock, noon, and I'm stopping in the middle of a leisurely, lazy, dreaming spring day, and the window is open and I can hear somebody in the yard below speaking peremptorily to a young kitten, and on the table in front of me is a tall bouquet of Easter lilies, also a very handsome Mexican earthenware pig which, with a slit in its back, represents a bank and contains one dollar and ten cents in silver—also a brown bowl containing apples, oranges, a lemon, and an oval silver bottle, also a little round wooden music box with a little wooden girl sitting on top nursing a doll. The tune is "Lullaby, and Good Night," played either fast or slowly as you turn the handle. This seems to be a still life I am painting for you.

Presently I have to prepare for a visitor, who is coming to pose for me. It is Julia, Toshihiko's beloved. She came

231

to see me the other day, and I gave her a cocktail, and in leaving she knocked a red geranium on the floor and broke the flowerpot in pieces, and then with her beret very much on one side she went, very primly cockeyed.

Today, after posing, I shall take her with me to a party in Charlestown, a party given by Mr. Edmund Quincy, a young painter, descendant of one of America's first Presidents, in whose little old house in Charlestown I lived the early part of this winter as a lodger. He calls me the tin soldier from some story by the Brothers Grimm, and tells me that according to the story I am to be buried in his garden, which comes to the fact that I feel this spring that the time should come soon when a small hole should be dug, in somebody's garden—and the tin soldier laid at rest. Every spring there is a new accumulation of springs to be remembered, when one goes out to drive in the late afternoon through the suburbs and hears frogs chirping in wet meadows and sees large gas tanks and billboards across the mist. And the springs get all mixed up—there are not enough, too many—it is quite perfect now—finished —and no more falling in love—very agreeable to look on such nonsense with a superior air—just laughing, because it is so amusing to remember it and be free of the sadness.

I should love to see you.

[To Catharine Huntington]

May 31, 1932

TODAY is one of those Castine days, so blue, with a whistling wind. I've been planting seeds in front of the house, but the wind almost blows the seeds all out of the earth as I plant, and I couldn't finish. We set out four rose bushes. Dan has moved all the furniture, and the effect is most refreshing. He brought in a great spray of horse-chestnut leaves, and apple blossoms and lilacs. He won't let me do anything at all. He cooks and washes clothes and makes beds and is *tellement gentil*. He also does the marketing, much more cleverly and economically than I ever could.

Dan has been having a cold today, and he has just come downstairs from a nap and is sitting on the pink sofa writing a letter. The first night, of course, arriving at the von Saltzas' about 9 P.M.; we both spent the night there, but Malcolm was sick, and the new maid elderly and nervous, and it was obviously not convenient to have us both there, but Beata said that I was to stay there as much as I liked, and she was so sweet and gave me a very comfortable protected feeling.

So Dan spent the next two nights alone in my house, and I slept *chez* von Saltza. The second morning, very early, about 7 o'clock, I telephoned from the von Saltzas' to Lorna (as my telephone wasn't connected) and asked her to go to my house and take a message to Mr. Hathaway. So after this fine diplomatic stroke I felt quite free to do whatever seemed most convenient. So, as I had to sleep in the room with Malcolm, and he was restless and uneasy, and I myself needed sleep, I came over to sleep here after that, and if anybody wishes to know who is the most *gentil* and tactful person in the world, it is Dan. We laugh because when he went to buy milk from Mrs. Bridgham on Water Street, just below, she said, "Oh, it is so nice to see you back again." He said, "Well, I've never been here before, but you probably notice a family resemblance. I am Miss Butler's cousin." And this may easily be distantly true, as one of the Almys married a Hathaway, and it's Warren's middle name. So now the news of my cousin visiting me has gone coursing over the town. Edward rushed up to me, and seeing Dan in the distance said, "Is that your cousin?" We have a very amusing time, laughing a great deal. He sends you his love, and I send mine, *beaucoup, beaucoup*—with this particular immediate sense of those letters, and such happiness and inexpressible gratitude, and trying in a dumb way to imagine for a moment the emptiness if I had never known you existed.

And to jump to the most recent details, the clothes are a great success. Every day I put on something new, and Dan exclaims and so do Philip and Beata. What a lovely dress! And every time I say that you gave it to me. Especially the gray linen which I wear with brown straw belt from Peck & Peck, and a little brown hat, and brown and white shoes. Also the brown and white embroidered dress Dan likes very much, and today I have on the funny dark red with white dots from Filene's basement, $.49, and it is *tellement chic*, with brown straw belt and brownish reddish big round brooch. And, of course, I still have others in reserve—your thin pale dress with little cape, for instance. In the evening I have worn the plaid, green black velvet which Dan admires. Dan gave me one of his special shampoos, and now Philip wants one for himself. His head has been so exposed to the sun it is turning to straw, he says. We all wake up early—about five or six—and seven seems shockingly late, and for the first time in years I am sleeping at proper times.

Why am I so lucky? So much pleasure and such lovely people around me.

Dan just brought a nice icy drink and a plate of thin round slices of brown bread, and put a big log on the fire, and we are both making a little scratching sound with our pens while the fire rustles.

It is five years exactly since Toshihiko came to Castine, and the mad cycle is finished, at last something is learned.

234

Mr. and Mrs. Muffet

IT WOULD ease me to know that things are better and your lonely holiday forgotten. I want to do something about it, and on the contrary all I do is make it worse by rioting away to the northern coast with Dan and being endlessly amused and charmed by watching him put this house into a new state of being. We have had a few unexpected visitors. One day Glovey and one of her gang appeared at the door, having come over from Lincolnville where the Russians have a house. The bootlegger called at the same time and brought us a gift, as a sample, of a bottle of Demerara rum, so we sipped rum almost all day and then bought a half-gallon. Glovey stayed most of the day, and yesterday Warren drove over with the young man called Bill whom I have known at Glovey's parties, and Dan cooked a superb dinner which we ate formally in the dining room. Usually we eat our dinner from the little black bench in front of the fire, sitting on the floor! It is amazing how energetic Dan is; he rushes up and down and has rearranged the entire house, and cleaned the woodshed, and now is building a terrace. There seems to be no end to his ingenious ideas. Also, we have got two kittens, which are quite a psychological care. The first was a present from the Greenbies, who live here now all the year around, and this kitten was a very beautiful Persian of a subtle strange color, very much like the one I had before which I adored so. Dan put on it a little pearl necklace and a bell, and we thought it was a lovely little cat. Then about a week later we rescued one of the much smaller kittens from the von Saltzas because Malcolm and Ingeborg were gradually killing them, and as soon as we brought it to our house, the first kitten became so jealous and horrid that we don't know what to do with her. The second kitten jumped this morning from the upstairs front hall down into the Japanese thing holding candles which hangs on chains, then fell, carrying two candles down to the floor below, causing a terrible clatter and shattering her own nerves, so that she has been crying ever since. The first kitten, Toupsie, stalked out of the house, hurt by our introducing a new pet so soon, and spent last night under the ell, and in the fields, and perhaps tasted life, as they say, a little too soon. *La vie est tellement compliquée, alors.*

Warren told me yesterday that Mother asked him if he could drive her up next week, although she keeps on saying that she isn't sure. I want so much to have her come, and Dan is so charming about her. I think everything will go well, and it will be a nice summer. Dan seems to be terribly happy and never seems to get bored or tired of thinking of new things to do. Surely nobody has ever dreamed of doing so much to improve the house.

This is a lovely quiet and rather hot Sunday noon. We had such a sumptuous Sunday breakfast we are not eating any lunch, except an eggnog with rum in it. Dan is sitting at the desk writing letters, wearing one of his Marblehead striped sweaters and pale blue cotton pants, and I am lying on the floor. We even do the washing, except the sheets and towels, and this afternoon I have to do the ironing. Dan loves to discuss the food, and I just stopped writing a moment to listen to his plan for supper, or rather dinner tonight. He just stepped into the kitchen to taste of the lamb broth he is making.

Now that the house is very nearly settled, I want to begin to draw again and work on my interrupted story of Haute Savoie.

July 5, 1932

You know how sometimes there is so much to say that one can't say anything. I have only been hoping that you knew

236

by instinct, but now I don't dare to trust wholly to that, because I am afraid there may be rumors reaching you which might hurt you, making you feel that I had confided in others first. I did confide in Philip one evening when I was alone, and rather *distraite,* and he was near.

Of course, it is about Dan and me. *C'était vendredi le treize mai qu'il m'a dit qu'il veut se marier avec moi—et depuis ce jour là c'est toujours la même chose—beaucoup de projets et de bonheur,* but all the time I have been feeling guilty toward you because you said to me, "Now, anyway, don't you marry him!" But he is determined, and he is sweeter to me than anyone has ever been. We can't do it, however, unless I can sell my house and get by that enough cash to carry us until he gets his job. But the Fabens are quite interested in buying it, and we are carrying on a correspondence with them. The suspense of not knowing yet, however, is rather terrific. Dan works furiously building a terrace. He has done so much and is so marvelous about my sentimental associations.

I am longing to see you, and I just pray that this news, rather uncertain news still, will not make you suffer.

My mother seems to take the idea amazingly easily, not, of course, easily, really, but quite gaily, considering how terrified she is of any sort of change. Of course Dan is most winning and tactful. Barbara's being here helps so much too. We spend very merry evenings, *à quatre,* playing games and laughing, and my mother seems very well. But I haven't spoken of it to any others in the family, except Lurana. It was so amusing in Peabody, when Dan came several times. Kitty used to deck us in lilacs and call us the bride and groom before a word had been said to anybody.

July 8, 1932

It's five o'clock in the morning, imagine! I woke up somehow, and I'm sitting up in bed on the porch. The weather turned gray and still overnight, with a little patter on the roof. Yesterday, Dan's birthday, was so beautiful, and we both felt so very gay and happy. We sent off a very fatal letter to Helen Fabens, setting a price on the house. My mother is marvelous, taking it all so easily, being so kind to me, wishing terribly that she could buy the house for me, but unable to, but praising me for having given it its charm and value, and helping me with suggestions about presenting it to purchasers.

By the way, when I said in my last letter I had been so afraid of telling you about the plan of marriage, I didn't mean that I thought perhaps I was stealing him away from you, because of course if you really had wanted to marry him you would have. I only thought that for me to step off with anyone in wedlock might seem rather boring and depressing to you. Of course it would obviously be an escape for Dan from a rather intolerable life, and for a long time I was kind of skeptical about his loving me as much as he said, but I just would be a fool if I didn't believe him now. He shows it in so many infinitely sweet ways.

Philip arrived two days ago and brought Harriet here. I wanted Kitty too, but her father couldn't bear to part with her. I expect others will come. Fergus isn't well again, and Gladys will probably bring him a little later. If I sell the house, I'll have to break the news to them all, and I hate so much to deprive them of this place, which they all adore and love so much, and if this thing happens it will be a farewell summer, and the minute the house is sold, if it is, Dan wants to get married and rush to Quebec and then go to live at 80 Myrtle Street, taking my room and the one across the hall, marbleizing the fireplace and painting the walls and hanging new curtains.

July 13, 1932

I WAS quite relieved to get your second letter today. Not that there was anything wrong with the first one, but I felt as if I had dealt you rather a shock, and you were naturally a little stunned. Well, it is all very curious about selling the house. I have thought of that in any case. I have the cold shudders in the night, seeing how deeper and deeper into debt it is carrying me. My mother is dreadfully burdened, and I can't ask her to help me. She couldn't do it anyway, and I think this is perhaps an exception in these times, one case in which it is more advantageous to sell. That is, if the Fabens decide to buy. You see, a wooden painted house in the country looks bad if it isn't kept up, whereas your brick house is always presentable. Dan has done wonders in improving this place, building the terrace, and setting out more and more trees, and with him to do things it costs me much less. But if winter comes, as they say, there are enormous coal bills. The running expenses, except for coal, are less with Dan helping me, but there are always the awful recurring necessities—repairs, painting, taxes, mortgages, etc., etc. It is such a big place.

As to marriage. I think it seems very nice. You know mature people whose lives have been hampered by immature marriages, but if it is turned around and one has had one's freedom and education first, and then chooses a person of similar experience, it is a different thing. If an affair begins as an experiment, it doesn't ever get beyond that stage. Everything has, with me, been so fragmentary and tentative, it seems wonderfully balancing to have someone who wants and insists on permanence, and on the ritual.

The house and place have never looked so beautiful. It is seven years I have had it. Mother happened to say, not apropos of that but when someone mentioned the significance of No. 7, that in the Bible seven is the symbol for completion. It ends a cycle.

[To Dr. de Forest]

July 26, 1932

MARY CAMP tells me that you have spent summers at Marblehead in the past, and I wonder if there you ever knew any of the Hathaway family, of Marblehead (Mr. Hathaway, an insurance and real-estate dealer), because I quite sincerely flatter myself that you will be somehow interested to know that Dan Hathaway (of Marblehead and Paris) and I are planning and plotting and scheming and hoping to get married very soon. Mary seems to tell me that you used to go to Marblehead before you were married so perhaps if you ever laid eyes on my Danny then (you see how silly I am now) he must have been quite young, because he is of course younger than I am, though not too much, and yet time passes so quickly that I think he may have been then just a beautiful boy with enormous blue eyes and dark reddish hair. Anyway, he is very beautiful now—everybody thinks—and sweeter to me than anybody else I have ever dreamed of. As we have no money and no job at present, getting married depends on the sale of my house; and my house, being always like a lucky talisman in a story, is capable of transforming itself when needed and is helping me now. Some friends of mine are anxious to buy it and are coming to Castine soon to see it again, and I hope that perhaps by September the sale will have been accomplished. We

240

haven't announced our intention to marry; we hardly dare to until it is settled about the house—that is, except to certain members of our families—but I wanted to write to you before you leave New York, as Mary tells me you are going to California.

I have thought of you very many times and torn up dozens of sheets of paper trying to write to you since your letter came, and I want to thank you and tell you that, regarding my debt to you and your extreme kindness about it, my chagrin and my appreciation are about equal, both enormous. If my friends buy the house, they are to pay by yearly installments, and in this way Dan and I will be able to live, probably in France, for at least two years, until things are better or else have gone completely to smash, in which case nothing would make any difference anyway.

This is a very brief letter compared to the pages I might write to you, but it is something anyway, and I know you must guess that it is a cycle which is ended, by the grace of God, somehow. How lucky I have been, I keep thinking, lucky in tears even, to have been blessed with the gift of knowing you and being allowed to shed tears under your compassionate eyes. Please don't think that I ever forget to be grateful—no matter how long the silences.

[To CATHARINE HUNTINGTON]

October 4, 1932

IT SEEMS like an allegory meaning I don't know what, to be able to come back to Paris under such different stars, mounting these beautiful old stairs and coming into this romantic apartment with the sweetest person in the world. Don't think I am too silly. If you won't laugh at me, I must say that my cup of happiness is full. We are so much in love with each other it is just silly, incredible. Morning,

241

noon, and night. I remember Henry saying once that getting married is like a vaccination—you never know whether it will take or not. It does or it doesn't. And I may add that the element in the vaccine which makes it take is X, an unknown quantity, which can't be foreseen by any brains or calculations.

We have our beautiful cat, our Toupsie, whose dark shadow and plumy tail sweep across the floor. We have our victrola, and we have bought some lovely pieces of old furniture, and the place is nearly settled. A stove has just arrived, which will be set into the black marble fireplace tomorrow, and in a few days our rugs and Taro's painting should arrive from Castine. Dan had already a lovely little bed which we find is big enough for us, and he had a little red iron sofa and a few chairs, and a bookcase built in the wall. We bought a writing table, more chairs, two *fauteuils,* a *poudreuse* for me, and a bureau— all lovely old pieces carefully chosen—a few little tables, especially a three-tiered table on which Dan has arranged our little treasures, little objects from Castine and Marblehead, and one of Dan's antique dealers gave us, for a wedding present, an old Russian brazier in the shape of a Russian lady with folded hands, like a figurehead, and to me they gave a beautiful fan. Dan had also already had a mirror and his marble bust of a king of Russia, and a long wooden barometer or thermometer on the wall, also his gilded Napoleonic placques, and some paintings.

We arrived last Thursday, less than a week. We were mad with excitement and joy and very busy getting the necessary extra furniture, and a few bottles of wine, and arranging little domesticities. I had written from the boat to Toshihiko without expecting an answer, not knowing if he was alive or dead. And the second day we were here, late afternoon, while Dan was asleep on the little sofa and I was half-dressed, mending a stocking, a knock on the door, and Toshihiko burst in, excited, amazed, and apparently very delighted. I took him into the bedroom because Dan was asleep in the other room, but Dan said something and I went in and said, "Toshihiko is here!" He said, dazed, "It's not possible!" He was dreaming that we were on a boat in the English Channel and he didn't think Toshihiko could possibly come to see us there. And then dazedly began to think that he had come out with the pilot. Well, while Dan was waking up, Tosh and I were madly laughing and talking incoherently in the bedroom. Then Dan came to the door and bent himself a little way through and asked Tosh if he would please hand him his pants because he had nothing on but a sweater.

They liked each other from the first moment. We sat together drinking vermouth in the candlelight. I got dressed and Toshihiko gazed out of the window with Dan and admired the place, the roofs outside, the wonderful stillness, and we just couldn't talk sensibly. It was really great fun to amaze Toshihiko so much. He evidently hadn't got a letter from Castine telling of approaching events, only the note from the boat saying, "Write me at 22 rue Visconti, Mme Hathaway." He was all apologies, very charming, for having done such a shocking thing as to come unannounced, but said he couldn't help it, and Dan was so charmed by him, it was all right. Toshihiko seemed to fall in love with our place, and with us, and was all amazement. His affairs were better, and he looked very well, although he says he isn't too well. He kept telling me, quite astonished, how well I looked, and how different, so much pep, he said, and he declared he hoped to see us a great deal.

Of course we haven't half told each other our histories. We were too incoherent, but we shall meet again soon, for that. He seems to think it is very becoming for me to be

PARIS WINDOW

Illustration from *Mr. Muffet's Cat*

married. Oh, well, I am so glad he is here. It adds a great deal.

Dan has just come in, and I have to get washed and dressed and go out to lunch. I am ashamed almost to be so happy.

November 12, 1932

WE ARE moving from the rue Visconti to 65 Boulevard Arago, into a little house, studio, dining room, bedroom, and kitchen, also garden and sunlight. We decided this mainly because Dan's mother decided to come over, and we'll need more room, also kitchen, but even if she weren't coming, I should like the little house much better, having more room to move around and no long flights of stairs to climb, and more cozy home life of cooking, etc., to say nothing of a fine place to work, big studio, rent

244

seven thousand a year, about what I paid on Myrtle Street, only minus heat and light.

We met Katharine Dudley soon after we arrived here, in the Deux Magots. Katharine thinks Dan is simply lovely, and a very rare person, and that we are both too lucky for these days. She likes his elegance, and they laughed a great deal together. It was such a pleasure to see her.

Our cat is increasingly beautiful—her tail is now a wonder. She is lying on top of me now as I lie on the floor. Dan and I walked for miles this afternoon, and it was too lovely. We went to the Musée Carnavalet near the Bastille, a very gray, still afternoon, and walked home across the bridges and along the quays, and at last in this quarter, stopping to have a nice hot grog in a café. On our way in one of those cheap sidewalk markets, Dan saw a little sweater striped black, white, and gray which he liked, although I remembered you told me never to wear them. However, we got it and it is most cute, with a silk scarf of Dan's to make it a little kinder, and I feel quite excited wearing it, as well as nice and warm.

We are waiting now for Bravig Imbs to come in. He asked about you, and said you were one of the loveliest people he ever saw. You may not remember him, but he met you with Elliot, he says. He is married since then to Valeska, the Russian girl. We see them both quite often. They are very intimate friends of Elliot and Camille. And all these people think they never want to live in America. Perhaps I have been, we have been, luckier than some Americans; it has certainly never been barren and dreadful in our secret haunts, behind the curtains in Pinckney Street, or in Castine or Hadley. I could never wish to become an expatriate. I really think I have lived about long enough, having so many marvelous things to remember.

Dan and I live a very retired cozy life, and after we are

settled in the new house I do hope to write memoirs and draw all the time, as I feel my cozy old age drawing on.

November 19, 1932

I FIND myself at the present beautifully protected, with observation sharpened much, instead of dulled, and going along the street or sitting in cafés, when I see some woman alone who has a certain thirsty and forlorn look, I feel ashamed to look at her unless I can forget my present self completely and look at her as if I were looking into a mirror, because I really feel I am she, or have been for so long that I can never forget it. And I miss my mother and am sometimes unbearably conscious of her pain, much more unbearably and sharply than before, as if all old bonds were so much more heightened and so much more precious. It seems as if a new and very definite attachment which gives a new pattern to one's life makes the other and older attachments terribly nostalgic, partly because the new one seems to force one to be, officially at least, at a distance, officially not belonging quite so much to the others. I have had hours when I could cry for Castine, and it seems as if someone had died, and my Kitty, I think of her so hard I can see her and hear her so vividly it really is a physical pain. But it is like the *"Sacré du printemps."* You can't get a new harvest without tearing the ground up, and it is an ecstasy of readjustment—ecstatic pain.

Now the candles are all lighted and the decanters filled, and we are expecting Bravig and Valeska Imbs, so I'll have to stop.

Paris
November 22, 1932

As ONE cannot ask for *de quoi écrire* when one is sitting on the *terrasse* of the café, only inside, I sacrificed sheets of my sketch book because I feel like writing to you. And it is so cozy here under the awning and close to the brazier that I can't move. Empty coffee cup in front of me, two saucers, and a fresh package of cigarettes, and I am alone, because Dan has just gone off to try to find a bed, and I was feeling a little tired so I stayed here. It is amazing what a lot of trouble and mounting expenses we are having moving into our new house. Somebody could write a book about the French people's passion for doing things in as complicated a way as possible. The rents may be lower here, but the proprietors haven't the slightest intention of keeping their places in repair, and it is we who have to make all the improvements. We had to install electricity, which means not merely hiring an electrician but getting permission from the proprietor, then paying a thousand francs to one's fellow *locataires* for one's share in the main current, then the proprietor signs an authorization and sends it to the electrician, who sends it to the main office of the electric company. Then we go to the main office to see if the authorization has been received and registered in a large untidy book, then we make out another paper telling our family history and pay several hundred francs for a guarantee, then we go back to the electrician and tell him this is done, or the company notifies him, and at last after three weeks he begins to do the work. At the same time we wait for a series of *fumistes* to clean the chimneys, none of them keeping their promises to come, so we keep engaging another and waiting hopefully for three or four days.

The painter in the meantime has been scraping the walls but doesn't dare to begin to paint until the *fumiste* has finished, on account of the soot, and the only thing that really is done is the bookcase and armoire by a very faithful and good little carpenter.

We are told by an old friend of Dan's to go to a certain

address where we can buy a stove to heat the studio for two hundred francs, installation free. We go there and find the price has gone up to two hundred and thirty-five and the installation will be one hundred and twenty. The friend was an old American painter who forgot to say he bought his stove about twenty years ago, which made a difference in the price.

Now we are trying to find a *lit-divan*. We have been sleeping in Dan's very narrow little bed, which we are going to put in Mrs. Hathaway's room. The price of the new bed, which we thought would be about five hundred francs, seems to be mounting *vers les milles*.

There is a cunning little baby all dressed in immaculate white wool at the table next to me, with its very charming smiling mother and rather tired father. The mother has on a suit of pale grayish tweed flecked with brown, with wide revers faced with dark brown velvet and brown velvet buttons. The short jacket all buttoned up very tight, a tight little hat of same, very much on one side, showing dark, shiny, scalloped hair. Very *chic* and also very maternal and rosy and happy. The father came first with the baby, rather forlorn, and they sat and waited for a little while, and the father ordered coffee. Then the mother arrived, and as soon as she came, very protecting and clever and gay, the whole family became organized. She brought a box from a *pâtisserie* and took out brioches and tarts and spread them out like a picnic, quite shamelessly making a little economy, ordering only another coffee and hot milk for the baby. Now they have just gone.

We went to see a mechanical circus the other night in the studio of an American artist named Calder, whose curious works of art, made of wire, used to appear in *Transition*. We were taken by a rather eccentric, affluent, and alcoholic couple from Chicago. We were about seven in one taxi, including the very amusing Tonny, Dutch

248

painter, former protégé of Gertrude Stein, and his friend a poet and the poet's mistress, a very gay and charming person wearing red crocheted gloves—a French countess turned Bohemian.

Toshihiko's Japanese girl friend left a collection of kimonos and obis, etc., with him to sell if he could, as I believe he paid her fare home or part of it because he had persuaded her to stay a little longer than she intended or could afford to in order to go with him to Spain, and he felt responsible toward her. Now he is so poor he is anxious to sell them, and I'm rather pleased because I have been able to help him to sell them. He has never mingled with people in Paris, except Japanese, and he seems to be quite astonished because by one or two introductions he has not only sold most of the kimonos, but met someone who likes his paintings very much and will introduce him to the manager of a certain gallery where there is a chance that he may have an exhibition for nothing. I'm hoping that I may have a chance in the same gallery later if I work hard all winter to do enough portraits.

Although everybody says it is dead here in Paris now, it seems to me more alive than most places, and as soon as one knows just a few people, one is constantly meeting more and more, and one's opportunities increase if one has anything at all to show. I suppose all this is due to the café habit, a very good and helpful habit, if one has an ambition to become known and successful and if, of course, one remembers to spend part of one's time at home working.

Dan came back to where I was sitting and it grew chill, so now we're home again. Dan has just been cutting the mauve *toile de Jouy* that we bought today for curtains in our dining room. It's lovely and cozy and warm here with our Salamandre, and a kerosene lamp and candles.

249

Christmas Day, 1932

THREE weeks ago we were moving into this little house, and Mrs. Hathaway was arriving from America, and Dan was going to Le Havre to meet her. So many things at once. Mrs. Hathaway wants to go to the Balearic Islands, and wants us to go, quite soon. It seems life in Ibiza is so cheap that if we go down there for two or three months, avoiding the heavy coal expense of winter, we would be doing rather well. But Paris has been in a state of spring-like weather steadily for two or three weeks. Every morning the sun is pouring into our little dining room, and people are working in the gardens, and Dan wears his summer sweater and old pants and rakes and digs in our garden, so it seems unnecessary to go south. We are waiting for a sudden crash of cold weather to send us off in a hurry.

In the meantime I am working quite hard, doing my book called *Mr. Muffet's Wonderful Cat and Her Trip to Paris*—forty pages done and seven illustrations. Toshihiko gives me criticism and is most encouraging. He keeps telling me I am improving. He is terribly flattering, really. Seems to be rather astonished in some ways, and he's very sweet and kind about expressing it. The light in our studio is marvelous, and I am so fascinated by doing the illustrations that I can't tear myself away to go out or do anything else.

I am quite proud of having, at last, one or two new clothes. Among the many beautiful kimonos we bought of Toshihiko, we got one which Dan admired enormously and wanted me to have a dress made of. It is greenish-grayish silk with a mauve leafy pattern printed on it. We ripped it all apart one evening and took it to the *couturier* who made my black suit last time I was here, M. Cadet and his wife, both *couturiers*, and very skillful. They were surprised to see me, and I introduced Dan and as soon after as possible Madame privately exclaimed, *"Qu'il est beau!!! Qu'il est charmant!"*

French people are extraordinarily sympathetic with Dan. They respond to him very much, and he is with them much more natural and at ease than with Americans. He drops all his defensive apparatus and is so much more a complete person. He told me this a long time ago, in Castine, and it is very pleasant to see.

Of course he sends his love to you. He always asks me, after I have written to you, if I sent you his love. He is lying down now, having just marbleized two rooms and a staircase since we had our Xmas dinner.

[TO DAN HATHAWAY]

DEAREST MR. MUFFET,

Here I am all alone in our house. Harry has gone out for the rest of the day, and I have to stay here on account of the laundress.

I want to write you a letter. Often I feel that way because I haven't the gift for talking, and I can express myself much better this way. And sometimes I feel awfully badly because I seem to be incapable of telling you things. Sometimes I have hurt you without meaning to at all. Oh, my dearest Dan, I never mean to hurt you, as I know you never mean to hurt me. I can see too well, by your great sensitiveness and your quick self-defense, that you have been so badly hurt in the past, I don't know by whom, that you are on your guard sometimes, even with me. Especially so on the subject of money, which is something I am absolutely determined shall not make us unhappy together. You mustn't think I don't understand a little something about you. I may be wrong, but I think somebody, I suppose your father, must have been much too severe with you on the subject of extravagance. Not understanding your nature at all, he must have hurt you terribly and antagonized you. Your mother, seeing how you suffered, naturally couldn't bear to see the effect of severity on you, and so she perhaps went in the opposite direction and tried to help you by always believing you were in the right whether you really were or not, which was what almost any loving mother would do toward a suffering child. And you still suffer if there is the slightest hint of reproach, and you get quite strange, defiant like a hurt child. Oh, my dearest Dan, don't you know that I realize this and try every possible way to save you from it? But I think if you understood really and truly the thing I feel about money, you would believe once and for all that I am never trying to hurt you, or deprive you or coerce you.

To me, money is alive. It is almost human. If you treat it with real sympathy and kindness and consideration, it will be a good servant and work hard for you, and stay with you and take care of you. If you treat it arrogantly and contemptuously, as if it were not human, as if it were only a slave and could work without limit, it will turn on you with a grand revenge and leave you to look after yourself alone. You have to control it absolutely, but with patience and love, and then what pleasure and comfort it will give you in return. It will even be glad to do charming and graceful things for your friends too. You know what an awful thing an uncontrolled servant is and, worse still, a rebellious slave. That is what we have had. Look at the history of the past year in our checkbooks and look at us now. It is our own fault, nobody else's. We had a very, very good servant in the beginning, and we let it get absolutely out of control. The other extreme would be just as bad too. A miser makes a fetish of the servant, falls in love with it, and won't let it work at all, either for himself or his family or friends. He sits it up in the parlor in its best clothes and kills it with adoration.

Now Mrs. Muffet has expressed her philosophy about money. And as she really has had fairly good success with past servants, she suggests that she should try for a few months to train this present one, and get it under control if possible, and working well, and willing to stay through the year. She cannot do it without Mr. Muffet's co-operation and faith in her.

It is obvious that we can't live without our servant, and we can't live tranquilly if it is threatening to leave every few months.

Mrs. Muffet loves Mr. Muffet very, very much. That alone is the whole reason for everything. The reason I am passionate, obstinate, and sometimes angry about money is because our life together depends on it. It depends not only on having it, but on not being tormented every day by little conflicts about it. You don't feel the anxiety that I do when we face a crisis because you are so lucky and something has always turned up for you. But I think maybe I am your luck now, because I have an absolute feeling that the moment has come for me to try my system. And if you will trust me absolutely for a few months, and give me a chance to see what I can do, I will be gay about it and very, very nice.

I cannot go on living the way we have done. You don't realize it, but for instance just last week almost four hundred francs went just for pocket money. I can have all the courage in the world if you will co-operate with me, but I haven't the courage or the strength to live a precarious existence, especially if it isn't a bit necessary really. We have enough still to keep us well and happy if we make a plan and stick to it. And I bet if you consent to Mrs. Muffet being the banker we will be able to *faire la bombe de temps à temps* as well, without either one of the Muffets feeling deprived or thwarted. It is all a question of balance and proportion, like architecture. There can be deviation and play and ornament, but the building has got to be symmetrical; if it gets lopsided again, Mrs. Muffet refuses to live in it, just exactly as passionately as Mr. Muffet refuses to live in a house that is not in perfect order.

[To Catharine Huntington]

St. Valentine's Day, 1933

WE ARE now on a very cunning little old-fashioned Victorian boat, all upholstered in dark blackish dahlia-red velvet and black leather, terribly soft and comfortable and shabby and cozy, crossing from Majorca to Marseilles, on our way back to Paris. While in Majorca I rode from the boat with Camille between springlike fields and blooming almond trees, arriving at dark at the primitive little Spanish inn where Elliot greeted us, very blooming in a costume of sailcloth, dyed pink, cerise shirt, red and white plaid necktie, and beret. We had merry hours in the smoky, shadowy little café where we sat with a rough-and-ready but very talented young American girl who is doing remarkable paintings under Elliot's direction; and her quiet Spanish lover, a painter, and the native habitués of the café, slouching around the tables wearing their wide-brimmed black hats and black clothes, made in the dim lamplight and smoky shadows something that was certainly very Spanish.

Majorca wasn't much fun. We all had terrible colds, and the *pension* was boring. Yesterday we had the nicest time we had had all the time. We met, with Camille, as we sat in a cozy bar, an American artist who asked us to come for tea and cocktails in the afternoon. We found a marvelous enormous house in one of the narrow crowded streets in the heart of the city. He had made over an old factory, and the huge white plastered rooms, heated with stoves and fireplaces, and the bare and businesslike studio were terribly nice and strangely cozy, especially his darling little five-year-old boy, very tiny and very bright; and nice buxom English wife. He had known Dan years ago, and when he mentioned Chicago I discovered he knew the Dualeys very well and Dan Reagan, and Dan Reagan's wife's first husband, etc., etc., etc., and we had very pleasant interesting gossips. His name is Jacobson, not very young, and it was kind of a reminiscence of Dorothy's Chicago newspaper atmosphere in *Forgotten Frontiers*. And among other things he gave us valuable hints about doing illustrations, having done many children's books and comic strips himself.

Here we are sitting at one end of a long table in the dining room, where one writes letters or looks at the magazines that are scattered around, while a *garçon* is setting one of the other long tables with gentle tinklings and rustlings; and as I write, Dan is looking at pictures of Czechoslovakia, and we think it would be fun to go to Prague some time. We haven't got much to read at this moment. In our cabin the Paris American papers worn to a shred, and a Mallorcan string bag full of Tauchnitz Editions we have finished; and a novel by an old Radcliffe girl named Marian Winnek, which was lent to me the other day by Eleanor Hosmer, whom I met on the tramway in Majorca.

After dinner—just a handful of passengers—just nine, all sitting at one table and talking in mixed French and American about Spanish food and hot-water bags. And the little boat so cozily puffing along, making me feel sleepy.

Illustration from *Mr. Muffet's Cat*

17 avril 1933

SITTING in our *bistro* having a *café crème,* and sending off some of Toshihiko's announcements for him, I send you one, as I am sure you will like to see it. But it's rather tragic, rather than anything, because he is risking his last cent on it. He is quite desperate. He came in the other day, and he was rather heartbreaking. He is living with

Mr. and Mrs. Muffet

a French girl, not too happily, and dreadful financial situation and defiance of family.

I WONDER what you are doing today. If it is as hot there as it is here, you are of course enjoying your cool, cool salon and just deciding to make a little tea and have it in the garden. I wish I were sitting there with you, two together murmuring about life. And of course, as usual, I would be wearing your clothes. Just the last two or three days I have been so thankful for the gray linen dress you gave me last year. A good deal of the time these hot days I wear almost nothing in this more or less rustic pavilion. But yesterday I had to go out, across the city, to mail my finished story of Mr. Muffet's cat to New York where Helen Faben's sister, who has worked years in publishers' offices and is now on literary staff of *New York Sun,* is undertaking to sell it for me. It was a most pleasant feeling to see it going off, all stamped and registered, and marked for *Ile de France.* In the meantime, imagine! Caroline was at a storage warehouse with Dan helping her to dispose of the contents of 6 Place du Panthéon. She came a few days ago, with Delteil and Sophie, but he couldn't stand Paris and left for Avignon, where they live now, and she came and stayed with us while Sophie stayed at the Reagans. It was so hot we sat late last night under the trees on the sidewalk of our local café. It seemed so curious, these repetitions of *La Vie,* sitting together on a summer evening, as in 11th Street, Pinckney Street, Hadley, but poignantly lacking you.

Caroline said she had written to you on the train coming up, so you probably know her present mood as well as I do. Fairly contented, I think. She and Dan got on together very charmingly; of course he was delighted to have a guest to take care of, to make an exquisite breakfast for, etc.

But speaking of these reunions in Vienna, Paris, or Oslo, I really find my desire is to reunite under the elms—that is to say, the return of the native is my idea of happiness. I am not a cosmopolitan, or at least I don't think so. This hot weather makes me all ready to fly to Castine. But it isn't just climate, or habit—it is just simple homesickness for certain people and certain houses. This doesn't include my own house especially. Another one in Castine would do very nicely. However, I think the nostalgia makes me work much better than I could at home. And if this book is accepted, perhaps I'd better stay here a little longer and see if I can do something else. I said the story is finished, but not all the illustrations. So I still have several weeks' work to do.

Dan's cat has had her first kittens, by a French husband, one kitten just like Peter. It is all in the book, the Franco-American romance, etc.

It is getting hotter and hotter while I write, 5:15. I must get dressed and go out for the first time today. We have a very nice *ouvriers'* café at the corner, where we sit under the cool horse-chestnut trees and have *apéritifs* before dinner. Caroline left this morning early, so we are alone tonight.

Summer has come over us so suddenly. I didn't know it would stir so many feelings in me, especially migratory instinct.

I wonder if anything good has been written in America that you are excited about. I have beside me a copy of the *New Yorker*, very rare here, which Mother sent me, along with *Atlantic Monthly*, *Scribners*, and *Time*, a delicious feast (imagine feeling that way about them). I find reviews in the *New Yorker* of new novel by Conrad Aiken, also a much-praised best seller called *As the Earth Turns,* about Maine.

Well, if we go back soon to live in U.S. there are little items of food I hope to continue with, new ways of making salad dressing. And with the beautiful big strawberries of this moment, pile a lot of sugar on them and a dessert-spoonful of wine vinegar (to about one-half box of strawberries), and turn it all over and over, as if you were mixing lettuce in dressing, and it is quite wonderful. Then cream, too. You don't taste the vinegar, but it heightens the strawberry flavor in a most mysterious way. And did you ever cut little cubes of very stale bread and rub garlic on them and toss them into the salad? The next book I thought of writing is *Mr. Muffet's Cookbook,* with still lifes from our kitchen and the little shops of this quarter.

[To Warren Butler]

July 30, 1933

Hurray for our operations—the *same* day! No, I didn't have any ether dreams, because I didn't have to be cut open deep, and I told the doctor I didn't want to take ether. I was scared of dreaming. So I lay very still, wrists and ankles tied down, and I heard the cutting through the local anesthetic—a sweet little French nurse holding a little cloth above my face and smiling at me upside down and giving me a pat on the cheek now and then, and then at last leaning over and saying *"C'est fini!"* They were simply sweet to me—a marvelous, world-famous doctor, and nuns in charge of the nurses, a big tree by the window, a lovely big courtyard and at sundown nuns sitting on green iron chairs on the grass knitting, and in the morning bustling home from market with big baskets of vegetables.

Probably I have written in my head as many letters to you, as you have to me, but I want to thank you for the two very nice ones which came visibly, and also for your share of something else I received which I shall repay soon I hope. But this letter isn't a substitute for unwritten ones. It is a too lazy Sunday afternoon, staying at a little pink house on the Marne over the week end with some friends we met in Paris last winter. There is a riverside café whose very much amplified radio is playing too much jazz disturbing an otherwise very peaceful place under an enormous rustling poplar tree. The word rustling reminds me you have written me three letters, not two—a letter written on a picnic drinking gin given by a lady.

We are having a marvelously happy life. Dan is so sweet to me—you can't imagine. The visible proof of it all is in the hands of Harper & Bros. They are very enthusiastic and are going to take quite special pains to make "a lovely book" of it—typographically, etc. I hope it will make up for some of the unwritten letters. I have still a good deal of work to do for it—more drawings to make and some which the engraver wishes to have changed so that they may be reproduced properly. I know I was ignorant about those requirements, and I am only glad that some I sent will pass without being changed.

I know it was hard for you to write at first—you probably felt as if I were changed—but I am not, only perhaps rather nicer, healthier, happier, and more productive.

Please forgive me for writing on a lazy day, when it is not my best, but I am tired of postponing, always waiting for a perfectly clear time because it is too long in coming. This letter has just been interrupted by a game of anagrams with our host and two callers. Now they have gone to swim in the river, and Dan and I have returned to our letters—sitting at a little table out of doors. *Alors!* here comes somebody along—I was interrupted before I wrote the path— Our host's mother and another French lady, and their curiosity about anagrams lying on the table, and

our teaching them to play—we had to play in French
naturally.

So please accept this poor fragment torn out of a lazy
day, the only kind of a day when I can write at all because
the others are all drawing days, and it is even harder. But
when the book is finished I will draw my breath and do
better—

August 14, 1933

HERE is a little card-trick to amuse a convalescent. Somebody showed it to Dan and me, and when we were doing
it the other night, it made me think of you, because it is
so mysterious. It is not a trick, really, but a mathematical
mystery.

Lay the cards out in the following manner. Take the
first card of the pack and if it is, for instance, a four, lay it
face down and, counting that card as four in the series of
thirteen (because there are thirteen cards in each suit)
lay the next nine cards in the pack on top of it, face down.
The next card may be a Queen, for instance, which, of
course is number twelve, so you just lay one card on top
of it. Keep on making piles of cards in this way, counting
to thirteen from whatever card you turn up each time,
until you come to the end of the pack. It doesn't matter
if you have a few odd cards left at the end—just lay them
aside. Then ask the person to whom you are showing the
trick to choose three of the completed piles, and remove
all the others. Then ask him to turn over two of the three
piles so that the bottom card of each is turned up. Add
the two numbers of these two cards, and to the sum add
ten. Take up all the other cards—the rejected piles and
whatever odd cards were left—that is, the whole pack except for the three piles that were chosen, in any order, it
doesn't matter. Count out of this pack the same number
of cards as the sum you got by adding ten to the numbers

of the two cards turned up. Then count the cards left in your hand, and that number will be the same as the number on the card on the bottom of the third pile.

If you can tell why this always works you are far brighter than I am; in fact you are the only person I know who might be able to explain it. The person who showed it to us said it was invented by a man who was serving a life imprisonment, which might perhaps be necessary for solving it.

When I first learned this trick I remember I wrote it to C. Huntington in my enthusiasm, knowing that she and Creighton like to play cards together, and I thought it might amuse them. But she was quite horrified by my thoughts being upon card-tricks, and she quite crushed me. Apparently she thought there was something very curious about bothering to send a card-trick so far. But I think it is rather nice to do it, and makes the ocean seem much narrower—to think that you will be sitting at a table some evening soon, saying, Here is a card-trick Kitty just told me. What! I thought Kitty was in Paris! Yes, sure she is, but she just showed me this card-trick just the same. When we were doing it the other night, we were visiting in a little pink house in the country, on an island in the Marne, underneath a huge poplar tree.

I am busily writing another story. I can't seem to stop having started on the adventures of Mr. and Mrs. Muffet and Toupsie. The adventures we have, the places we go to, the people we know, and their animals, seem to furnish such amusing material, all ready-made, for a continued story—like the Married Life of Helen and Warren. So I am hoping that Harpers will welcome the idea of a Muffet series—the Mr. Muffet books. We are thinking, very vaguely, of going to Algeria for a few months next winter, which of course will give me very exciting material, and probably fascinating for illustration. The friends whom we visit in the pink house, an American woman with a French husband, are thinking of going to Oran for the sake of some venture in the wine-business—the father of the young man being a successful wine-merchant in Paris—and wishing to establish a branch in Algeria. They want us to go along if they go and it is surprisingly near, and the climate of course better than Paris winter. But perhaps you had better not speak of this since I don't know whether Dan has mentioned it to his mother or not. There isn't any antique business here, or anywhere of course, and there isn't likely to be any, but our coming to France seems to have been justified by the simple fact that Dan insisted on bringing Toupsie along with us. Don't you think life is rather whimsical? I can't tell you how much fun I have writing this kind of thing, and doing the pictures, and I really feel it is just the beginning, all depending of course on whether the children of America say so or not. I work every day, sometimes almost all day, and Dan takes the most marvelous care of me. I really couldn't possibly get along without him, if he had to go out to some job every day. Besides if the Muffet product is remunerative we will need to be free to go the places that are amusing to write about. I want to go home too, because I miss you all so, but since the book was accepted, and I've begun the new story, I must make the most of the opportunity, and if this vein continues best abroad, I must stay a while longer. It is a most wonderful feeling to me to have become suddenly professional. Doesn't that sound awful! But it is really such a cute little profession, making children's books, that one can't be too solemn about it. Dan seems to enjoy it so tremendously, I don't feel too selfish in having, as it seems to me, most of the fun. Of course, he is my leading character, Mr. Muffet, and his whimsical ideas, and the fact that he developed such a remarkable personality in the cat he loves so frighteningly, and that he has such an eye for the humorous in all animals, is the thing the book is made of. And he naturally attracts as friends other people who are fascinated by animals, so now we have a collection of friends and their pets, that is very interesting—and Mrs. Muffet is their Boswell.

[TO CATHARINE HUNTINGTON]

September 17, 1933

I THOUGHT you would be pleased about the book. We got the news of acceptance, by cable, the morning after I came home from the hospital. You can imagine how happy we were. It has given me so much confidence. It has made a great change in my feeling, really. I shall be perfectly satisfied, absolutely delighted to keep on doing children's books, writing and illustrating. It gives me all the scope I want. Like the puppets, you can express a great deal in a minor art if you like. I have had most magnificent letters from Harpers, all nonsense to take seriously, except as a grand opportunity, of great value, to make the most of the editorial phrases; way of praising and patting on the back. It goes back to Radcliffe days, Copeland, *Atlantic Monthly*—only it really doesn't for me, because I know I write differently, much more easily, ever since Dr. de Forest. And I adore the feeling I have now, of having a profession I can really claim. I have more and more plans in my head for continuing the Muffets, for drawings, etc. Harpers ordered me to stop making drawings before I had finished them all, because they were making estimates on costs, and thought they might want a different kind of technique for better reproduction, but now they tell me to go ahead in just the same way, so I have still to finish the drawings, two or three full pages, and a lot of tiny decorations, which I shall adore doing, and a cover design.

Mr. and Mrs. Muffet

HERE it is the eleventh of March, and you wrote on New Year's eve. I have had it in my mind so much, the desire to write to you, and there isn't any excuse except the days simply aren't long enough. I work nearly all day, writing or drawing, then the light is gone and I am tired. And of course there are certain letters that I have to write, to my mother, and to Harpers, etc. They are always asking me something or other. (A transatlantic business correspondence is so clumsy and long.) For instance, they sent a few papers to show me the type (very nice indeed!), but to my horror and despair a word in the text had been changed; if you please, the word "last" was changed to "previous." No wonder I had to write a letter for the next boat.

This is what I am planning to do. I started a second book, which seems to be quite amusing, and Harpers' childish and inexplicable enthusiasm makes it seem worth while to continue. I don't dare to leave France until it is done, writing and illustrations, because I could not possibly do it away from this spot, and mutterings of war and revolution make it seem probable that once in the U. S. we might not be able to come back here at any moment. On the other hand, I don't know whether we can possibly live in America on the same small amount of money, in spite of the exchange, on which we live so contentedly here. That is the important question, and I can't find out by writing to people. Nobody answers such questions, and things have changed so in the last year and a half in the U. S. that I am in the dark. So, after I finish this book, I want to go home (I can't be so far from my mother such a long time, either, at her age), and find out for myself about living in the U. S., and if we can't do it I will come back to France, and if we can, Dan will come and bring our things.

Maybe I'll be ready to go by June. I hope so. Dan will be happy here in this house in summer with Toupsie, and the *jardin* to work in, and it's the best time for me to go. So you see I am looking forward to seeing you this summer, earlier or later. I wish I still had a key, so that I could walk in, as of old, and you would open the door of the salon and give a little scream of surprise. Then we would go down into the kitchen and make some tea and carry it into the garden and tell the story of our adventures, for hours and hours.

I must enclose my poem, "Miss Vague and Mr. Penny." These names have, I must explain, a significance which I suppose might be called pornographic. I suppose it is Dr. Tyler who makes me think of that—remember how you asked him what that word meant a long time ago in Lexington? This is the poem:

> V. *"I want a boarder, I haven't any.*
> *Someone like you going in and out*
> *Would give me something to think about."*
> P. *"What are you, an old maid?" said he.*
> V. *"Oh, no, no!" She laughed roguishly.*
> P. *"Whereabouts do you live, is it far?*
> V. *"Just up the road and there you are*
> *There's a very high wall, so when you come*
> *Just sing or whistle or even hum,*
> *And I will hear you and know it is you*
> *And then the next thing you have to do*
> *Is ring the Sonnette beside the gate*
> *And I'll try not to make you wait."*
> P. *"I know what I'll do, the best of all!"*
> *Cried Mr. Penny, "I'll scale the wall."*

266

Mr. and Mrs. Muffet

V. *"Don't let the ivy catch your toes,*
   You've no idea how thick it grows!"
P. *"Don't you worry," he said, "my sweet,*
   Your boarder can jump without catching his feet!"
V. *"Oh!" Miss Vague gave a joyous squeal,*
   "I wonder how that will make me feel!"
   They had a lovely time, I hear.
   He stayed with her, off and on, for a year.

We were having a very gay time the other day with Katharine Dudley at her Deux Magots, her first appearance in Paris for over a year, and Dan made me say this poem to her, which made her laugh so much that I thought it must be quite funny. Then Harry and Dorothy came along, and it had quite a success again. I have an idea of doing something which might be rather gay and original. A narrative poem of Miss Vague and Mr. Penny, a little novel in humorous rhyme. But there are other things that interest me so much more. I am aching to get to them. I don't know whether it is Dan, or France. No, it isn't France because it didn't have the same effect before; it must be Dan. Anyway, something is working in me as never before, and I'm trying to make the most of it. The time has come, as far as I'm concerned, for concentrating on work, in peaceful surroundings with peaceful company, writing one's memoirs. Those crazy stars that did such strange things to me seem to have moved away to somebody else. It's all very amusing to remember, very charming, and curious, and no longer tragic.

[To Toshihiko]

April 24, 1934

I am quite changed. I am not ashamed of being changed. I would be ashamed if I could love anybody so much as I loved you, and then lose you and not be changed.

You say at last you have made yourself simple and humble. If you did love Julia, then you must be suffering now, and I am sorry for you. If you really did love her then you must be changed too. Love leaves a mark.

And yet I am separate from you now. You would be surprised. I am not "in love" with you. It is something else. It is that queer thing that lasts. Nothing can kill it. It is like some part of the earth. It is a hardness and it is a softness, both together; it is rock underneath and soft ground on top. If you wanted to lie on it you would find it soft, and the rock underneath would make it solid under you. It is connected with the earth and with the stars. It is quite strange.

In a way this everlasting thing isn't so much selfish love going toward you, but love going toward everybody and pity toward every creature that lives. I feel as if I were going toward death, and in that way I haven't desires for myself, so the love must be something you can take. You would take love from somebody who was near death, wouldn't you? You would know it must be pure then, "without sediment," intrinsic value!

Sometime we will both know.

Please sometimes when you are with somebody you love, or perhaps alone, remember the black bench and the cold nights and the little short dream life. We were both happy then.

[To WARREN BUTLER]

May 10, 1934

LAST year you wrote that you had had a secret plan to come and see us last spring, but that you had been obliged to postpone your visit for a year. Now it is May, 1934. Is there any hope of your coming?

I wish very much that there might be. If you want a

reason, an excuse to come, it can be that I need you. I do
need you. I have been sick, and it is taking a long time to
get strong again, in spite of Dan's devoted and wonderful
nursing. I want very much to go home, but I'm not yet
strong enough to go alone, and we have decided that it
is best for Dan to wait here until we know what the doctor's opinions are. (All this question about climate, and
the Island of Jersey.)

If it would be a pleasure and a rest to you to come and
stay with us for as long as you can, then we could go back
together. I'm not strong enough to suggest that you bring
a child with you. I'm afraid it would have to be a very
unexciting visit. I get so frightfully tired over nothing.
And it has been very hard for poor Dan to have all that
responsibility and anxiety and constant care. He does all
the work in the house, besides cooking very special things
for me and washing and ironing and waiting on me like a
nurse. You will perhaps like this absolutely eventless life,
composed of only house and garden and market and café.
It's not a pretty old village, only a big growing suburb of
Paris, but our corner of it is quite nice. No, it is old, very
old, with Christian martyrs' bones in the church, but it is
so grown and suburbanized. Don't expect it to be very
paintable or quaint.

I'm writing as if you were coming. Oh, I do hope so! I
do need you. The doctor here has written to Fergus, so if
somebody can be found to translate it, you will know
what has been happening to us, more than I do, probably.
But I know one thing the doctor may not know—that if
only the Atlantic Ocean were smaller I would be better.
It is small when one is well, but grows horribly big as soon
as one is sick.

Can you let me know quickly, as soon as you decide,
whether you are coming or not? Perhaps you haven't
thought of it since you wrote that time, but please let me

know because if you are not coming, and I should feel suddenly much better, I might start suddenly for home alone. But if you should be nursing the idea secretly, perhaps this will give you the necessary, to your conscience, excuse to carry it out.

This letter, however, worries me. I don't want to be urgent for fear of frightening you, and yet I want you to know how much it would mean to me if you could and wanted to come. I have had such a longing and need for you. Dan is more and more an essential part of me, but you are and have been for so long, it's different. I'm different now too, you will see. Perhaps you will like me better.

Dan says if you come and you and I go back together, how bewildered the officials will be at seeing our names together, Warren Hathaway Butler, Katharine Butler Hathaway. He thinks we ought to transpose them somehow so they will match, then we can share a stateroom. But we can anyway.

Please let Mother know you have had this letter, because I haven't written since I wrote her I had been sick. In fact, I enclosed that letter in one to Lurana in case it should be disturbing. Things always seem so much more disturbing when one is far away. I don't want you to worry about me. I just must be rather patient, that's all. I was tearing along pretty fast, so excited over my book. Now I feel the way I did when I made the first trip to Castine. You took me, and the love-birds, and got me settled in the Brophy. Probably this is Castine's revenge on me because I went away, after it had made me so well and strong.

May 15— Just received letters from Mother, and have decided not to be so heroic about suppressing my moments of panic-stricken homesickness, having heard that you were struck that way in Essex, and walked home to Salem in the middle of the night. I'm not so crazy, then.

Mr. and Mrs. Muffet

[To Dan Hathaway]

DEAREST MR. MUFFET,

Another midnight letter. I have had the light out for a long while but can't sleep, thinking of my Mr. Muff and missing him so terribly.

The facts have now boiled down to this: I have seen Dr. Tolman three times this week, and each time I have questioned him very seriously in order to make our plans, and he tells me very firmly not to make any plans for this winter other than staying here until he finishes working on my throat. I asked what about going back to Creteil in case he gets through with me, and he said No. Not under any circumstances am I to go back to Creteil this winter. He and Fergus have talked the whole thing over together, and that is the ultimatum.

These moods come and go, and it is hard not to write everything as it comes. But I know this, my most necessary one, that it is only you I need, and just as quickly as possible.

Come, Mr. Muffet, come, Toupsie! to your poor lost and loving Miss Muff. Separation is poisonous, it is like a disease that eats into one's life.

I have many things to do here just as soon as you can get here and fix a working place for me in our house, somewhere around here for the present; I am dying to get to work. I'm just bursting with work, but I need Mr. Muffet, and only Mr. Muffet to help me. We will never part again, unless you get too tired of being so necessary to Miss M.

I was getting pretty frantic without my Mr. Muffet, but if I had gone, then I would have missed Dr. Tolman's return from Europe, and the whole business of the tonsils would have been postponed indefinitely, whereas they both, Fergus and Dr. Tolman, seem to consider it very important. I would have also missed the debut of the book, which Miss R. wants to have me stay for.

Reading your two letters yesterday, there is such a change in them. First you are most eager and impatient to come here, and second you think Jersey is better after all.

It would mean everything to me to have you here as soon as possible. I need you very much. There are so many things I haven't been able to tell you in a letter. Difficulties for your Miss Muffet. I know more now about my position in relation to the others. The difficulties are much better now, but I want to tell you the whole thing so that you will understand what your poor Miss Muffet has been up against, and how hard I have tried to do the best thing. And you, too, my good patient one, I know you have tried too. I wish I might take the next boat and see you within less than a week, but as I can't without going against strict medical orders, I can only pray that you will get out of your difficulties as quickly as possible and come to me. We've got to afford to be together, or we might as well not be married. After a few months we will surely know whether to send for our furniture, or whether to go back to Jersey. Apart from doctor's orders, it is a decision which I don't care to make alone. Although you keep saying so very generously that anything I decide will please you, I do not feel that I am the real Mrs. Muffet when I am without you.

If you feel very strongly that you want to bring our French furniture, do bring it. But my idea was that during a (perhaps) temporary stay here we would be very occupied with looking over our books and getting together our possessions here, and would be able to scrape up enough to keep house with through the winter. Please use your *instinct* about this. It's the best way. My instinct fails me now. I only know that I need you, and that in the present circumstances we had better not make a final move until we know the result of this tonsil business. If we bring the furniture, we certainly can't afford to take it back again. But we could leave it here where it would be safe and if necessary we could sell some of it.

September 12, 1934

No, DEAREST Mr. Muffet, cunning one, I can't take care of my nails properly, because it makes me miss you too frantically. Although, on the other hand, if I am not too nervous, sometimes it is a pleasure because I know you like to have me do it. But I'm beginning to know how the Salem and Marblehead wives used to feel when their husbands went off in ships for months of voyaging—much worse, of course, to have no chance to cable, but nothing is much worse than not being able to touch the hand, and there isn't an invention to accomplish that yet, across four thousand miles, or even less.

You were very good and clear and sensible in your letter, and I myself had thought of the same thing, the possibility (if Flo went to America) of our staying out our second year there, but now—

We are fearfully crowded in Peabody. One can't possibly do any continuous work there where there are so many people, so much interruption, and really nobody but one feeble girl to do the housework. You would be shocked if you saw such terrible shortcomings in the way of housekeeping. So I am just existing until you arrive and we can be alone somewhere in Muffety neatness and regularity.

You are a sweet, sweet one, Mr. Muffet. I reread your letters, and you are so patient, and there isn't a word of reproach or anything except most patient attempts to

273

solve our troublous separation. As you didn't mention my idea of leaving our French things there temporarily, I am afraid you thought it was a horrible idea, and that you felt you couldn't bear to be parted from them. But you didn't say anything, so I don't know what you thought about it. I don't want to make you sad. Please tell me your feeling.

But it's definite now that I must stay here for a while. And I need you as soon as possible.

9. *Back in Maine*

[TO CATHARINE HUNTINGTON]

Blue Hill Falls, Maine
July 14, 1935

I HAVE been slow about writing because I was *quite* tired and also found to our surprise extremely hot weather here, for Maine. Every afternoon the mercury, as they say, rose into the eighties. I stayed a great deal in bed the first few days, in fact until today, and my impression of the place was colored by my seeing too much of the interior, especially the bedroom.

Now I hasten to try to tell you what it is like. It is a house of the same period as the Douglas house which was next to mine in Castine, but neater, fresher looking, and with more trees around it. It has just been newly shingled and painted, white with apple-green trimmings, and new screens on all the windows. In the front yard, where I am now lying on a blanket with a very fine breeze rustling in the tree over me and a glass of ale beside me, there are four trees, a horse-chestnut, a willow, a poplar, and another which I cannot name. Directly opposite the house, across the road, is a level hayfield. On the horizon of the hayfield we see the tops of poplar trees, the ridgepole of a cottage, and a flagpole. These indicate the shore where

275

the owner of our house has his cottage, and where we are supposed to have our "private beach." It is a little too far for me to walk, and we haven't yet driven down, although I think it must be very nice, and I expect we shall get the habit of going there. Beyond the hayfield we can see a strip of blue water, and above the water rises Mount Desert. Almost directly opposite, I should say, is Seal Cove, where the Morisons' place is, and I could go there quite quickly from here in our landlord's cruiser. Around behind our house is a field, sort of a pointed shape, which stops at the edge of a wood, quite a frightening low dense wood. On one side of the house is a little pond, bronze color, with long grasses growing round it and alder bushes and a few little old apple trees. There is a tiny waterfall that rushes out of the pond, and dragonflies are always darting over the surface of the pond in the daytime. At night the field behind the house is quite ghostly, filled with moonlight and fireflies, and bull frogs keep twanging their G-string in the pond.

Inside, the house was as awful as possible in atmosphere, mostly caused by a forest of terrible stuffed chairs and many large photographs of relations hanging on the walls. Mrs. Hamilton gave us permission to remove everything we didn't like to the attic, and practically everything has been removed. Dan worked steadily for about twenty-four hours, hauling and pushing and heaving, getting incredibly large pieces of furniture up the long steep staircase and out of our sight. Now we live in chaste, quite simple rooms. Enough, however. We have retained the patent rocking chair, and the organ which Dan loves to play. Dan is marvelously delighted with the place. The first two or three days I was horribly homesick for my lost house and Castine. It reminded me of it so much, and yet was so terribly unlike it. Now I am getting used to it.

The roads around here are lovely, of course. Yesterday

we drove to Ellsworth, which is only eighteen miles away, where we bought two bottles of gin at a state store. Liquor is not sold in Maine except in these state stores, which are like post offices. It is very governmental and seems neat and nice, somehow, just like going into a nice post office and buying stamps, only the stamps are bottles of gin. Also one can get all sorts of wine, not very expensive it seems to me. Probably much less than where the merchant makes his profit. You would love it, I know.

Our neighbors are farmers, not too near. Not so much style as Castine. It is really quite nice, and expect to like it more as time passes.

We hope to hear from you. We hope very much that you will come. I think the easiest way is to come by train to Ellsworth, where we will meet you. Bucksport and Ellsworth are about an equal distance from here, but you said you did not want to come by boat.

September 8, 1935

WE ARE in the act of buying an old brick house on the shore, in the village of Blue Hill. It is unbelievably like, in some ways, my house in Castine. It is unbelievably its equal in grandeur, but considerably smaller and cozier. It can be paid for in installments lasting nine years. I hope you won't be horrified and displeased by this decision to plant ourselves again in this remote region. It is somehow impossible for me to give it up, and it is partly on account of the effect that the climate has on my health. I can breathe here much better than farther south. And Dan adores it. We took a little package of sandwiches and a little cocktail in a bottle to the high side of Blue Hill late yesterday afternoon just before sunset, and sat on a field and had our supper. Dan was so overwhelmed by the beautiful sight of the bay and islands, so very grand and dark, just then like something by Rockwell Kent, that he couldn't begin to drink or eat, while I was busily absorbing sandwiches and cocktail. He really has fallen in love with this country and wants to live here all year round. Of course we *must*, having bought the house, as we can't afford to pay rent in Salem too. Also, our things will be simply too beautiful in the brick house. We are most eager to have you see it. One of the first utterances we made was to say we knew you would like it.

The house is hidden from the road by standing at the end of an avenue of *thick, high* cedar hedges, and behind the house the field goes down to the shore, our own land. A little cove, in fact, belongs to us. On the left the boundary is made by a brook in a deep ravine and some very ancient willow trees, like Castine. The fields are big, four acres in all.

[To Warren Butler]

September 17, 1935

I HAVE just got your letter and poem. They moved me so deeply that I can't answer them properly. I was afraid you would feel something like that, but not *nearly* so much.

I want to re-assure you. You mustn't be afraid of my getting "more and more habituated to turns, corners, textures and surfaces of a new life, establishing a new intimacy with myself that you will not share that will be unknown to you, living in another world." That can never happen again. I have always had a terrible craving for new experiences, but now at last my hunger and thirst have been satisfied. I have had enough. I am perfectly content, and now my one function is to sit in the chimney-corner and tell about my adventures. I feel as if the

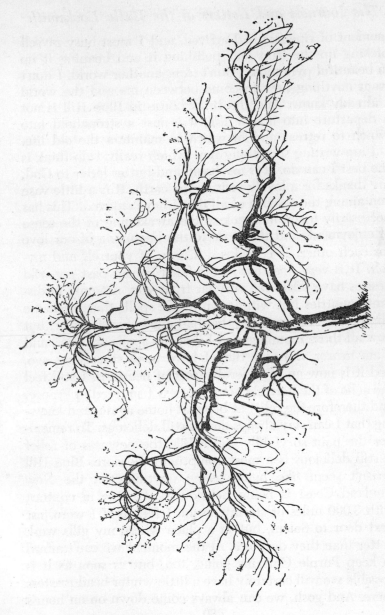

APPLE TREE, BLUE HILL

moment of ripeness had arrived, and I must busy myself picking up the fruit and polishing it and heaping it up in beautiful pyramids. I don't *want* another world. I don't want anything new to come between me and the world I already know. And the brick house in Blue Hill is not a departure into a new life, it is just a stronghold into which to retreat and in which to maintain the old life.

I am writing something now which really I do think is the best I can do. It is my bread-and-butter letter to God, my thanks for a lovely visit on the earth. It is a little vase containing the essence of all that I have enjoyed. This has necessarily taken me back to the awakening of the sense of enjoyment, and therefore to the beginning of our love for each other. It contains a history of yourself and myself. It is very fine that in the fairly recent past my wild desires have taken me very far from you, not only in distant countries but withdrawn under spells that made me almost forget everything that had once been familiar; but now all those roamings and Kilmeony spells are over, and I am nearer you now than I have been since long ago, and it is now an invulnerable sort of nearness. I still feel the ache of the horrible homesickness I suffered in France, and therefore the relief at being at home again, and knowing that I can stay always now is still delicious. To remember the pain so vividly still, while the newness of relief is still delicious is a most voluptuous pleasure. Blue Hill doesn't seem like being away; anything on the New England Coast is being deliciously at home in contrast with 3,000 miles of stormy ocean. I feel as if I were just next door to Salem, but in a place where my gills work better than they do there. At the moment we can't afford to keep Purple Curtains going, too, but as soon as it is possible we will certainly have a little winter headquarters there. And gosh, we can always come down on an hour's notice, and stay with you, or in Peabody, or at the East India. I know you did become very fondly attached to our cute little Purple Curtains, and so did we, but we will have a Purple Curtains the second as soon as we get the Brick House on its feet.

I don't know whether *I* have said what *I* meant to—it is exactly the opposite of what you said. You feared that "at our age" there is more and more danger of our becoming separated, alienated by divergencies of experience. And to me the contrary is true. I can never be lured any more by any divergencies on my side. I am back again—the circle is finished. I am a contented and jolly old woman now, writing my memoirs. Safer than ever before from anything new and alienating—completely banked fires, all self-contained, spinning a web out of a thread that comes out of me and all that I remember. I tried to tell you before we came away that the chief reason why I was so inexpressibly happy in our return to Salem was the fact that you had been so imaginatively sympathetic and loving toward Dan, therefore knitting us all together. That for me was the great step toward our happy life in America, and you did it, accomplished it. Now nothing can undo that, and I feel secure and, as I said, invulnerable, in my nearness to you in a way that moving to Blue Hill can't affect except to give us times of added pleasure.

If you could arrange to come here *now*, immediately, for a few days or a week, we will go on with this. Telephone us in the morning anytime until one o'clock, or else in the evening after nine. Sedgwick 37-2. We will meet the boat at Bucksport, or the train at Ellsworth—much easier for you than long drive.

Your poem is a lovely one.

Dan says to tell you that the missing will not be all on your part, or on my part. He is always talking about you and missing you and wanting to see you, looking forward to visits from you.

[To CATHARINE HUNTINGTON]

November 23, 1935

WE ARRIVED here about one o'clock today—Warren and Mother and I. The last week or so has been so bewildering that I could not even answer your postcard, and before I knew it the bewilderment and chaos had resolved itself into departure, and now the journey which began yesterday morning is finished. I did not even telephone to say good-by because I thought it would be better luck not to, and gave me more the feeling that you and Creighton were coming so soon that it wouldn't matter. If you thought that our rooms in Salem were nice, I wonder what you will say when you see Sarn. I was perfectly astonished when I came in today. It is infinitely more charming and beautiful than I had expected. Dan made not only the curtains, but the bed cover and bolster covers for the little guest room, and it is perfect. Nothing could have been nicer to go with the wallpaper and furniture. My mother is really enraptured with the house. Warren says it is much more beautiful than Castine, the house and land both. Mother and Warren are staying at the hotel, the Blue Hill House, as Dan is not really established enough for guests, chiefly because the kitchen stove is waiting for a missing part and can't be connected.

It is evening now. Mother has gone to bed at the hotel. I am sitting in a white room (with purple curtains), and Warren is sitting reading, and Dan in bed asleep in the next room, fires burning in the fireplaces. We stopped and called on Henry Beston yesterday and saw his wife and two very exquisite and amusing little girls.

Back in Maine

[To Dr. de Forest]

December 8, 1935

Did you get a very crazy letter from me about two weeks ago? I gave it to a young man to mail for me whom I scarcely know, and perhaps it got lost somewhere between here and the Blue Hill post office. If not, and if it did reach you, I have been wanting to say that I felt contrite afterward for having sent even you such a letter.

I have to admit, however, that I feel a—sometimes quite desperate—need to see you, and I should like to plan to come to Boston at some time when you will have perhaps a little time for me.

The doctor here is a most civilized person, very understanding and gentle. He doesn't approve of the new skipping trick my heart has got, and he is trying various things to control it, but as yet unsuccessfully, and of course I am feeling that a few periods with you could be more likely to cure it.

But I try to remember how busy you are, and how many other people have claims upon you, and how it is easily possible that you can't have me come at all at present.

If it didn't sound so purely selfish I should like to invite you to come to Maine sometime during the holidays. If only I didn't *need* to see you so much, I should be bold enough to ask you because I think you would like our house very much in winter, and also I think this landscape in its present winter version would thrill you. But the fact that I need to see you makes me think it isn't much of an invitation. Sometime, however, I shall invite you when it is for pure pleasure, for peering into the harbor at schooners instead of peering into the gruesome depths of a patient's Unconscious.

283

I HAVE felt so ill I haven't even been able to write to *you*. The doctor made me stay in bed for three weeks, for a heart rest. I'm beginning to get up a little now and move about very gently and carefully. The heart is better, but every day several times, usually, and at night, there comes a mental distress that is almost intolerable. At the same time I feel as if I were understanding many more things. My brain seems to perceive so much more than ordinarily, and I am furiously eager to write it all down. But the margin of physical strength is so terribly small. I can't walk any length of time without the heart getting bad again. The margin of finance is almost nonexistent too, so I feel caught in a trap—as if I could not move in any direction.

My brother Warren came here for a day not long ago, not, I think, because he thought there was anything wrong with me, but he had to go to Portland and came on the rest of the way. It was an opportunity for me to consult him, but it is not easy or natural for me to tell him of any trouble of mine. I have scarcely ever done it. He becomes remote and evasive, and I always change the subject quickly and feel as if I had overstepped some mysterious boundary. He urged me to come back to Salem with them in order to have more time to talk and try to settle my affairs, but I had only just got out of bed after three weeks, and I could not stay up more than a hour or so without feeling exhausted. So he began here to study my situation, or rather to plan a solution, *without* much preliminary study. His first idea was to show me by making out a budget on paper how I could live on what money I have. He seemed to me like a surgeon so intent on cutting out whatever seemed to him unnecessary in my way of

284

living that he hardly noticed whether or not the patient happened to die on the operating table.

I tried in a most faltering, inarticulate way to convey to him the nervous pressure and difficulty involved in making a drastic change in one's way of living, especially if it is already as limited as mine has been lately, by pointing out to him how dependent he is upon cigarettes and whisky and asking him to try and realize that living on the very minimum would be for me perhaps even harder than for him to give them up. His answer was sharp and angry: *I* can afford them. If *I* couldn't, I should be able to give them up. Which does not sound as *if* he were inclined to relieve my distress by opening my cage, but by pointing out to me from the outside just how possible it is for me to make myself contented in it. He suggests that I do not need a car, yet there is no other possible means of transportation here, and I would be absolutely imprisoned, because doctors always tell me I must not walk any distance, never, never to the point of fatigue. My brother doesn't even know that I have got a thing called chronic myocarditis. He evidently can't let himself think of me as weak in any way. If I show any sort of weakness, either emotional or physical, he becomes hostile at once. He can't help it.

We talked of my mother, but he feels my mother must not be disturbed on any account.

Can you imagine what I felt during one of my hours of terrific tension since my brother was here, when I happened to open a certain famous little book and I read, "Not as the world giveth, give I unto you." "Let not your heart be troubled, neither let it be afraid." I read the whole book—the Gospel according to St. John—and I felt as if I hadn't known it, but that the cage door had been standing open all the time. I simply marveled at the amazing sayings and actions of that man. I kept finding the truth

285

of psychoanalysis in it too, which was one reason why it struck me so. It is wonderful never to have read or known anything about the teachings of Christ until you have found that in spite of your proud intellect and your worldly experience and your artistic insight you are defeated and helpless. Then they do seem like the flowers of spring—for freshness and miraculous beauty, and so much more besides, one can only fall back on his own oriental imagery to express it—as when he says, "Whosoever drinketh of the water that I shall give him shall never thirst; but the water that I shall give him shall be in him a well of water springing up into everlasting life." And toward the end he keeps telling his friends that after he is gone he will send a Comforter which he calls the spirit of truth.

That is what you are trying to teach also—that the only solution and way toward happiness is to learn to receive the truth. Isn't it?

I want so much to talk to you, and I should like to come for a few days if I could arrange it, and if you are there. I have a small store of money left which I owe for necessary things we had to do to the house, but I haven't dared to part with it. Of course, it doesn't cover many journeys. I would rather come alone, which means coming by train. I don't feel well enough to risk a very long drive in winter weather, possible intense cold and storms. I can stay with Catharine Huntington, although I will have to engage a maid to come in by the hour and get meals, and I will have to buy the food. Except for breakfast, C. is not there. I will manage something or other.

I am terribly unstable. I make up my mind over and over, first one way, then another. Since I read St. John I have felt a more authentic sort of peace, and I have felt that my *own* business is with the seeking for truth, rather than trying to settle money affairs. I decided yesterday that I would not compromise. I would stick to my book, it is perhaps my real salvation, and let the money situation solve itself.

It is when I feel paralyzed by mental distress and cannot seem to move a step in any direction that I feel I must be really *sick* mentally and need help from someone wiser than I am. There is one thing which never changes—it is the belief that I must express something that's in me. . . . I must follow it. I had never undergone the test of losing my financial stability before, however, and that is something I have to deal with now. If I don't deal with it myself and find a way out, then I can scarcely consider myself equipped to write anything of great value to anybody. So I am seeking for the way out which is really the truest way, the way which is harmonious with my creative instinct.

If I decide not to come after all, you will know it is because I am trying to solve the problem alone, or rather with the help of this little book which I am now reading and rereading. Yet I feel that it would help me to know truly what my solution is—even though it is and must be in *myself,* if I could come and hear myself telling it to you.

As usual, I have written you one of those terrible letters, all confusion and craziness which I could not possibly write to anybody else.

[To a Family Physician]

December 30, 1935

This is in the nature of an S.O.S., if that means a distress signal. It is to ask you if you would be willing, after reading this letter, to see my brother Warren and tell him a little about me.

Do you remember one day last summer when we were in your private office, and I was feeling rather upset because I had not been able to accomplish in my life as much as I wanted to, and you surprised me out of my wits by telling me that people who have had Pott's Disease often accomplish even less than I? You spoke particularly of the shock it gives to the nervous system. Well, that information has not dampened my ambitions, but it has explained for me certain ways in which I seem to have (and always have had) no endurance. One thing has never been demanded of me, and that is that I should earn my own living, and the question of money has always been abnormally terrifying to me. I have often thought that the lack of it would finish me up very quickly. I have felt rather ashamed of that weakness, but I couldn't help knowing that it was there. My mother, you see, has other people dependent on her besides me, and there really isn't enough to go around. Well, for some reason it has always been frightfully difficult for me to talk with Warren or any member of my family about the effect this has on me, and so I keep it locked up in me until I am about ready to break. Something seemed to break about two months ago. My heart kicked up in a way it never has done before, and I had idiotic floods of tears, and the doctor here put me in bed for three weeks' heart rest.

Warren was here yesterday for a day, and I managed to open the subject of my finances. I do not know whether Warren is in a position to help me even a little every month, or not, but at least his only solution of the problem was to urge me to try more than I have ever done to become independent by my own work. He is very fond of me, but he always urges me on to more and more effort, and more and more responsibility and struggle. He is never willing, for some reason, to think of me as being in a way handicapped. Probably partly because I haven't been willing to think of it myself. But lately I have felt the edge of my limitations rather sharply, and yet I can't explain it to Warren without seeming to be making excuses for myself and being a weak character. Not being a doctor, he doesn't observe anything of that kind and just tries to spur me on, while the doctor here urges the opposite.

In my own way, and at my own pace, I am working at a piece of writing which I think is the most interesting thing I have ever done, and I'm having correspondence about it with the editor of the *Atlantic Monthly,* who is very interested in it. Of course, that is a grand opportunity. But I can't do it under pressure, or with any burden of financial responsibility on me. I can't seem to carry those two things, which I know is very weak. Nevertheless I am afraid I have got to be a parasite in order to amount to anything. Eventually, of course, I hope this will bring in some money, but it can't now. What I hope and pray for is that my family can give me just enough security to safeguard health and nerves until this thing is done. I know it will repay them. But, of course, they won't do it if they don't understand the need for it.

If you feel that I am being unreasonable and spoiled in this letter, please just tear it up. I have tried my damnedest to get the sane view of the situation and not to baby myself. If you think it is asking too much of me to expect me to undertake to earn my own living or even part of it, because of certain physical and perhaps nervous limitations, would it be a natural and easy thing for you to give Warren your medical slant on the matter? I wouldn't want you to do it unless it is your own honest-to-goodness feeling. But I only imagine from what you said last summer that it might be.

I know it would surprise Warren very much to hear what you said to me that day, and I think it might alter his attitude toward me in a way which would be a life-saver to me. I don't want to add to his responsibilities, goodness knows, and please believe I don't want to take advantage of my disability. I have always tried to do the opposite. But I think perhaps Warren ought to realize what he is asking of me now.

If you feel like speaking to him, can you make it casual, not as if I had written this letter?

You are an angel. If you think I am a silly cry-baby, please tell me so. Maybe that is what I need. Expecting too much in a cockeyed world.

[To Catharine Huntington]

January 14, 1936

"There is a time of Snow in all endeavor." This line comes back to me always as the one line in literature that expresses the idea and can console me when I am blocked in my endeavor. I have been in bed for three weeks, with the brain almost crazy with productiveness while the heart was behaving ill and the body had to submit to complete inactivity. Now the convalescence is almost equally maddening because so slow. Such penurious hoarding of strength and such mean little outlays permitted, while I feel myself actually bursting with creative riches. To say nothing of magnificent correspondence with Ellery Sedgwick, with his sympathy and interest in the thing I am writing, or rather not writing, because I haven't got the strength. Add to this financial penury and the fact that there is nobody in my family whom I can go to for any help. That is the real trouble with my foolish heart, which can't seem to understand or adapt itself to sudden loss of "security." For the first time in my life I have felt done for, defeated, utterly swamped.

In fact, in this state of mind one is hard to please. So

far I have found reality in E. E. Cummings' *him,* as fresh as daffodils after how many years, and as consolingly crazy as ever. And in the Gospel according to St. John, read for the first time, and in Faber, or *The Lost Years,* by Jacob Wasserman; and in *The Bible in Spain,* by George Borrow. I have just got Hemingway's *Green Hills of Africa,* which seems as dull as dull.

I am amazed by the sayings of Christ. They seem truer than anything I have ever read. And they certainly turn the world upside down. They are rather decidedly akin to psychoanalysis as I've experienced it with Dr. de Forest.

Probably I am just going crazy, like many other people who live in Maine all year round. In this state there are more different kinds of religion than in any other, I believe. These long cold solitudes incline one to meditation.

As soon as I am stronger, I think I shall go to the West-'ard, as they say around here, meaning toward Boston. I am dying for conversational refreshment. Dan has had the monotonous life of a devoted nurse, and I haven't yet been strong enough to carry on conversations with him. He adores his monotonous life and has no wish ever to leave. He has been invited to play bridge regularly on Monday nights with the only contract bridge players in town, very exclusively consisting of the barber, the high-school principal, and another young man named Osgood. He has great fun playing, he loves bridge. The wife of the barber comes and spends the evening with me when they play. She is the librarian and a very remarkable character.

May 9, 1936

I was trying to get a number in Ellsworth, an oculist with whom I needed an appointment. They didn't answer. Blue Hill operator said, "Well, they never answer over there to

Ellsworth. I think they must all take a vacation on Sat'day. It's a good fishin' day today, and I think they must of all gone fishin'." (Say this with that caressing, indulging, cosseting intonation which we used to notice in Castine.) Yesterday I gave a number to the operator and she said, "Thank you. It's been a lovely day today, hasn't it?"

The smelts are runnin' up our brook at night now. You can catch them in your hands, pails full. They taste awful good.

It is a good fishing day today. Very still and quiet, fine mist falling. I have been over to the neighbors, Mr. and Mrs. Munroe, and got Mr. Munroe to come over and talk about our brook. "She needs some digging out. She's got out of her course." We saw a plant on the edge of the ravine. We asked him what it was. "That's Ragged Sailor, that is," he said. "This other is Creepin' Jenny."

My, it's a beautiful life here. Dan has done a magnificent lot of work cleaning the place up. He says he has never been so happy in his life. It looks wonderful, and he's busy every minute, all day long. Yesterday had three of the volunteer firemen burning out our ravine. Dan working with them. It was very exciting. The ravines had been used as a dump for thirty years—old furniture, automobiles, stoves, toys, dead trees. The chief of the firemen is one of Dan's bridge friends and calls Dan "Dan'l" in the most attractive way, a very handsome and *gentil* young man of great charm, who reminds me of Frederick. Dan is very proud of the fact that there are three or four men in the town who call him "Dan'l." One is quite an elderly neighbor whom Dan calls Frank.

I have made johnnycake myself twice since I came back. I am very proud. Next thing I intend to learn to make bread. Dan doesn't know how to do anything of that kind.

Back in Maine

REG. was so very *gentil* to me the evening I left, I am going to try to bring him some smelts from our brook for breakfast. Going smelting tonight at midnight with the funny librarian whose letters you liked. We go down to the mouth of our brook with flashlights and catch the fish in our hands, very silvery and mysterious, like a poem by W. B. Yeats. Otherwise our spring is far inferior to yours—that is, its progress is very halting. Sitting here, looking between purple curtains, I can see our mound-shaped lilac bush and its spikes, the same color as the curtains. Dark and unawakened still. One lily-of-the-valley is out, that's all. But we shall have crowds of them later. Everything froze a few nights ago.

Something like the miracle in *The Two Beans* is happening to us. Two magic little men came from Salem gabbling incessantly, running over our house, taking measurements and writing down plans. Then hopped out again, and presently we have been given to understand that they will come back with armfuls of radiators, pipes, and a heater. Also a bathtub, toilets, and washbowls, which they will come running in with, install, and run out again. This caused by the fact that Warren bought four or five houses to tear down and had the wonderful idea of giving us equipment found in the houses and having them installed for us. Greatest luck we could ever have dreamed of.

June 24, 1936

MAYBE you went to Washington on Monday and are not at home yet. I hope you did go. It always seems something like going to Paris, rather foreign and hot in summer, scandalous and exciting. I mean it sounds, rather than seems, because I don't know how it seems, not having been there since childhood. I'd like to know really how it does seem. From here it seems exotic and flowery and feverish, and full of intrigue, and very romantic; private yachts and Jamestown and Mt. Vernon and dark laughter. I must say I am for Roosevelt. I should hate to trust my fate to that Landon face. Those smug Republicans, they all seem revengeful against Roosevelt's good breeding. They are so boastful about Mr. Landon being very plain, and his wife's artless modesty. She will not write a column about her day, they tell us over and over. How they do hate anybody who has any brain or remarkable enterprise, or intrinsic superiority!

We're having a very cool and gentle and monotonous rain. It is evening. I can hear the water trickling into the cistern in the cellar under the floor, and the raindrops banging on the tin porch roof over the front door.

I've just got a marvelous workroom established upstairs, where I intend to seclude myself from now on and not waste any more time being sick, or dashing about. It is the best working place I have ever had in my life. A square room with four windows, southwest corner. Old wallpaper, brown stripes—just brown, very odd, but quite studious-looking. A fireplace with quite nice mantelpiece, and a chest of drawers, daybed, wide oval table covered with all my pencils, erasers, pen knives, drawing pens, blotters, drawing ink, paint box, charcoal, etc., a low bench beside the couch where writing case and work in progress, as James Joyce calls it. Other side of couch is table holding victrola to call up past. There is a huge closet with shelves piled high with manuscript and notes and typewriter and typewriter paper. Also, portfolio of drawings, all of them. It really is wonderful. Windows look out into apple trees and across flowery fields to harbor.

November 19, 1936

HURRAY for Roosevelt! by the way. An election has taken place since we parted. I was thrilled. I have Mother's radio now, and I adore it. I listened to Roosevelt's Madison Square Garden speech, sitting here all alone in the dark, and I was thrilled. Then on the night when the returns came in it was marvelous to hear the roaring crowds around the streets of New York. Since coming here I promptly subscribed to the *New York World-Telegram,* so between that and the radio I get a few electric currents from the outside world.

I wish I could express better what I am feeling. Distance, being so far from the places where things happen, and my own ignorance make me feel like someone who is blindfolded, but intuition acts like a very powerful sense and brings me a most extraordinary feeling that under the surface of ordinary life now very great things are happening, as if some great powerful *"Sacré du printemps"* were going to revolutionize the world, and it seems as if Roosevelt were the instrument.

Dan sends his love and says we're just wondering when you are coming up here. He says tell you we are having venison for supper tonight, shot by the Blue Hill barber. Dan looks marvelously well. He is so peaceful and easy and countrified. This life is perfect for him. He thinks so himself. Rather, he thinks no other kind of life is any good at all.

January 15, 1937

THE weather is still so nice here, I don't think we will go to Boston for the present. In fact, when I remember the

295

terrible times I used to have last year making my daily trip to Dr. Morris in the snow and ice, I think it would be more sensible to spend the bad months of the winter, if there are going to be any, here where there is no need of my struggling to go out, cozily working on my book, then go down in the spring when it would be a pleasure to be roaming around Boston, and all much simpler and less expensive as to transportation, since in bad weather taxis are a necessity, and in the spring I could perhaps drive myself.

I am quite deep in my book, Obma,* as I call it for short, you know. These letters are the initial letters of the first line in the Song of Transformations, which is my theme song. I often wish you were here to glance at a page or two and give me a criticism of it. I found it very sloppy. I remember you said it wasn't really "written," and I found it so myself. I am "writing" it now, I hope not too much. It was lumps of ore only. Now I'm digging out the metal itself, or I think I am. I am just getting on, just having the wonderful sense of continuity, of being for the first time since I began this book quite free from despair, of long heartbreaking interruptions.

[To Dan Hathaway]

March 22, 1937

You are so sweet and good and patient with me. But I cannot endure the way I have been feeling lately, and I can't bear to inflict myself on you in this condition. My instinct for self-preservation keeps urging me overwhelmingly to go away somewhere alone for a while, as if that might cure me. Certainly it would be easier for you than to have me here. There are times when solitude, like starvation, is necessary to get rid of one's poisons.

* *The Little Locksmith.*

Back in Maine

[To Dr. de Forest]

April 14, 1937

UNTIL yesterday it seemed more and more hopeless to think of combining work with Dr. Morris and work with you. The expense of living in Boston, and of keeping my car or taking a great many taxis, and of Dr. Morris' treatments and of the analysis all at once made a deadlock. Then yesterday out of the blue came the loan of a furnished apartment in Boston during the month of May, including room enough in an alley beside it to keep my car.

Now your note saying that you have from 12 to 1 o'clock free every day except Friday. If you will let me come just one day a week, I shall feel very lucky indeed. That—with transportation back and forth until I get bold enough to drive alone—I can pay for as I go, thanks to the windfall of the apartment. I could easily pay for more than one period a week if I could spread the payment over three or four months, as my income is now adequate, and when I am in Blue Hill our expenses are not over $150 or $200 a month, so it is quite easy to save for extra things.

I have just finished paying for a bathroom and have saved up enough for an artesian well, which is now being drilled—enough, at least, unless they have to drill more than one hundred feet! However, I do think I would rather begin with one period that I know I can pay for. So how about Monday, May 3rd? My address will still be East India House for another week. I forgot to say that Dr. Morris wants me to come every day at 10, which makes 12 to 1 suit me beautifully.

July 27, 1937

I HAVE hesitated to write to you again until I could announce my decision as to going on with the analysis. You

297

said you thought I should think it over and feel it over a long time before deciding, and I am doing that. At least, I find that Dan feels no objection to it, which removes what I had expected would be a very difficult phase of the matter. So it is really only up to me now.

I could not write you the angry letter after all. As soon as I wrote the sentence, "Shall I write it down and send it to you?" my own question, implying trust and confidence in you, broke down the frightful feeling I had had toward you since leaving you the last day, and melted it away, for the time being, at least. Until then I had felt so hostile toward you that I wondered if it would be possible to go on with the analysis. In fact, I was ready to tell you that I had actually lost all faith in you and wouldn't dream of coming back. It seemed as if you had cruelly and wantonly injured me by letting me come for those few weeks when you knew it was bound to leave me utterly confused and suffering. For at least a month after coming back here I felt so sick I thought I would never get over it. I wonder how much of that kind of experience I can stand.

I must admit, however, that little by little I was aware of benefit that I had got too, a little dawning light here and there. Then followed a month or so of extraordinarily happy functioning progress in writing and now another spell of awfulness, such mental confusion and torment. During the good period I saw Mary Camp for the first time this year, and she told me with enthusiasm that she thought I seemed better than for years—speaking psychologically—referring to the fact that I had been seeing you and having some periods of analysis. So it is rather up and down, and contradictory, and most difficult to arrive at a decision. However, I shall arrive at one and tell you of it as soon as I do.

In the meantime I'm writing something that is sort of a dividend from all this torture ... quite nice, I think ...

Back in Maine

Aus meinen grossen Schmertzen, Mach ich die kleine lieder. I don't know very many words of German, but those two lines I've always known and said over in my head semiconsciously—always underlining, in my mind's ear, the *grossen*. I have only in this moment come to realize, in writing it down for you, that I did emphasize it so.

[To Catharine Huntington]

November 21, 1937

I HAVE been terribly occupied, not merely with book writing, which was reaching a climax, but with a new development which threatened to be a booming money-making enterprise on my hands, but of which I've now relieved myself, partially. My little friend, Griselda was in a jam, and needed money, and began to knit some rather homely striped mittens for the visiting nurse, who had asked her to do them for her to give away as Xmas presents. I thought how nice to do embroidered mittens and attract a more fastidious eye. And so I decided to give mittens to all of my friends and relations for Xmas, for which I made the designs, and Griselda started to do the work. Then I got excited over it as a possible project, a native industry, and behold! it is now started. I got too excited and fatigued, and have just spent a few days in bed, and am now better. As soon as Xmas is over I hope to do some more elaborate and interesting designs. We had limited time for the Xmas presents, so she had to stick to the three simple designs I made first. We have received orders from other people to whom we have showed them or to whom I wrote about them, and soon got as many orders as could be done in time for Christmas. I can't resist telling you about yours. For town wear, black mitten, gray, white, and yellow embroidery. They fit so well that they are really quite smart-looking.

Tonight I feel rather lazy and pleasantly relaxed after a spell of dreadful gloom and nervousness. It's strange and delicious how it suddenly lifts, for no obvious reason, and one is happy again.

[To Dr. de Forest]

February 25, 1938

I WANT to come and see you if I may. I expect to go to Boston about March 1. I can't tell the exact date because of an impending visitor who won't, however, stay more than a few days.

Although I've had an extremely happy winter, the bad days that come and eclipse the happiness and even the memory of it are so confusing and dreadful that I know, of course, that something is wrong somewhere. I want to tell you about it and talk about the possibility, if any, of doing something about it.

You said in your last letter, Isn't my "endless faith" in you a hope, a wish! I should say it is much more, it is something that has been built, very slowly, by you and by me, and I don't believe I have really lost any of it. But all that is a most difficult thing to write about—unless I took pages and pages. When you wrote that, I wanted to write you a long letter about faith; I discovered I felt very passionate about it, but I was afraid it would be too long—almost a book.

I will telephone to you when I get to Boston, if you are going to be there.

March 6, 1938

THANK you very much for your note, which was forwarded, as I left Maine a little sooner than I expected.

Back in Maine

I am at this moment in bed at the East India House after a wild journey and several days of rather too exciting experiences. Yesterday I felt *too* exhausted, and the best thing seemed to be to take a rest here for a few days, so I shall stay in bed three or four days, as I have often done before when in this state. It always reminds me of a cistern that needs to be replenished with rain, or a battery that needs to be recharged. I suppose there must be some way of preventing my heart from getting so excited and then getting so very tired, but as yet I don't know what the way is, and so I can only let it happen and then restore it afterwards. I'm feeling in a very happy, easy sort of mood, and full of very interesting and hopeful ideas about you and things I want to say to you, and consequently I am very eager to see you. I think a little light is beginning to dawn on me here and there; only a little, however. But enough to give me a strong desire to go on.

I am hoping, then, that this rest may fill my cistern, or recharge my battery, enough for me to rise up and come and see you toward the end of the week. Since I have no car, and Dan is not with me, I do not know exactly how I am going to get to Cambridge, but I think I'll find some sort of method such as is used by the handful of people still left in the world who haven't got automobiles.

If the style of this letter sounds rather eighteenth-century, it is because I am reading Jane Austen, as I almost always do if I have to be in bed, and if I am lucky enough to be anywhere near a set of her works. There is nothing I adore so much as Jane Austen's works, especially for reading all day long in bed. I have just begun on the second volume of *Mansfield Park*. What a lovely book!

JUST now I was doing my exercises—which are, as always, essential to my health—and thanks to the train of thought you started the other day, I was conscious of how I felt while doing them. As often, I did them very calmly and patiently, but with a fury inside. I had never really known before why I *had* to be so extraordinarily calm and good and patient to make myself do them. Today I found out that they made me want to yell and scream and throw the dumbbells at somebody, just somebody. I want to run and play tennis and be wild—instead of being so patient and good and doing my slow, silly, feeble exercises.

This morning I woke very early and felt such suffering and confusion. And after a while suddenly the confusion resolved itself into this—a terrible surprise to me: I want to get a divorce from Dan. I can't bear being married. I was horribly unhappy the first year, and I *knew* it, and used to wish he would die. I wanted to escape. I knew it was a mistake; but I made up my mind to make something good out of something bad. And superficially that has been accomplished. It is infinitely better than it was, but still falls far short of what it should be. I have been an invalid ever since I got married. Before that I traveled alone, lived alone, took care of myself after a fashion, quite badly, but still I did it, more than now. I was horribly lonely sometimes, and life didn't seem worth living—that is, after I lost Toshihiko. But I did not have the heavy, unwilling body that I have now. This morning, as I imagined being free again, going back to my lonely and rather dreary life, it seemed to make me feel young and well again, as if a frightful burden were lifted. Since I began to pride myself on *creating* a good marriage, I have fooled myself, and

302

a lot of our "happiness" has been synthetic. Miraculously enough, there has been some of it that has been real.

Spring, 1938

HAVING achieved Katharine and Dan instead of Mr. and Miss Muffet, let's have courage and get down to bedrock. Oh, Dan! I feel wild and tortured, there are devils inside of me. There is an ordeal ahead of me because I've got to face them. Can you go through it with me?

[To DR. DE FOREST]

Spring, 1938

I MADE myself, as entirely as I could, humble and un-critical because I thought it was the only way I could learn. I laid aside what I consciously think of as the "tall" part of my mind (the part which is authentic—speaks with words, authority, self-assertion—poise). I deliberately humiliated, degraded myself—lowest common denomina-tor, took off all my clothes—previously always spoken with a question-mark after every sentence. This is a sign of a weak position. I did it because I was not *tall*, but depro-cating. Now—the way your face looked—I thought I might give, or teach, you something.

Don't try to understand everything, interpret every-thing. But I think about you and often write a long imagi-nary letter. Now there are certain thoughts, ideas, consid-erations which for a long time have been present in the conscious part of my mind, and I want to try to tell you about them. They are rather difficult and subtle things to express, and I have been too lazy to try to do it.

That is, the abstract philosophical religious questions which are so much a part of me and my daily thoughts

303

and yet so rarely, rarely put into speech that they are buried in a deep silence and solitude like fossils buried in a rock. But I feel as if my not telling you these things might cause a misunderstanding that might waste a great deal of our time. It never occurs to me that it is possible to tell anybody, even you.

June 3, 1938

WITH next September only three months away, it is time I wrote to you. My belief that I should come back to you then has begun to slip. When I felt it begin to slip a little, I watched myself very carefully because I was conscience-stricken about you and your time, and I didn't want to make you lose, or some other patient lose, the chance to have that hour. But it is only since the last day or two that my uncertainty has got to the point where I feel I really ought to warn you of it and give up for myself the claim you have allowed me.

I want to come now just as much as I did when I told you I wanted to come. But since I came back here I keep feeling that it would be an almost unjustified self-indulgence on my part to disorganize my life with Dan, and Dan's life, for an indefinite length of time, and for very uncertain results. If I were alone I'm sure I should not hesitate. Also if I were really sick and suffering, or if Dan and I were getting on badly, I should feel justified in doing it. But without having some really desperate problem to get solved, or an illness to cure, I think I ought to be free and alone before starting out on such an exacting and lonely journey. I *hate* to do it in dilettante fashion, as I have so far, and I am afraid that to do it with the absolute absorption and single-mindedness that it needs would mean, in my case, throwing my marriage right overboard. And I am much too happy to do that.

I love you, Izette. And I have lately a new reason why I

304

want to come back to you. Lately I have felt a changing
current in myself toward you. Instead of *taking* from you,
I feel a need of giving to you. I feel a need in you for
something I have that I think you have not. You see, even
in the midst of my chaos and despair and blindness, I have
sometimes something that more than balances all those
things, and I have been bold enough to want to give you
some of this joy. The first time I came to see you this spring
I talked sitting up, looking at your face. I had seen you
look sad with compassion before, but I never saw you look
sad with an inner private sadness as you did that day, and
it made me feel a strange and unfamiliar longing to help
you. And I thought that if I came back to you maybe
through me you might get a kernel of something that even
Freud doesn't understand. It is very hard to describe or
explain that joy; I only know that it is the most extraordinary happiness I know, and I am sure it must be the
same thing the mystics feel and call God. And when it
comes, there comes with it an absolute conviction that
all is well, even that suffering, agony, death, cruelty are
all forgiven and changed into harmony. I longed to tell
you this and have you feel it, too.

But this is a terribly stupid letter. I haven't been capable
of saying a quarter of what I wanted to and already it is
too long.

I can't possibly say good-by to you, and I hope it is not
necessary. I intend to write you many more letters.

[To Catharine Huntington]

July, 1938

Now I am grieved about your horrors and your sad disappointment in your work. And then I must go back to
the essential and say that in that you are certainly not
unrecognized. What the hell for professional recognition

if you haven't got satisfaction for the heart, and how many of them have? And how many of them are there that wouldn't be glad to—well, I don't know the rest of this sentence. There *are* successful ones who are happy in love as well. You and I both suffered from wrong beginnings, and it seems to me we represent something and can express something that is valuable, and you have, and will again. Don't despair. Everybody does despair, though. That is one of the symptoms of being an artist. The more sensitive and well endowed you are, the less likely that you will be understood as you wish to be. I bet that fame and praise are often horrible because it may not be really intelligent or understanding praise. I have just read a most revealing book by poor Thomas Wolfe, telling about his writing of his first book, and of the awful ordeal of his sudden fame, the cruelty of the publicity, and the hatred and bitterness of his home town. It is called *The Story of a Novel.* It takes away all the charm of fame. And I must say I had been having my suspicions that it might be just like that. The horrible exposure of laying one's life bare for everybody—everybody, the dumbbells, the gossipy, the vicious, the snooping ones—to read. Terrific. I think I would hesitate a long time. And maybe not publish it until I was well out of the way.

I have been terribly crazy lately, dreadful nerves, nightmares, horrors, despairs, jitters; but it comes and goes, and that is merciful. I do manage to beat them all off, like a gang of dragons, and make myself a fortification inside of which I write in the morning. It is only by steadily working and holding them off with the other hand that I can keep them from knocking on the door and scrambling through the cracks. And if I keep this island of safety for three or four hours per day, that is something. Oh, it isn't so bad as all that, but when it is at its height, it is almost unbearable—a sort of hideous tension all over. They say

the *changement de la vie,* or Dr. Bliss says anyway, is the cause of such franticitude. It has something to do with struggle to persist, something like that. Kind of a second adolescence, a flaring up of all one's energy and *joie de vivre,* but chaotic, too much, more than one can contain, it seems. And with me, I haven't enough physical ways of working it off.

August 1, 1938

WE HAD a pair of celebrities to tea yesterday. I told you, I guess, or did I? Charles R. Kennedy, who wrote *The Servant in the House,* and his wife, the actress Edith Wynne Mathison. They liked Dan very much, and his muffins and tea. We had a very cheerful, amiable, and quite charming time. Mr. K. said Dan looks like Gerald du Maurier in his youth. And I look like two other people. Dan also looks like his marble bust of Alexander I of Russia, they all said, as many do. Only these added that Dan's face was even better than Alexander's. Lots of compliments flew about. And stories of Cornish prize-fighters, and of Lord Chief Justices and of Lord Byron, and so on. They were very nice indeed, these celebrities, and very *gentil,* and loving, and sympathetic.

November 28, 1938

I HAVE had a mean, horrid cold for the past two weeks, and have been in bed a good part of that time, and now I am ready to screech with impatience and boredom. We had an invitation to the Whites, of *The New Yorker,* for tea this afternoon. Mrs. Newberry was to be there, and as I hadn't been out except for a few minutes in the sun, and still cough myself to pieces in the night, we decided that I had better not go. It is a long, cold drive out where they live, and after yesterday's blizzard there is the chance 'of getting stuck and having to sit in the cold and wait to be hauled out. This is one reason why I feel like screeching. To long desperately for a little change, and gaiety, and talk, and not to be able to take the chance when it comes! I must say I want to live while I am living, and not perish from inactivity and seclusion. But because I want to live I take boredom instead of more cold, at the moment. And during the past two weeks I have read four volumes of *War and Peace,* of which there are six. It is a grand experience I never tackled before.

There is a little cat lying so close to me I can hardly write. She is a kitten, and very much like Toupsie, except that she is definitely my cat, my pet, and very affectionate. She is a long-haired mousy cat with white ruffles, a little foundling that was given to Dan in the village. I named her Trouvée.

January 21, 1939

NOBODY could have imagined or wished for a more serene night for traveling than the one I had. It is queer how often the completely unexpected thing happens. After my nervous apprehensions of a blizzard and getting stuck somewhere, the only unusual feature of my journey was my going rather early in the morning to the ladies' room and finding the door of the toilet open and the conductor sitting on the ladies' toilet. When he saw me coming in in my chemise and sweater, he made some kind of embarrassed sound, and I went back to my berth. In a moment I heard him outside my curtain mumbling, "All right now, I'm sorry." Later, when I was sitting outside my berth, all dressed, he came along and leaned over and said, "I hope I didn't frighten you. We don't generally expect people to get up so early. I was afraid I might have kind of embarrassed you or frightened you." He had a wide, jolly face, and when I said I wasn't so easily frightened as that,

309

he laughed and went away quite relieved. I knew I must be in Maine.

Another letter from Mr. Sedgwick today, saying he "dislikes exceedingly" parting with my manuscript. He says it seems the only link with reality in the whole project. I don't know why he feels this, and I wrote him a letter saying I thought there was reality in the fact that I had stuck to the idea of the book through all sorts of obstacles and delays and interruptions for such a long time. It is five years since I first began, and I think I have been quite stubborn about it. I fought with Warren about it, for one thing.

I felt all right after I got on the train, and thanks to my beautiful visit with you, I have come back refreshed and ready to work again, for once after an absence not at all tired.

April 2, 1939

I AM continually admiring myself in the long mirror as I see myself shrink around the middle and see my stays need further and further reefing in. I have lost from five to ten pounds, and everybody notices the change and the improvement. The effect of losing weight has been miraculous on the heart—*much* less consciousness of it and much less difficulty walking and going up steps. Practically none, in fact. The other night I went out smelt-fishing with Jack and Dan, and for an hour I was scrambling around in a brook, climbing in and out of the water, over stones and up bankings and down again, leaning over constantly, almost standing on my head to see the smelts and catch them in my hands and toss them into the lettuce drier which we brought to hold them. And I was not in the least tired afterward, when we stopped about 11:30 P.M. I couldn't possibly have done it before without dreadful discomfort of the heart and fatigue that would have lasted several days.

I am passionately convinced of the danger and folly of eating too much. I still have to pause when going up any sharp, steep banking, or any long hill, but nothing like what I did and have done for the last three or four years. And that is just the time when I began to add weight. Before that, of course, I couldn't climb magnificently, but ordinary things didn't bother me, and I feel as if I had got back to that phase again.

[To Toshihiko]

September 26, 1939

I suppose that since you left Europe and returned to Japan you have perhaps become Japanese again, or at least more Japanese and less European than you were a year ago. And as it is now a very long time since I have been with you, or Taro, or Hirota, I suppose that I have lost a great deal of whatever Japanese understanding I once had. I suppose I am now much more an occidental than during that short time when I believed I had found something that belonged to me, the time when I learned from you a little of the Japanese way of thinking and feeling. I could never really possess it, not being born an oriental, but I could recognize it poignantly and know that I felt happier and strangely more at home in the Japanese atmosphere than I did in the American. Now, although I can remember it, I feel that it is no longer a part of me, as I did feel then. And I feel extremely sad, as if I were losing, or had lost, something essential to me. I am worrying for fear you, being now very un-American, will find this letter too foreign to your way of thinking, too unreadable to trouble with.

But if I have once known you and once a little understood you, I must think that you still remember at times every person who has ever meant anything to you. I think of how in Castine, sitting at the desk in a New England house, you used to cover pages like this one on both sides with Japanese writing, and your thoughts and feelings were certainly five thousand miles away from the room where you were sitting. And sometimes it was not merely space that you ignored, but time, too. You used to remember suddenly an episode of your childhood and completely forget the present.

There was a boy in your school who had a very poor pair of chopsticks, and you and other rich boys made him feel unhappy because of his poor chopsticks. When suddenly you remembered that boy one day in Castine, you said you wanted to go back to Japan and find him and tell him that you had suddenly realized how you had made him suffer, and you wanted to apologize; and because I know that you used to send your thoughts very far away from the place where you were sitting and let them dwell intently on a person you had not seen or thought of for years, I think it isn't impossible for you to think now of me with that sudden intentness and perception.

Please remember me. Because I want to communicate with you. And don't, please, remember me the way I was in Paris, because I lost myself for a while then. I think now I am more the way you first knew me, in the very beginning—just intent on being an artist, not asking for anything else except the freedom and solitude in which to do the best I am capable of. Well, now I am writing. You reminded me once when I stopped being an artist for a while, that in art is the best happiness, and I know it is true. I believe that now, and I am lucky enough to be able to follow it. What I am writing is the story of my getting free, of the almost miraculous way in which I learned to be free from a great physical handicap and deformity. One important step in the learning, the most important, was the Japanese way of thinking and feeling: the honesty and frankness and intuition of a Japanese influencing a New Englander. I have not nearly finished writing it. There is a great deal to tell besides the Japanese influence. There is a description of a childhood in Salem, of the town of Castine, my neighbors and friends and family. It sounds terrible as I describe it now. A book about myself sounds terrible, but I don't think it is terrible. I think it is good, somewhat good; not bad, at least.

I have shown the first few chapters to Mr. Sedgwick, chief owner of, and for many years editor of, the *Atlantic Monthly,* and he liked it so much that he has written me dozens of letters about it and asked me to come and see him at his house twice, and tells me he wants to publish it when it is finished. It happens that he is very deeply interested in Japan. When he went there, he said, he felt at home there as he never has anywhere else. He owns a Japanese statue which Hirota told me about. He lent it to the Boston Museum for a Japanese exhibition and Hirota said it was marvelous, the most beautiful thing in the exhibition. The next time I go to his house I shall ask him to show it to me. But he has not yet read the part of my story which is about the Japanese influence, because I haven't come to that yet. And when I do write it, I want to send a copy of the manuscript to you, to read and criticize if you will. And I want to ask you if you still feel, as you once did, that I might do something toward making Americans understand Japanese better than they do.

You know there is a tremendous prejudice here now against the Japanese because American sympathy is with China. I have just been reading the opening chapters of a book by a very popular American newspaper correspondent, John Gunther, called *Inside Asia.* He begins by describing Japan, the Japanese Emperor, and the Japanese people. And although he is unprejudiced, so far as I can see yet— I haven't come to the part about China—I am struck by the lack of subtlety or true insight concerning the Japanese. His obtuseness concerning them annoys me, and it makes me wish to write something myself. But I have lost too many of the details I once remembered. I may be still capable of understanding a little of the Japanese feeling and way of thinking, but I should need to refresh my memory before attempting to write anything except that story I now have in my head. Do you think I could learn something more if I had a chance to go to Japan? Could I be of any use in explaining Japan to America? First I must finish my present book. Mr. Sedgwick wrote me in his last letter, just the other day, "I am confident that the book will have a practical as well as an intellectual success." If he is right about this, if it should be a success, then I might be of some value as an American writer, and then the thing I should like best to do would be to go to Japan and live a little while and learn more about Japan and the Japanese way of feeling and thinking.

I could never be content to do this as a tourist, or as a professional observer. Having had in you, and in Taro, close friends, I could never feel that I was learning anything real unless I still had your friendship and unless you would help me. It all depends on whether or not you still think of me as a person of understanding and of sufficient insight and talent to be able to write something true and valuable about Japan. It would be a long time before I could actually do this. It will take me another year, I think, to finish this book, as I work slowly. Besides, we can't possibly see what is coming, what destruction and what great changes may be coming very swiftly with the European war. I wish I knew what experiences you are having, and how you feel about the things that are happening in the world. I am having a happy and interesting life, and if it had not been for the Japanese influence that came to me, I don't think I should ever have come the way I have, nor had nearly so much to be grateful for.

[To Dan Hathaway]

Spring, 1940

Because I am so inarticulate in conversation, and am constitutionally incapable of telling even my closest friends and companions about most of the things which matter to me, and yet can, luckily, do better on paper, especially since I have found the medium of Obma, which takes care of almost every subject. Because of this, Obma * is a help to me, and it is a help to me to have had you read it and also John and Nela and the various members of the family. Writing it was, and is, for me a process of discovery. It has showed me things I didn't know, and it keeps on showing me new things as I go on writing. And there is one thing of greatest importance which it has shown me, something that hasn't been written yet into Obma, but I hope will be. But I can't wait to write it into Obma before telling you what it is, because I want you to know it now. It is simply that I have come to believe in God, the God of the New Testament, and I wish to try to live according to the teachings of the New Testament.

I have felt this ever since the autumn when we bought our house, when I read the New Testament as if for the first time and saw how great and wonderful it is. Since then I've lost my way over and over, but every time when

* *The Little Locksmith.*

315

I yield my selfish desires and put myself entirely in the hands of God, everything comes smooth again, and especially with Obma, every page, every paragraph has been written when I had a clean sense of God's guidance. I can't receive this marvelous gift and say nothing about it to anyone, not show my gratitude. When anybody praises Obma I feel that I want to say, "Don't praise me, I didn't do it." To you, who say Obma is wonderful, and to John and Nela I just want to say that from being just like you and them in my attitude toward Christianity up to five years ago, a complete transformation has taken place in me, and out of it has come this book.

Therefore I want to have it understood openly that I am a devout religious person, although untaught and ignorant concerning it, because I grew up in an entirely irreligious generation. I hated it violently when I was young except for the two or three brief periods, one I described in Obma. I used to be drawn and attracted for a little while, then full of disgust and scorn. And I never for a moment thought of letting anything of that sort influence my conduct of my life. That idea just made me sick.

But now I realize that even before I knew it I was being guided by God, in order to reach this place, where I feel an unmistakable vocation.

I feel terribly shy indeed, writing you this. As somebody said, it is as embarrassing and difficult to use the word God in our generation as it was to use the word Sex in the previous one. But I am telling you because I must, and because I know that once you realize how deeply I feel about it, although you may not feel it at all yourself, or be at all inclined to join me in it, at least you will regard and respect this feeling in me, and not hurt me by saying mocking things about the Christian religion.

Back in Maine

[To an Artist]

Spring, 1940

I AM afraid I won't be free on Sunday. The fact is, Dan seems so terribly exhausted that I am not making any plans for the next few days so as to be free to do what he may want. Often he likes to take a long meandering drive on Sunday into the back roads, exploring, etc., and I wouldn't like to go off if I knew you were coming, and he won't go alone. Let me call you up some day soon when I know I am going to be here. And no doubt we will be dropping over your way almost any time.

Out of my own experience I think that the best and most lasting and most healing thing is work, even if in the beginning it seems terribly lifeless and forced. If you are patient and quiet enough, and not rebellious, it comes back, the way sleep comes, when you don't know exactly.

I, being rather an ardent kind of person, have felt frustration and despair such as I couldn't describe to you if I would. Now I've discovered that the wild rebellion one feels is terribly destructive. And the answer is simply to channel one's energy into the other sort of love; it's all the same thing really. I mean, being in love with what your eyes dwell on, and your aesthetic sense receives, and expressing it with writing and painting. I have that little verse from the *Muses Plantin,* in Antwerp, dated 1588, and it has quieted a frantic feeling and made me able to work and have as wonderful days, over and over many times. It is this: in old French—

Un labeur courageux muni d'humble constance
Resiste à tous assauts par douce pacience.

The best things, I am sure, and you know this, are done in that mood of sensitive, receptive quietness such as appears so beautifully in your pictures.

317

Won't you take out your brushes and your paints and handle them again, even if you don't do anything with them at first? They are your best friends.

I think I have in me an instinctive sense of obligation (for some reason or other) toward sensitive, talented, and misunderstood people—those who have great capacity for happiness if properly adjusted but who have not yet succeeded in struggling out of their essential loneliness. Van Gogh's life is a record of such a person who never was able to get the personal happiness he needed so badly. I know from experience what a frightful nervous tension one can suffer just from the lack of companionship of one's own kind. Now I have been lucky—long ago I did find what I needed, and also I have had the freedom that is provided by a regular income which is enough to take care of physical needs. And I never can bear to see anybody else who has the kind of temperament and both mental and physical needs which I am acquainted with, starving and tormented by being entirely misunderstood and *not* valued by the people around him. Sometimes almost more important than sexual love or money to live on is, I think, somebody who can accompany you in your mind's experiences.

[TO CATHARINE HUNTINGTON]

May 18, 1940

IT IS wonderful to come out into the country, and yesterday was typical of the nicest things here. Katharine White (Mrs. Newberry's sister) came, bringing me the fleece from their black sheep, which I had said I would like to buy to have made into yarn and knitted because of its wonderful color. She carried it up high in her arms, a huge mound of solid wool, rolled up in a bundle, weighing seven pounds. I have found a woman in East Blue Hill who spins, and she will spin it for me after it has been cleaned and carded. After K.W. came, Robert and Christine Weston arrived, having been fishing in Walcott's brook, and brought us six or seven trout, and a bouquet of arbutus from the Walcotts' woods. A black fleece, brook trout, and arbutus, all in one day! If that isn't a poem!

June 5, 1940

THIS place looks lovelier this year than ever before, it seems to me. Such a mountainous lilac bush all in bloom. The house filled with their fragrance, and I have been picking lilies-of-the-valley. Our own that we set out two or three years ago are now so thick and full of blossoms. I adore them. They always remind me of Patchin Place, and Taro.

If this existence is going to be crushed out, at least it's lovely while it lasts, and I insist on enjoying it as long as we are allowed to. Enjoying it more intensely and realizing it more intensely, because of this cancer that is growing so fast around the earth. But I believe in miracles, and I think there will be one. But we will never be the same again. We mustn't be.

[To DOLLY —]

June 9, 1940

I AM feeling better, but it was and is always chiefly emotional crises that knock me out, and a foolishly hysterical kind of heart, and at present I don't believe that anybody can be serene. Tom was quite right about the evil in the world, against which we should rise out of our apathy.

It is not the crises that are bad, but the damned New England suppression of feeling—to which I was fatally trained—which make all the subterranean trouble, exploding now and then in a much-needed and very wholesome crisis. I had some very helpful conversations with a psychologist at the Harvard Psychological Clinic in Cambridge.

[TO MERRILL MOORE]

Summer, 1940

I CANCELED my appointment with you because I wasn't ready to tell you anything. You see, although I value all the knowledge you possess and so generously give me, and I want to use it whenever I can, the ultimate decision on any really important thing has to come out of me. I have a relationship with something invisible: the well into which I let down my pail, the well out of which I draw up my pail filled with the stuff which makes Obma. I have found it inescapably necessary that my personal life and Obma must come up out of the same well. It was not until after I had been writing Obma for some time that I realized this necessity. At first it was only letting down the pail for Obma, but I've known lately that the discrepancy between using one source for Obma and something much more shallow for my ordinary life was the thing causing such discontent and such a sick feeling in me.

I have been dodging the necessity to use the same source for everything because it meant something too hard to face. But sooner faced, the better. I have to believe fully, wholly, without compromise, in my well, and act according to what I believe.

Dan and I spent a lovely day at Corea, with Marsden Hartley, a painter who is also a poet, a friend of Hart Crane, Carlos Williams, etc. His newest volume is *Androscoggin*, Maine poems published last year. He was thrilled when he heard that we know you because he has always been interested in you as a poet. We have sent him

320

our two volumes of M. M. to read, as he does not know them, and then he intends to write to you. He is a lovely person. I fell in love. He has the bluest eyes I ever saw.

Warren left yesterday after lots of work and inspiration. Dan was absolutely exhausted. He can't take such a supercharged being. We will stay alone and quiet now. He needs it, and also I couldn't work when Warren was here. I was too much on the alert to forestall explosions and trying to protect one from the other. It was very difficult and fatiguing, yet a great deal of good came out of it too.

[To WARREN BUTLER]

October, 1940

SINCE you left I have had thousands of imaginary conversations with you, written you thousands of letters. The reason for this torment is the feeling that there is conflict, there is a huge mountain between us that I am trying to push away with all my strength. When I talk with you about a third person and his situation and problems, you always listen to me with great attentiveness, and I know you value my opinion and you believe I have a certain amount of insight; you are even swayed by me sometimes so that you act quite differently toward that person than you had planned to. You tell me sometimes that you like to have me tell you when you are "wrong" as you put it touchingly humbly. Yet when I am driven by some difficulty of my own to try to describe it to you and present it truthfully, everything that I hear myself say to you sounds like weak and incoherent and despicable foolishness. On the subject which I know most intimately I feel it is impossible for me to speak to you, as I can of other subjects—why is this? Do you know? I think it is partly because when we are talking of a third person we are talking (and may we be forgiven for it) as if we were superior beings, Gods looking on, weighing this and that. When I am in distress, I am weak, I am not superior. You are a God looking on, weighing this and that in me, and my alter ego, my detached self, cannot then be my advocate as it would be the advocate of a third person. You can't stand weakness, confusion, emotion. It makes you feel hostile in spite of yourself. You condemn me from the first word of my weakness, without meaning to, I know; but because you can't help it.

It is easy enough to sympathize with and sponsor in another person thoughts and feelings which are like our own—it is like approving of one's self—but giving your sympathy and your understanding and your love to a person who is in the throes of thoughts and feelings that are *different* from yours, and different from anything that you personally have ever experienced, that is another thing—and I don't think you can possibly do it unless you are able to surrender your *self* completely—throw away everything out of yourself—empty yourself completely for the time being, while you yield yourself to that different person, and absorb his thoughts and feelings into you until you know what they really are intrinsically and quite separately from the way they happen to affect the critical part of you.

Anger, for instance. Now, I am very glad to say I am married to someone who also erupts once in a while. And I have come to this belief, that when a person gets angry with you he says things about you that are like white-hot chunks of lava—they are absolutely crude, and if you happen to be like you or me—nonerupting—your instant reaction is cold distaste, and sudden conviction that your relation with the person is hopeless—he is saying about you the opposite of what you complacently believe to be true—he simply doesn't understand you or appreciate you. Well, throw this *all* overboard, and after those precious chunks of lava have cooled off, run around and pick them up humbly like a scientist. They may not look like much to anybody else, but if you let yourself become as selfless and free of preconceived ideas and as patient and as humble as a scientific research worker is, you can translate those awkward lumps as if they were cuneiform inscriptions. And you will find, to your surprise, revelations about *yourself* on them, which are more important and precious to you than anything they may tell you of him. You can find in them usually that *you* are the one who has been at fault, you because you were so uncritical of yourself, complacent, self-absorbed.

People say, I believe, that in anger a person says things that are a caricature of the truth; but in that caricature you can find truth about yourself that you could never find any other way. And if you will value those lumps of lava they will help more than anything I know of to strengthen the love and understanding between two people.

I feel that there is the same significance and value to be found in the other emotional outlet—the crying and blurting out of crude sentences of a person who is in distress. The cool listener usually feels superior, and considers it so much weak babble; but it is also lava; it is crude because it is coming direct out of the person, hasn't been molded and made presentable by the artist-brain. I am appealing to you to yield yourself to this letter sometime when you are lying on your little pallet in Beverly alone; let it play over you like the music of the music box, listen to it, and see if you find any tiny grain of treasure in it— anything to save and use.

One reason why I have written this—very badly and fast—is because I feel an inevitable conflict between us. I know that before I am able to push away that mountain, which I hope to do—I mean the mountain that lies between us—a difference of point of view, emotion, life-illusion, whatever it is—I know that in my struggles to push it away, I shall cry, I shall blurt out foolish sentences, I shall appear weak, and I may even be driven by the feeling of impotence to anger and I may say cruel and hateful things. I am appealing to you to understand that I want you to consider the possibility of your doing for me what I would do for you under the same emotional stress—I would pick up those shapeless lumps and hope to find precious meanings in them. I want you to do it because I know from experience that it is a crossroads at which love either grows great and indestructible or else allows itself to be defeated.

I can't ask anyone, unless I do it without knowing that I am, to do anything that I wouldn't ask myself to do, and if possible I think one should ask less rather than the equal, because we are so unequally equipped, and the other person may find even the equal demand too much for him, for some reason. One should always assume that, rather than the opposite, certainly.

What I'm asking you to do in this letter is what I've done myself many, many times, and without the benefit of being forewarned, as you are now.

I need you—I need your love, and your compassion. Something is troubling me almost more than I can bear.

[To Catharine Huntington]

December 5, 1940

We have had a perfectly lovely time in Salem and in Peabody; all the family so harmonious and gay except Warren, who had one sad moment with me, but got off at last for his tour with Philip and is probably happy now. Lurana gave us a Newfoundland dog with whom we both are absolutely entranced. Miranda is her name, and she drove to Maine sitting up between us just like a person, and her calm reassuring nature is exactly what both Dan and I need in a dog. Never a cry or a bark, no nervousness such as is so tiring in other dogs, she is a perfect delight to both of us.

Stahl's Tavern,
Waldoboro, Maine

I WANT you to see this address, where I am spending the night, because it shows you that I got safely past Brunswick before I stopped. My anti-Brunswick sentiment carried me through. I had the horrors when a traffic light halted me just in front of the house I lay awake in on the way down. It seemed as if the bearded lady, who kept clutching at my arm and shoulder, would spy me and drag me in. It was really a wonderful escape to feel the Pines of Bowdoin College behind me. I thought there wouldn't be any traffic now, but I've never seen so many huge crawling trucks, and just enough other traffic to prevent passing the trucks, until we came into the next town and a broad main street. It has been very hot. I am now delightfully sleepy and have had an early supper and am going to bed. This is a really nice old-fashioned inn. The old proprietor sits at a cardtable in the living room, quite elderly and bronchial, in his slippers. On the walls hang great ship paintings in rich gold frames, his father's ships, one painting of his vessel by a Chinese painter in Hong Kong harbor, another a big watercolor of his ship in Melbourne harbor. The Chinese one is beautifully done. On the white marble mantelpiece is a cribbage board with a brass face on it, a hunk of amethyst quartz, a tropical shell, a pair of rather swell vases. There is a large dark-green wicker rocking chair, upholstered easy chair, this desk, and on the wall at the foot of the stairs, which go up out of this room, there is a wooden board

325

hanging on a nail. On the board there are four rows of hooks, five hooks in each row, with large old-fashioned keys hanging on the hooks, and to each key is attached a huge oblong brass tag with the number on one side and on the other in old letters, STAHL'S TAVERN.

Did I tell you that I asked Merrill Moore again to tell me the word meaning of a number, or a word which is the same backward or forward, like 101? The word is palindrome, "palin" meaning same, "drome" meaning run. It runs the same. Merrill also pointed out that "revere" is, all but the final "e," a palindrome also, which entrances me, and makes the name of palindrome unavoidable. May it bring you luck! It certainly ought to. Anything that can run the same backward and forward should be utterly unbeatable. 101 Rever 101 Rever 101, A rose is a rose is. I hope this won't make you feel wild. I find it perfectly soothing. Some say that when letters and numbers begin to have power over you, you are fast plunging into total mental disarrangement. But people have liked palindromes since the beginning of everything. They represent balance, eternity.

I feel very happy and pleased about everything. This is a lovely beginning of a month.

January 7, 1941

SOMEHOW when you say the most heartbreaking things you say them in a way that makes them so funny that I laugh my head off. Your New Year's resolve should certainly work if it strikes you as funnily as it does me. But I know what you mean nevertheless, and I think it does work. "Assume a virtue if you have it not" is what Hamlet said to his mother, and he argued that chastity would work in from the outside, and I think this is sound psychologically. It certainly ought to come easily to an actor. I

don't mean chastity as in Queen Gertrude's case, but any
virtue you want to assume, any virtue you feel you need.
It is perhaps the core of the British endurance, it is the
opposite of the nonenduring Latins, who moan and beat
their breasts and collapse.

[To ELLERY SEDGWICK]

March 28, 1941

I AM the disappointed one because you didn't respond
at all to my idea of a ceremony. I thought you were so
Japanese in love of ritual that you would like to see me
come with my helpers, and bow very low with a speech,
and hand you the oblong package, which you would receive with another bow and oriental speech. Then I
thought there would be great merriment and a tray of
sake and rice cakes. I thought that something you had
waited forty years for, even if it is worthless, as in
oriental fashion I am obliged to insist that it is, would
require some little decoration of this kind. Now I have
decided that, although you are patient and trusting and
infinitely believing, you are greedy, and all you think of
is the inside of the package and not at all remembering
to think of the hand and the patient person who has made
it. This is too American; it is disappointing.

I would have had my secretary come ahead and play
on her oboe to all the office at 8 Arlington Street a very
familiar old song—Victor Herbert I think, but I'm not sure
—with the words of the chorus. "And when I told them,
As I certainly have often told them, They didn't believe
me, No, they didn't believe me, That I would ever get
my story done."

Well, maybe I will send a Western Union boy over with
the package, to sing the song for them.

It is all very bleak and grim, this way of doing things.

April 2, 1942

Perhaps I will risk boring you to tell you complainingly about my chief and most annoying symptom, because I am sure it is something that couldn't happen to you. I have neglected my abdominal muscles, those good sustaining muscles which are so all-important. Years ago a famous specialist who took care of me told me I must never stop doing certain exercises which kept my abdominal muscles strong. He said I would always be all right if only I did them—because in my particular case things are so out of balance that without that reinforcement and underpinning, everything goes haywire with heart and lungs, as they begin to slump with the slumping of the underpinning. And I've neglected my exercises now for about two years. I did notice getting shorter of breath than usual, with queer sensations of constriction around the neck, and there were also these ferocious headaches in the morning on waking. Then, after being in bed with a cold, etc., after the wedding, the relaxation of that little sickness was just enough to put the finishing touches on the neglected muscles, and since getting up from that spell of bedriddenness I have scarcely been able to navigate. The midriff keeps caving in, and I grab for pieces of furniture to lean on. But I've begun humbly to do my old doctor's exercises, and I think I see the beginning of improvement. I do them three times during the day, with rests between, and it requires quite a lot of patience. I can't do anything else very much, as one's best energy has to be saved for the exercises. It is like training for a prize-fight. A very secluded life in deshabille, and boring in the extreme. I read an article by Gene Tunney in the February *Readers' Digest* describing this very subject—the importance of keeping the abdominal muscles in good condition because of their relation to heart and lungs, and he described the dreadful results of neglect, which was a perfect description of me, even the headaches. There, now, that is the subject, disgraceful because I allowed it to happen, with which I am occupied. But I am grateful for my little house in Boston, which is very cunning. The walls are shiny white paint, woodwork cream, floor dark red, curtains ruby red leaves on cream background, rug red, flower-painting in white frame.

This scribbled drawing makes the room look twice as large as life. It is really very small—everything close together. Dan looked like a giant when he came in here, and he felt too large, he said. This little salon is directly on the street, and the people and taxicabs going by often seem to come right into the room. Not that it is too noisy, because it is only a side street. It is merely very sociable and neighborly. Three doors farther down the hill is the great big street full of traffic and excitement, shops and shoppers, a church and a jail and a hospital a little farther down, and the Charles River Esplanade only a step away.

[To CATHARINE HUNTINGTON]

May 15, 1942

THE journey was simply lovely. Pat was a perfect companion and nurse and chauffeur. She was so sweet and good and did everything—carried and lifted and arranged and all, after finishing my packing at the Lincolnshire in the morning. We both enjoyed the journey very much. I rested in bed two days afterward, and now I must tell you that each day I am definitely better and stronger. I can see it by certain advances and increase of things I can do.

Our carpenter has put up my head-traction board and pully, and Dan helps me do it twice every day. Also the carpenter has put up an iron bar for me to do my stretching exercise on (Dr. Chapman's idea), and that is great fun. I walk up and down on the terrace, and I can tell that my lung capacity has increased a lot already. Breathing is much better.

June 8, 1942

TODAY is exactly one month since Pat and I drove out of Boston, on just such a fair, sunny day. And I can really feel satisfaction and cheerfulness when I realize how much more I can do now than then. At times during the past four weeks I have felt secret despair many times when I felt as though permanent damage had been done, and I would never get back to the way I felt a year ago. There had been a curious new feeling of breathlessness ever since the illness in Peabody which seemed very sinister, but it grows less and less, and comes less and less frequently, until now I go upstairs here three or four times a day without any breathlessness at all. And I began to do some work last week; the pleasant feeling of excitement began to bubble up again. But I have still to be most economical of each day's ration of energy, or the fatigue is bad and most disheartening again.

For the first two weeks the rain and fog were simply beautiful to me with the beautiful late spring proceeding almost imperceptibly. It was the most perfect dreamlike feeling, like a delicious opiate. I felt such perfect contentment and relaxation in doing nothing, only watching the shapes of things and the color, and feeling the softness and moisture of the air. Dan has been terribly sweet and good, and we have been happy and peaceful all the time.

July 8, 1942

I HASTEN to tell you that I have completely recovered now from my bronchitis, and ready to welcome you whenever

330

you are ready to come. I know you said it would probably be toward the end of next week, but if you know that I am all well, maybe you will come a little sooner. Anyhow, just let me know what day to meet you.

There is one most uncomfortable symptom of my improved health—that I begin to be very restive and feel frustrated and mad because I am not doing anything, and because I am so passive in this menage, and must be in order to preserve peace. When I am not preoccupied with work, then I want to stir up something else and take command and have a houseful of guests and great activity of every kind. Claire Evans, as I've probably said, has urged us to come and visit them in Arizona, and Dan is shocked and horrified because I would like to go. You would think he had never traveled or done anything except live in this village, from his sense of injury. He makes me seem like an insatiably restless, dissatisfied one, so difficult to please. If you have a house like this, you stay in it, you are mad if you want to leave it ever. I am so grateful that you can come, and he looks forward so eagerly to your coming, as I do. He has discovered something new about bread-making which has improved his bread very much, so he will make extra loaves when you are here.

How grateful I should be for all that I have! And my good luck at being really better. It will be wonderful to have you here. The weather is better now, too. I sat out in the sun today at last.

[To KITTY HAWKINS]

August 12, 1942

I HAVE had you so much and lovingly in mind it has been difficult not to write. I have followed you from place to place, writing down each new address in my address-book, and only thankful that you at least are only a night's journey away—not out in Ottawa, or British Columbia, wherever that is. Now, with one of the darling Portuguese tumblers in one hand, in the cool of the evening, and a great autumnal wind roaming and tumbling around in the trees, I hasten toward you.

My brother is here—Warren Butler—my nearest in age, and always extraordinarily close to me in thought and feeling. He wanted to be near me during several weeks' holiday from his business—the family business which gives us our bread and butter—because he has had some ideas uncoiling in his mind a long time which he wanted to get onto paper, and he felt that he could do it best if he was near me. I didn't think we could both work on our two books under the same roof at the same time, because I am so devilishly susceptible to any other temperament than Dan's in the house when I am working. But he, my brother, has done so much to give me freedom to work that I wanted to give what I could to him even if I had to let my own go for a little while. But I see that Dan is getting too tired, and I think I'll ask my brother to go to the inn for a little while. He has got started on his book, and if he can see me often he is all right; he really hardly knows where he is, he's so wrapped up in what he is doing. Dan is very fond of him and he of Dan, otherwise it would be impossible, of course. He will have to finish it soon and go back to his business unless he turns into a writer instead. When I think of an intellectual gentleman writer I suddenly see your word-picture of your distinguished uncle in his Jaegers. My brother isn't quite like that—he would adore you and drink whisky with you with gusto. It, whisky, is a very great friend of his. Also he is an amorous one—not dried up like the men in Montreal. Goodness, I am not suggesting anything—my brother isn't handsome enough for you. He looks too much on the intellectual side perhaps.

Back in Maine

I must tell you how changed is the front salon at Sarn. I inherited some furniture from a very beloved aunt of mine—it arrived last night. You can imagine how eagerly Dan knocked the crates off it and got it into the house. It consisted of what we needed most—comfortable things to sit on—a wicker armchair with dark red velvet cushions for the guest room, another cunning little wicker easy chair for my workroom with its cushions instantly covered by Dan with the flowered linen you gave us in Paris, and for the front salon a little cozy plump sofa with two arm chairs to match, covered with faded green satin—all three *most* deliciously comfortable and relaxing.

We instantly found that the room became delightfully magnetic, as never before, lacking the furniture. It is fun. We said, "Imagine Kitty Hawkins sitting here!"

It is now, amazingly enough, 4:30 A.M. I woke suddenly and couldn't go to sleep again—heart racing uncomfortably. Too much moonlight on my bed too, so I moved quietly into my little back room where I sometimes sleep. Now I hear Dan moving around downstairs. A few weeks ago I couldn't write or read at all because of a sinus in the forehead which flared up and affected my eyes, a vicious pain across the forehead. I couldn't write to you then, or do any work. It's much better now, and now my book has been hanging in midair because of my brother's visit, and it is quite painful, much as I love him and am so thankful to have him doing what he wants to at last, after spending half his life looking after the rest of us. But, as you know, having one's work stopped short is very painful.

[To Catharine Huntington]

September 27, 1942

YESTERDAY Warren telephoned from Salem to say that he had bought the October *Atlantic* at the airport in New

York and found me and *The Little Locksmith* at the very beginning of the magazine, the opening piece, and was much impressed. He said it was very beautiful. Glovey said the same. Well, I really was thrilled, having felt pretty skeptical. Last night Pat telephoned the same from Cambridge. At the same time, yesterday, the proofs for the second installment arrived. So I have been busy today working on them. The second one has not been nearly so successfully cut, I feel, and I am changing it a good deal. I wish you were here to give me your judgment. However, I must rely on myself and return it tomorrow or next day.

I am feeling very well, a little wobbly still but so much better, and yesterday went to the hospital for check-up, and Dr. Bliss gave me a good account of myself, although he still wants some improvement in heart action which he says will come in time. I asked him how soon I might go to Boston, having an overpowering desire to take my autumn trip, and he surprised me by saying any time now, certainly by the end of next week. Mrs. Herron is driving down with her chauffeur, and I can go with her, which is so cozy and reassuring.

Today I walked in our driveway, and I am delighted to find that I walk better and more easily than I have done all summer. This is such a good sign. All thanks to the little sapphire pills, I believe.

October 1, 1942

In spite of Dr. Bliss's approval, I don't yet feel quite up to the journey and excitement. But do not be dismayed. I have been having so much excitement the last few days that I feel like absorbing it slowly, instead of getting into any more quite so soon. Letters began to arrive congratulating me, and the first was from Dr. Chapman! Then

Katharine Day wrote extravagant yet very nice praise.
Povla Frijsh came to the door and rang the bell while I
was resting and looking horrible—*I* was, I mean, undressed, unwashed, in old gray pajamas, after working
all day on the new proofs which had arrived. She came in
all bursting with emotion, tears in her eyes, saying, "What
you have written! It's wonderful! It's beautiful. Such restraint. I had to come." She came in and sat down and
went on talking about it, and really in tears, and then
said she hoped I wouldn't think she was too forward, but
she felt she must give me something to show her gratitude. She said, "After all, I too am an artist, and I *know*
when something is real," and she said she wanted to give
me one of her bracelets, which she had brought on purpose. She took it off her wrist and put it on me, and I
began to weep myself, almost. She did it with such honesty
and urgent feeling. Simply strong human sympathy and
experience and recognition of a fellow artist. Imagine how
touched I was and how much reassured, as I had begun
the day with dreadful misgivings when I learned that the
Blue Hill supply of *Atlantics* had arrived at the little store,
and I felt embarrassed and shamefaced as to the effect on
people near at hand. Povla's bracelet on my wrist since
that moment has fortified me against such misgivings. It
is a silver and turquoise, heavy Indian one, which looks
very well indeed between my other two silver ones. Betty
Anderson called me up last night, and she was so enthusiastic. She said she couldn't possibly tell me how much
she liked and admired my story, and how vividly it re-
called her own experiences, having suffered as a child
from the same horrors. It does make me feel terribly re-
warded and happy to have people near by, ones who
might have felt bound to say something, yet not really
liking it, speak so much from the heart.

You will think I am maudlin. I am just rather awe-struck.

You sound so pleased about my coming now that I feel badly not to. But I do know what it would be—how excited and tired I always get arriving—and I feel like building up a little larger reserve first. Also, something came over me last night concerning the book, a solution for the end of it which I must work on for a few days because I might lose it by a sudden dislocation. This new idea is not so much for the book as for my own peace of mind and a solution of these panic fears, and this dreadful division from which I suffer so much. The book is so entirely a part of me, however, that it is just as much for one as for the other. It certainly all ties up together, the idea of transformation, of evil into good, of undesirable things into desirable. And it belongs particularly to our time, this present time, when there is, as Clifton Fadiman says, a "Miltonic struggle" going on between heaven and hell.

Dan is just going to the post office with your fountain pen and the valuable stamp which I happily found in the little cupboard of the desk.

Dan has been keeping the little coal fire burning steadily in the dining room and in the bathroom, which keeps us most comfortable, and of course wood fire in back parlor when needed. He doesn't seem to mind all the stoking, but really enjoys it.

Reading your letter again, I feel you will be disappointed by my not arriving the fourth. But I feel comforted by your saying you would come back with me the minute I felt I must come. I realize that just knowing that I can go now, that Dan doesn't mind and Dr. Bliss consents, relaxes me! Idiotic necessity. It is not idiotic, though. There are all sorts of prisons, mostly self-made.

I feel beautifully relaxed today and staying mostly in bed to make the most of the sense of relaxation! Yesterday we drove far out on the coast and called on some very nice, attractive people. Then Mrs. Herron came for supper, and we had a really wonderful time, a great celebration and conversation and my check, $250, arrived from the *Atlantic*, and we all got very excited and silly over it. Mrs. Herron has been waiting almost two years for her "dividend"—the appearance of the book, that is. You remember the joke about her putting money on me when M. Moore told her I was going to be famous, and she took me to T wharf and kept a taxi fabulously waiting while we had tea, and she promoted our friendship in view of later on enjoying my fame. Then nothing happened for so long it seemed like a lost investment. She talked in a remarkable vein last night, about the war, good and evil, her children, families, the idea of a family, Roosevelt, peace, Christianity. We spent an exciting evening. I feel so grateful for the few yet life-giving new people I've discovered and become attached to lately. Here in this lonely place there is an intensity about relationships, so much importance in any taste of real communication. Mrs. Herron, like Povla, doesn't waste her time on the conventional ones. We went to tea at Povla's the other day, and her house, a summer cottage, had such a clean, Scandinavian polished air, and a restful emptiness.

October 8, 1942

I STILL feel the need of the journey. Somehow it seems as if a change might break up this invalidish attitude which clings to me. And now the plan is that I shall go in my own car, the best and most comfortable one I know of, and we have got one of our friends here to drive it for me. He is a good workman, a mason, and he plays bridge with Dan in the winter; of Danish descent and, curiously, he always reminds me of your brother Frederick. I wonder if you would see any resemblance. Dan, of course, can't bear to go. Besides, it really is a ticklish time to leave the house, when he is keeping the three coal fires gently going. And I would really enjoy this more or less impersonal companion. He can best go over a week end, and we are tentatively planning on the seventeenth, as the coming Saturday is not so good for him. In the meantime I've had proofs flying back and forth, and more manuscript is due now for me to work on.

Dan gives his love to you, Miss Huntingdog, as he now calls you. He has just made a big package of hollyhock seeds to send to somebody. Oh, another letter about *The Little Locksmith* came from Merrill Moore, out in Denver, and he sent a cigarbox packed full of presents.

[To Mrs. Dahlgren]

November 9, 1942

You may have seen the *Atlantic Monthly* with little extracts in it from my book. The first installment came in October, and they will continue through February, I believe, under the title of *The Little Locksmith*. There has been such a long delay since the *Atlantic* editors first read the MS. and expressed great enthusiasm for it about two years ago, until now when it has just begun to appear, that I had quite lost faith and did not anticipate anything except chagrin and mortification when it did finally appear in print; therefore it has been an extraordinarily happy surprise to receive many, many letters from people who like it, and to hear from the editor that he also has received letters from readers who were pleased with it. This has been very exciting for Dan and me, and now I feel very eager to go on with the next book. Also, as you said in your letter, transportation is so difficult now it seems best to stay at home, *especially* if one is not very

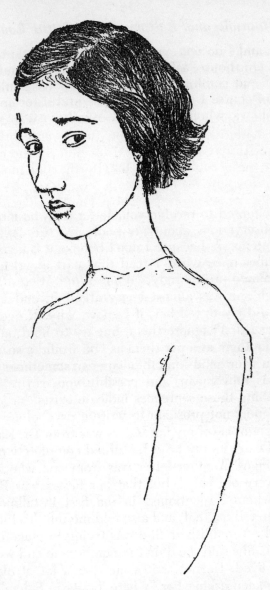

ELIZABETH KEATS BUTLER
Katharine's Niece, Libby

athletic, and I do not expect to go on any distant visits at present. Our house, as managed by Dan, is so much more peaceful and comfortable than any place I could go to, though of course I miss my brothers and sister and nieces and nephews, whom I love and usually visit in winter if possible.

[To Libby]

November 11, 1942

I was delighted to receive your letter with its most interesting observations about my book. Do they still ignore those sentences?—because I don't believe it is a good idea. I remember once when I read that part aloud to Ranie, she exclaimed protestingly, *"Why? Why? Why* did they?" as though she was almost angry about it, and I believe I never did try to tell her, if I knew, why. If ever I hear any now, I don't ignore them, but try to hold onto them and stroke them and pet them as you would a scared bird caught in your hand—and then you can sometimes find out what it is they mean, and possibly you can relieve the hidden thing those sentences indicate exists.

But I must not presume to write a psychology lecture. Even though one of my fan letters was from Dr. Karl Menninger, I can't let my head be turned completely now and off its hinges. Another letter was from one who said she was "a very old lady," but that her father was Professor Morse, whom I mentioned in the first installment. She wanted to tell me that, and also told me that his biography has just been published. She was trying to make out who I was, too. She said she didn't remember me and wondered where I lived. Harriet writes me that a lot of old ladies in Salem keep asking her "where 'bouts in Salem" I used to live and what my father looked like. Apparently they're *all* reading the *Atlantic Monthly*. Ranie wrote me the other day and said that what she calls my *Atlantic* has been kept under glass in the Radcliffe college library, with other recent publications by old Radcliffites.

Today Mr. Weeks, the editor, sent me what he always calls the block of marbles from which he intends to quarry the next installment. It begins with the sun and air that you like, but he had deleted the little paragraph about "not thinking," and I suggested, solely on your account, that it be restored. They limit me to eight pages in the *Atlantic* for that January issue, so they *have* to take out things, and I don't know whether you'll find it when you look for it or not.

I am most pleased of all because my nieces seem to approve so highly of this story. It was written for them, for the nephews and the nieces, more than for anyone else. It was, as I said to Happy in a letter yesterday, kind of a biological instinct; it is the turtle's eggs dropped slowly into the earth; it is something I had to say, and there's a lot more as yet unwritten; it's to make amends for what I *planned* to do in Castine and didn't stay long enough to do and perhaps couldn't have done anyway.

[To CATHARINE HUNTINGTON]

November 17, 1942

IF YOU see De Lany, will you tell him I appreciated his letter very much, and that I have simply been unable to answer. I got a beautiful one yesterday from my father's old friend, Bliss Perry, saying, "I believe you have written something that will live a long time." Please write me again as soon as you are able and tell me what you are doing for Thanksgiving. Something, I hope. We are having the Latours.

The Journals and Letters of the Little Locksmith

[To Mrs. Ann Watkins]

Blue Hill Hospital
December 6, 1942

THIS is just a report to you to tell you that I'm afraid we'll
have to take some time out from working on the book's
publication because of an ill-timed caving in on my part.
The doctor here thinks I should go to Boston, and we
are just waiting to see when I will be able to lie down
so as to go *en* ambulance. At present, my only comfortable
posture is on the knees with head bent down in front of
me, like a snail or an unborn child. Only then can I
breathe. Even if this strange posture doesn't fit very well
into an ambulance, I think I may get sick of waiting and
go down in a day or two. The purpose is to find an ortho-
pedic hospital, since the reason I am in such a state, we
suppose, is because I have neglected my exercises, which
if I would take them all my life faithfully, my famous Dr.
Bradford said, would keep me all right always.

K. B. H.—*Born* October 2, 1890—*Died* December 24, 1942.

10.

From the Journals

FIVE IN THE MORNING—A REMINISCENCE

How still it is, to wake at dawn
And in half-listening dreams to lie,
To hear the first birds on the lawn,
And see the last stars in the sky.

And in the stillness is a pain
A memory of long ago—
Groping, I wander back again
Past sounds and scents I used to know,

Only to find a little child
Who wakes when all the sky is white,
And lies impatient in the house
Where hangs the hush of summer night.

I know the smell of morning there;
Of new-built fire in kitchen stove,
And dew-wet lawn, and breezes rare
That from the clear, cold mountains rove.

All is familiar in that room;
The fragrant square of window wide;
And, one by one, the shapes that loom
Where shadows can no longer hide—

I watch the long sought things appear—
The chest, the chair, my little dress—
And far across the room, the bed
Where lies my mother, motionless.

I was a seed in the depth of my mother's body. The words confound me in their unreasonableness. I—this breathing, wondering, commonplace, amazing creature whose hand is on the page—I—the beginning of myself, was a seed sown in darkness by an unguessed (?) hand. Alone, yet phenomenally confident, I took the breath of life. I absorbed her vital fluid. Yet through my self-seeking, she grew beautiful and conversant with sorrow.

Sometime write about this:
I belong to a nice family. We are comfortable financially and mentally . . . cheerful evasion of any unpleasant subjects . . . a surface of decent behavior, a great respect for self-control, pleasantries, a sensitive enjoyment of nature and poetry. There have been tragedies before my brothers and sister and I were old enough to understand them; but they were never spoken of.

I belong to a family of Caspar Milquetoasts—I don't know what began it. We never quarreled—children's as well as grown peoples' quarrels generally having their origin in a dispute over the possession of some object or other. Probably the reason we never quarreled was because the possessive instinct had never been developed in us. We were always busy, unprepared for anger. The urbane frolicsome sophisticated people who are really immature, who can't cope with real emotion . . .
Bertrand Russell's theory that creative instinct will eclipse the acquisitive—but unless one becomes Gandhi and abjures all possession there is sure to arise even in the life of the most creative persons a crisis in which there is a struggle for possession, a struggle in which the emotion of anger will play a part.

Reading in a box of old letters, making me a separate magic sort of person. Warren in Cambridge telling me

346

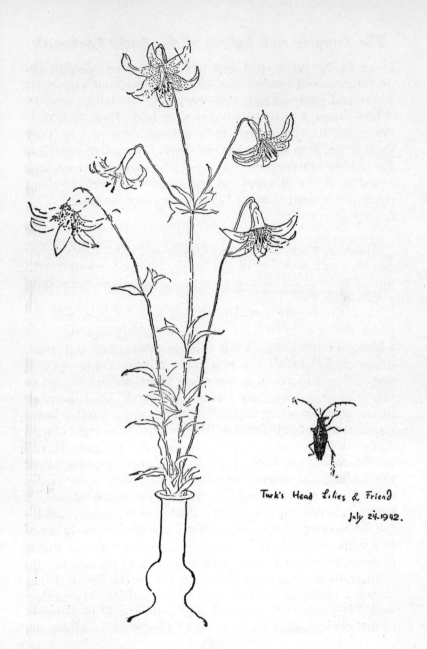

Turk's Head Lilies & Friend
July 24.1942.

I can be "a great woman," full of great praise and expectations—and giving me as an example—a spinster—active and professional. How curious!

Since then, I broke the image they had of me—and they don't like it. The locksmith is a symbol to people, they want it.... It is something precious to them—the virgin—the nonhuman person—the physically maimed is precious to them. Why? It seems to represent something to them purer, freer than they are—something extraordinary. This is very interesting.

Ancestor-worship in our family—all our relationship sacred, every member of the family beloved, treated with utmost respect and tenderness, made to feel precious, rare, yet humble.

How the family felt—that I was too precious and too much theirs ever to have the usual earthly experiences—a being set apart. And I felt in an invisible cage, deprived, different. When all the rest were talking about getting engaged and married, it was never mentioned in regard to me. Silence instead—yet I felt that I could beat them all in my understanding of passionate emotion. I felt I knew much more about *l'amour* than they. I scorned them. About doing other things—they played ball, ran, played tennis, rode horseback. I could only *watch* them, never the feeling, the *release* of physical exercise; never really acting, being...no earthly, bodily existence at all, it seemed...no participation...snowshoes once...driving Betty once in a while...Yet I rebelled, fiercely, once in a while—took them by storm—except for that one thing, *l'amour*, in which I felt myself too marked for hope.

In Danvers, when we drove on the North Shore, I had always a yearning toward the world of fashion. My mother said, "The only way you will ever enter it will be because of artistic successes on your part." One Sunday afternoon

348

From the Journals

I saw two girls, older than I probably, driving together in a smart sort of carriage, one of them driving, the other sitting beside her in a slouching attitude such as I had never seen. It was wonderful to me. She looked utterly world-weary, either broken by a great and glamorous love affair, or else simply drunk. This sight suggested so much to me I have never forgotten it. I prized it always and aimed to enter that world—it was akin to me.

I have always believed that happiness and goodness are one. The happiness I mean is a sense of delight in being alive ... delight—joy within one.... If you are happy inside yourself, you are a sign to others that life *is* good and that it is possible to be happy. I have always thought that such happiness was unassailable. It didn't depend upon possessions, but it did depend upon freedom.

The stuff, or element, in the child was so alien to me that it would not even mix with the stuff or element that was in me. It would not even adhere, not even for a minute—like trying to stick on a postage stamp that drops off again and again. The same with the stupid pity; it ran off like water off a duck ... we were not affinities ... the jolly visitors— There was another kind of feeling toward me, its effect upon me—my mother ... My father's effect on me, making mo feel like what sort of a person. My sin—being saucy.

I felt a continual sensation or craving for something, I didn't know what. It was so continual that it seemed an inherent part of life to be hungry, to feel a perpetual irritation of desire—never to be able to rest in contentment and peace. I suppose that craving was the work of the mysterious little instinct that continually seeks a balanced ratio of experience, seeks to make a work of art out of one's life. It was this craving which was the driving force behind everything I did ... so that one's whole life shall be

as far as possible a complete fulfillment of one's capacity
for living...

The young are often encased in a shell too, even more
difficult to get through. The person who is irresistible,
however, is the shell-less—if it is a nice person—the real
inner self is visible—and yet selfless. To be truthful and
without a shell... How can anybody be interested in the
outside case—polite nothings meant to hide what is real?

In the scene with Warren driving at night with Betty
near Beverly—in summing it up, say how it was a lost opportunity, because of my fear and shyness, because of
caution. This opportunity became failure to learn something wonderful... something about the mystery of attraction, of intimacy—of love—the essential thing which is
always near, always possible, except for self-imposed bar-
riers.

A thorny child—a thorn in my mother's flesh—her feminine quality made me fierce and masculine—unbecoming
role on me. I was young—it was all new—no compromise—
everything pure and whole. Strong and invalid could not
exist together. The solicitude of my mother diminished me
instantly to the dimensions of a protected invalid child;
the mother of such a tormented child. Injury—it hurt—as
if somebody had actually laid hands on me. She tried so
hard, naïvely and humbly, to restore me to what she
thought of as my real self. I was sometimes bewildered
by our family of dissimilar, assorted selves—all under
restraint. New England restraint never giving any experience or understanding of volatile nature... embarrassed to show changes of mood—sensible. When my
mother was feminine and placating she seemed to oblige
me to feel as if I were a man—sulky, irritable, tyrannical

at the same time. I, inside myself, felt shame and love toward her ... loving her, touched by her almost beyond endurance—in love with her. . . . Here was a bitter conflict between us of which our minds were scarcely aware.

To make such a sacrifice, undergo such discipline, deprive my mother and myself, of so much happiness ... and add to this—failure. No great success story. What reward? Ease, happiness of a great kind ... compensation for love ... at home in the world—or at least in my own world ... learn to bank the fire. Nietzsche ... the horse waiting to be ridden.

I was the black sheep. I had a blind craving for experience. I wanted to get into the heart of things. I was always going away, then coming back.

Finally I had got so deep into the heart of experience that when I came back the pleasant surface of family life struck me as being like a blank wall. Inside myself I was crying out to them. I loved them devotedly, and I wanted to share with them all that I had known and discovered—the happiness and the torment. But I could not pass that implacable, invisible barrier of pleasantness and niceness. Moreover, I had come home to find myself faced with a very baffling ethical problem. No solution in any of my experience ... Again I battered against the blank wall.

Then I discovered that the whole comfortable nice world is the same. I found that the newspapers and the intellectual magazines that our nice world reads maintain the same implacable evasiveness of intimate personal ethical problems. One seeks and one does not find; there is a debonair arrogance of self-sufficiency something or other in all their writings and comments. No simple Christianity. Why isn't there any help for an intellectual person in distress? They (intellectuals) are helpless and ignorant when it comes to a simple question of goodness. There is nothing for them; nobody but Mary Pickford, and the woman's page in newspapers and confidential columns, ever deals or tries to deal with these things, and the intellectual would think he had gone ga-ga if he ever found himself reading any of these.

I read the description of Alexander Pope (?), "He was shaped like a pair of scissors, and he had the face of a child—but it was the face of a child who had been in hell." I thought, I *knew* that I also was a child who had been in hell. Because of that sense of disaster, somehow I had been initiated into an awareness of things my parents did not even dream of. I carried a load on my *chest,* heart, and mind all alone. The load I carried was a constant awareness of the principle of imperfection, of accident, of mutilation and obstruction which exists in the universe side by side with a design which appears to be symmetrical and as flawless as a snow crystal. In me the war between those two elements seemed to be having one of its most concentrated battles. The terrific silence in my family on crucial subjects and a misunderstanding of my own possibilities that lasted for twenty years, because of this inarticulateness. Even in the daytime I knew it was always lurking. The memory of it would flash through my veins like some secret horrible poison.

In the beginning, the first autumn in Castine, with all my plans and ideas for my house—what kind of a person I was, tranquil, gentle, mild—not chattering—talking how much, in what manner—the tranquillity most people noticed—calmness—when excited all inside torment. . . . The sense of disaster in the child, like a sixth sense—awareness of the element of disaster in the universe—that most people take for granted only to shudder at it when it happens near by—and forget the rest of the time. Grownups too innocent and too cheerful. . . . It seemed to me they have never thought about it . . . I had to carry the burden for them as well as for myself.

It is all very well to talk of being unhurt, keeping yourself clear, triumphant; it can't be. It isn't true. To give your faith, that is the risk. Then everlasting hunger, wistful shabbiness on the street—nobody notices—cruelty in me—my power to change her—unstable love—cruel love—destroying.

It was years afterward that I discovered what grief my parents had suffered and which they had hidden from me so bravely. They had, like most parents, misjudged the extent to which I was instinctively aware of my disaster, and they tried to divert me from the realization of it by giving me creative resources. . . . If only they had not hidden their grief from me—if we might all three have wept together, then I should not have had to bear the burden of it alone in a distorted form.

In every family of gifted children there is always an aunt in the background, an unmarried aunt who urges the children on as soon as they show signs of talent. It seems rarely that talent comes to children through their mother; more often it seems to come through the aunt. The mother gives the essential things to the child, it is true; the child would always prefer to live with the mother than with the aunt. But the aunt gives the extra, the super outside glimpse of life. She is like the joker in a pack of cards which, placed here or placed there, can change the whole aspect of the game.

I am going to tell you the story of my aunthood. First, something like Maeterlinck, I want to tell something about the life of the Aunt, aunts in general. The true aunt is the one who is unmarried—owing to some predicament,

physical or psychological, she is different from other people—very different from mothers. Very different from other
unmarried ladies who have no nieces and nephews—certainly different from a person who has nieces and nephews
and doesn't like them. That kind of an aunt is an aunt in
name only—not an aunt at all.

Today I had a new feeling—the supersensitiveness of
aunts, mothers, older people . . . a sound of strangers walking into my house, new tenants looking over the rooms . . .
taking possession. Why, this is what Aunt H. used to feel
—and Mother! But it is not our fault, it is not the supersensitiveness of elders, it is the arrogance and cruelty of
the young.

Like a daughter of joy, the maiden aunt belongs to
everybody and to nobody. She has no need to barricade
herself with any of the prejudices which people must
depend upon whose first concern is security. She has nothing to lose, therefore she can be radical, unprejudiced. She
has no husband's opinions and feelings and illusions and
vanities to cater to; she can be truthful and hurt nobody;
she lives an abstract life, not a personal one.

Aunthood was the relationship I liked best among those
which were possible for me. I was not a very good daughter. My family, liked me *as I was,* they liked me as a person set apart, a symbol. I did not like myself *as I was* but
as I *should have been.* I fought against my family accept-
ing and loving that caricature of my real self.

Aunts and Mothers—Genuine thoroughbred aunt is a
virgin. If married she becomes too vague, contented, easy-
going, like a mother, to be a real aunt. Auntism diluted
with other feelings, preoccupations, emotions of mother
and wife . . . Aunt has the pure passions and beliefs of a
person who, like a child, has not compromised—all or
nothing—pure dedication—strict standard—Jeanne d'Arc—
saints, fanatics . . . Nohant. Combine Flaubert single-

minded artist, G. Sand. I had been Flaubert, now I wanted
to be Mme Sand—her love of children. My house and
land, nephews and nieces. As though this wish were not
enough, I had two other wishes ... on the grand scale—
generous, lavish, greathearted, for love and for art. Desire for immortality through the coming generation.

It is stupid to ridicule the so-called dangerous age, as it
is stupid to ridicule any sincere thing in human life. Thank
goodness for people courageous enough to be ridiculous,
if they must be, in order to balance their lives. The greater
the maladjustment, the more prolonged the long silent
suffering and starvation, the greater and more violent and
spectacular the reaction must be. Courage, to those who
do not fear it, and who take their taste of life rather than
go on respectably and tragically trivial and virginal without ever having lived.

Mothers who have devoted themselves to their children
to the exclusion of other connections, their lives are dis-
jointed. The support to one's personality by friends. A part
of one's self and a real foundation and existence. The
things that one person can do to another, the stronger one
influencing the weaker, hypnotizing, calling to live or
crushing. Selling the personality—the essays—like Ring
Lardner—or Will Rogers, or Mary Garden, or any other
successful public character.

A person needs at intervals to separate himself from
family and companions and go to new places. He must go
without his familiars in order to be open to influences, to
change.

The desire to grow, the right to live and to blossom is
stronger than filial love and consideration ... terrible con-

flict. The sin is on the parent's side, for not teaching, or knowing, true values. One must *pity* the sin, after it is over, but fight against it while it is in power.

My house in Castine was not for vacation but for a way of life, permanent for myself ... a writer, mature, resolved ... zip, will, sudden strength, passive for a long time then suddenly awake and aroused and active. I was angry and rebellious; my family had failed me in some way. I felt homeless. I must express in my house my anger and my scorn, my pure feeling, my sense of values—most precious possession of every scrupulous person is his sense of values—spiritual misery at home in Danvers. Homelessness—something essential to me was not recognized there, and therefore I felt homeless.

I had never tried my hand at housekeeping. It was one of the things people talked about too much and did badly, I thought. I had always liked knowing as little as possible about it. A tremendous amount of self-righteous labor and boring discussion usually brought nothing but the most uninteresting and commonplace results ... I kept scornfully aloof.

The idea of transformations—the song of transformations—this is the charm—the magic idea underneath this story—the power to disguise—to change the appearance of something into something else, ugly to beautiful—the toad —the princess, the bird into a woman—"The Black Pearl" in old tales—this is the thing that is always happening, and in psychoanalysis, in the unconscious, it is always happening. This is the universal solution for every human difficulty.

I have always been fascinated by the idea of transformation—changing a house, taking some house that didn't exist and making it enticing. My conception of love—in the beginning—was idealistic, a literary idea, and snobbish —only for the rare ones.

Writing is unsocial, solitary work and the one safety-valve sort of reaction from it is contact with people. Otherwise the writing and the writer both suffer from lack of aeration and contact with material of art. The impulse—it is the conscientious purpose, or rather the fierce and vital purpose, to function at one's best. It is unfair to my present generation to accuse it of selfishness. The fact is that we understand life better than our parents did. We understand better the mysterious elements that contribute to happiness and health of the mind, and we are idiots if we do not use our knowledge to change unfavorable environments.

The artist is usually unconscious of religion. He is single-minded, intent on his problems and his delights—intent on the objective world. His *self* doesn't trouble him. Intensity—amazement, noticing consciousnesss of the artist instead of the mild acquiescence, mild, heavy, acceptance of things like the average nonartist. There are no blanks, no holes in his life. Trained to incessant alertness, he is always experiencing something while he is in health. Yet when he is older and something tests him and plows him up—then what? Perhaps he discovers religion.

Desired in writing of fiction: Significance which is not merely local. Values—significance raised to the nth degree. Separate, organic life as that of a flower—perfect and complete in itself. Intense realization of character and of place. Gathering material like a bee gathering pollen ... Gratify the aesthetic sense—form, style—crystal-clear—intention— carried along also by a controlled but unflagging intensity

—passion . . . Difference between amateur and true artist possibly his attitude toward completed work. I gloat over and enjoy my pictures, but I cannot bear to see my writings after they are finished. Beauty and mystery—unfathomable—surrender of the ego!

Polishing—burnishing—repetition is polishing—giving value. Significance—in life, repetition of a scene, of certain roads, certain houses, gives either a nausea of boredom or a mystical devotion—people—places.

If your mind is living and creative, you see more every day than you saw the day before. You see the miracle that is in everything. And nothing is *horrid* and *nothing* is ridiculous unless you choose to make it so by seeing it so. Each thing has its own sacredness and its own essential importance. You should be so sensitive and flexible in understanding that you should know how to respond to each thing according to its essence. No rigidity . . . no prejudices.

Writers and artists to be themselves with dignity, not to be always feeling apologetic toward the normal people and trying to explain and adapt themselves. They are guided, therefore their conduct should be all the more respected. Writer—half child, half very old and knowing; exultant, half apologetic. The humiliation of the artist, the discrepancy between the outside and the inside which is disintegrating and weakening and drives him to despair.

My idea of sublimation for the local girls and boys. Why did I want this? A very important reason of self-protection against all that spate of sex.

Between the coming of Tony and the time when I found my house, five other miniature members of our family had made their appearance,—my younger brother's and my sister's children—four little girls and one boy. . . After learning how to win them the predicament became an advantage—all the things we had in common . . .

Where the Deep Waters Flow—The aunt my nieces imagined was one of these special aunts. Some children don't care about aunts, my cousins didn't so much, but we adored our aunts. My Aunt Lettice, or Letty, Litty, Littley, Literary, Littie-lettie—she was better than any because she wasn't married; she belonged to *us*. Nevertheless it is the house more than the aunt which is the chief character in the story.

The age of the Aunt is passing—the unmarried, virgin aunt who puts so much of her suppressed desire, passion, gift into stimulating and encouraging nephews and nieces. She will not exist any longer. Virgins—nuns, dedicated lives . . .

There are virginal people who should remain virginal, but they have lost their dignity. They have given up their peculiar quality, and they have lost hold of their own meaning and their place in human life. Nobody believes now that anybody else is a virgin. So, if not obviously mated, people say that this person is homosexual, if not in actual practice then in inclination. People tell stories about nuns and priests. There is always an escape somewhere necessary, they think juicily, and they tell you about it. They won't let you think anybody can be really and truly a virgin.

This vigorous unmarried lady writer, wearing tweeds and low heels, transforming her unlived love life into fairly true and beautiful works, she must have, they say, a warped nature. Something sad or wistful is hidden away; something went wrong with a love long ago, and these works of art are only passionate compensation, and she would erase them all to have her chance back again.

As years pass, her face becomes more solidly noble-looking and her carriage more masculine.

Maybe this isn't true, though. Maybe there is some reason for having certain people set apart, as priestesses, confessors, nuns, whose innocence gives them a kind of calmness that is needed for a balance to cool off the rest of the people.

The Aunt, before having her own experience, had friends who told her about their affairs. She always used to champion love and marriage—also dumbness; she championed Fanny Brawne—against those who thought a genius ought to be understood. She believed in free love. She was very passionate in her belief in liberty. The Aunt, with and without cushion ... without, and sitting alone in public place—the feeling of looking odd and quaint, noticeable ... and submitting to this impression although feeling inside anything but odd and quaint. Walter de la Mare character.

Arguments back and forth about whether or not sex is very important—Galsworthy vs. D. H. Lawrence. "Sex is not very important—the body is not very important only as it reveals the soul," says Galsworthy. It is not very important, if it has been satisfied—dinner is not very important after you have eaten it—but if you are starving it is rather important. If sex isn't very important, look at the old maids—look at sad schoolteachers—look at defrauded women—look at defrauded men—look at all the substitutes —look at wrecked lives.

Whenever I caught myself using childish fascination I knew that I was losing my sexuality. But nobody is grown-up all the time. What is it to be grown-up?

The most tragic thing that can happen to a sensitive human being is to have his world destroyed. His world is the world he has chosen and made himself. It is his expression, his poem, and the adherence to it is his sacred right.

My world—the first successful essential of my world is peace, building my hours of work. Knowing one's tastes.

Reading *Roman Spring*, by Mrs. Winthrop Chanler. Such terribly charming and satisfying society for a person to grow up in. And compare the desire to find out the worst, to share and understand the degraded and despised. *Haute Savoie*—this comes from sense of inferiority of locksmith. One can't mingle with the beautiful ones. Love laughs at Locksmiths.

You have to lose your identity or anyway feel unlimited. You lose your identity in nature, with people, especially family, your identity or your historical identity is fastened on you, terribly irritatingly. With a lover one escapes again into a feeling of non-self.

Solitude and love and art—like going about naked—with some person following you holding out your clothes and saying these are yours, you must put them on.

Obey—I have to obey these deep tides—I have to go where they take me. Dreaming! dreaming—I have to obey my dream. I can't resist my dream. To resist is to violate all of life.

I learned it was possible to live in one room, and the cold hall and stairs, and the public w.c. and all their secrets, social, domestic life crowded into one room—the distinguished visitors and the beggars—and yet it was such a dignified life. I had never seen such dignity and sense of ritual before. To most Americans it would have been intolerable...Patchin Place...E. E. Cummings, dos Passos...Charley James.

The people—humble, friendly, amorous ones. It was as if the shell, the armor my family had encased me in for my protection and my prison had been unfastened, turned back on its hinges, and removed, and I myself had appeared—a person they could all recognize and I could recognize even if my family couldn't; the person naked, feminine, personal, soft, vague, shell-less, anonymous, desiring—without vanity—without pretension—or ego. I was incognito to family and old acquaintances—but at last I was cognito to myself and to the simple people of instinct ... and not of thought—like a cat. Those simple people seemed to know me—the barrier was gone, but not with the intelligentsia.

I felt as if I were nobody at last, merged at last, fused with all the rest ... not an individual, a mood, the mood of love—of humble love, without words. Going to dinner at Charles Restaurant. Nobody knew me—until Taro came. .... I felt so changed—I moved differently—with the secret consciousness—contained in the Japanese manner—of preciousness—value—not scattered, stupid, foolish, loud-talking like most occidentals. I moved—aware, with a sixth sense, of the Orient, aware of the precious gift I carried. The woman is nothing as an individual—but the precious gift she carries is everything ... she moves like one who guards something sacred.

The so-called selfishness of moderns is partly due to the tremendous amount of stimulation received. They are aroused and drawn into experience by theaters, books, automobiles, great cities. The current is quick and strong.

One reason, maybe, why Americans die so young—in middle age—especially in cities, is because they do not know their own bodies. They force themselves to live and do things without any psychic acquaintance with their bodies. Their instinct is deaf to the language of the body, which would tell them how to live if they would listen to it—they are absolute strangers to their own bodies, shy and self-conscious toward them. What about this relationship? What could it be? Is it a conscious pleasure and satisfaction, but never put into words, probably.

There is an awkwardness in American women. Awkward, jerky movements indicate lack of inner awareness of the value of dignity or submissiveness of one's female body. Sometimes you see that awareness in some insignificant girl—a salesgirl in a five-and-ten-cent store or a waitress or a hairdresser's assistant. Rich American women do not have that sense. Their movements are harsh, ugly, unaware of their own sex.

CREATIVE NONBILI

THE Japanese word *nonbili* means something horizontal like the earth. It is also, maybe, female, like the earth—also pregnant, like the earth. *Nonbili* is the stuff out of which new forms come. It doesn't know what is coming and it doesn't think about what is coming and it doesn't scheme and force what is coming—any more than the earth while she is sheltering seeds in her womb knows what a full-grown tree looks like. *Nonbili* is absolutely submissive and passive and empty of any feeling of impatience, coercion, or prejudice. Into quiet, waiting, breathing, receptive *nonbili* descends the creative spirit, like a miracle, like a god entering a temple which has been humbly prepared and kept sacred. This *nonbili* is like sleep, because the body becomes unconscious and forgotten. You can't watch yourself go to sleep. No more can you watch yourself receive the creative

363

spirit. Also the mysterious and grand forces which intermittently visit a human being—like sleep and love and artistic creation—are absolutely incompatible with coercion. It is frightfully arrogant and conceited to believe that you can grab these things when you want them. The only way you can receive them is to cultivate humility forever and ever and ever, world without end. Also, you must be as patient as the earth.

In order to have a foundation for your life to rest on, you have to have a sense of devotion in your life. You have to make this, too. It won't happen itself. You will be even more humble in front of your own poor possessions, and in humility you will be absolutely glorified. You will not necessarily choose asceticism, but you will see Divine mystery in each manifestation. To see in the kitten a most lovely and important mystery—to see in you the beauty which is, in a sense, your own, but in a greater sense not your own but the beauty created for you by all the mysterious forces both external and internal which have ever touched you and to be aware even in myself of another mystery and another sacredness—even in my body because it represents truthfully the principle in Nature of imperfection. The inexplicable cause behind all the burden and the irony and the physical, inexplicable, and cruel torment in human life.

The change of life is the time when you meet yourself at a crossroads and you decide whether to be honest or not before you die. Yourself, your whole life, up to now, is gathered together, gathered up in a knot. All the different sides of your nature seem to assert themselves at once, as if every part of you were striving for recognition and striving to be one whole person—all recognized and all acting together in good harmony. So your old angers rise up, and you can't be meek and mild any more because you are awake suddenly and being meek and mild would not be sincere.

One can describe all the minor though so important love affairs without reserve. But the one which has to do with the person who has grown into one's life, one must leave undescribed—let it be implied in the manner in which one's life has flowered, in the deep contentment and richness and creativeness of one's later life.

The amusing contrast between those who protested against my marriage, and the reasons for their protests (wrong); and those who saw it as desirable, wonderful, and the reasons *they* had (wrong). The true inwardness of it was utterly different from what anybody knew or thought.

A theory about divorce is that usually a couple have been potentially divorced for years—it is only the third person who sets off the explosion. One falls in love and learns suddenly how unhappy he or she has been all these years. Until then they have endured it—not quite realized what a hell it has been ... I was thinking people oughtn't to be so stupid, so unself-conscious that they have to learn from somebody else—that they are unhappy. Preserve your intimacy with God. It is much more important than a human love affair—then you know where you are.

There is nothing more infuriating and torturing between two people than to have one of them interpret basely something that is sacred to the other.

A person with a deep, mature, argumentative face who wears a childish, innocent white muslin dress with ruffles, white stockings, and black ankle ties ...

A man whose tenderness is never demonstrated. He loves profoundly, but in a time of stress to a person he loves he cannot caress her. He is very deeply, thoughtfully

365

tender, but he is not a lover. He has no ardor. But his love is deeply rooted and built into his life.

A person makes a sacrifice which affects and limits his whole career. He puts aside the thing he loves and accepts what he conceives to be his duty. This is a serious, heart-breaking affair. Ever afterward he seems to be trying to compensate himself in some way for what he has re-nounced—but he can never afford to regret his action. He is constantly justifying it—and the spectacle of someone else ruthlessly cutting through obstacles in order to obtain his prime desire always annoys and disturbs him. He main-tains his principle always, and always puts the single-minded one in the wrong.

All human existence based on desire—every act, every thought stimulated by desire.

A woman, self-frustrated physically, emotionally. She can't exercise her artistic talent as she desires on account of an inner check. She does not accept life. Temperament, mind, body all deformed by hesitation and denial. Yet she is beautiful. She is the goddess of chastity—sexlessness—morbid abhorrence of physical or emotional surrender. Instinct of creativeness is baffled, strongly inclined toward renunciation and suffering. A person who doesn't under-stand the passionate reticence of people who are in love—she asks them what it is like. She asks the married for their true opinion of marriage, and they won't tell her.

Rigid, unforgiving, shocked, sensitive, self-conscious people in relation to one more violent, instinctive, entire, happy, passionate, unreliable, uncontrolled, devilish, cruel, ardent—

Two people, one proud, one humble. They annoy each other and hurt each other's sensibilities.

A woman with a difficult temperament, highly emo-tional and terrible temper. One man, her husband, is in-finitely tender, and he is subject to her moods, completely

366

yielding—suffers when she suffers—is *afraid* of her. Another man, equally sympathetic, is *not* afraid of her—goes to the bottom of her troubles. Powerful—overmastering.

Taro—the end—something is wrong. I was unmasked—failure in what? Sense of guilt and sense of having deceived. He said I would cling to a swimmer and drag him down. Why this insatiable hunger for love, passion, which naturally repels? I repelled by my heavy sinking. It is too unequal . . . a heavy, drooping, clinging person. I am like that in love.

I want to say something about *l'amour*. *L'amour* has nothing to do with talk or ideas. It ought to come silently without any explanation, and I still think that it is a miracle which descends suddenly on two, in silence, and should be received—oh, and obeyed—almost like prayer, beyond words. It must be mutual, desired by both, and spontaneous, with no explanations, no ideas, no talking. The wind bloweth where it listeth.

Integrity is something else, quite different—can you live alone, mentally and spiritually alone? How can you do otherwise, unless it is ever probable or possible to find another person who wishes to guard the same thing in you which you secretly wish to guard above all? That would not be living alone.

VILLANELLE

So shall I be lying again
  As I lie now—still, so still!
While drowsily beats the rain!

With never a thought or a pain,
  With never a wish or a will
So shall I be lying again!

367

In my ear is the loud refrain
  Of my heart's old constant trill
While drowsily beats the rain.

When at last o'er my breast and my brain
  Shall have crept the lasting chill
So shall I be lying again.

Shall I wish for the world in vain
  Or shall I have lived my fill?
While drowsily beats the rain.

Ah me! how long I have lain!
  Will Dawn never come o'er the hill?
So shall I be lying again,
While drowsily beats the rain.

An essay writer has his pencil in his hand wherever he goes. He lives on the surface of daily existence, whereas a novelist or a poet is blind to half that passes him. Except when it feeds his particular need. He lives in wider reaches of the imagination. He lives according to his own tempo—free, timeless—"high, cloudy symbols of a high romance." We have got beyond ourselves; we have created fatal discord.

I can't say that I really know enough about psychoanalysis to speak with any authority. I am in the kindergarten stage. But I have never heard anyone else mention the things about it which struck me most forcibly. First, consenting to surrender for one hour a day all one's preconceived ideas of the kind of person you are. You cling fiercely, resentfully, and with utmost vanity to the belief that you are a nice person, a sweet-tempered, generous, good person. And it is, oddly enough, nothing that the analyst says which contradicts that agreeable belief of yours. You contradict it with your own lips—when you have become humble and unprejudiced enough to lie on that pallet and let those huge lumps of truth come veering volcanically out of the dark depths of your breast, in such a complete purging of the heart and the mind that it is unimaginable to a person who has never experienced it.

There are several kinds of truth. By omitting certain things you can make certain kinds of truth—artistic truth, polite truth, congenial or expedient truth, the truth of one's training, bringing-up, breeding; convenient truth, and the savage, primitive, awkward truth of psychoanalysis rebelling against the other kinds—and sometimes being the most remarkable, most beautiful, greatest of all—like the *"Sacré du Printemps"*—plowing the earth—out of one's unknown depths—the depths of the race—sometimes like symmetry of pure mathematics, startling beauty of symbols.

The unconscious. . . . Psychoanalysis since it deals with fundamental human nature must be capable of being explained in simple human terms. If we understand the murders and other crimes which we all read about every day, we ought to be capable of understanding psychoanalysis. The unconscious is like a black dog. And psychoanalysis simply teaches the human being that his happiness and success depend upon his attitude toward the black dog—his beast, his property—his dog. It teaches that the best way is to make friends with the dog and to understand his nature, to conciliate him, not to be ashamed of him, not brutal to him, nor overindulgent to him. But most of all, to *know* him.

People are shocked by the unrefined disclosures of psychoanalysis. Refined sensitive people refuse to allow these disclosures; they feel that psychoanalysts are outraging their ideal. But when all this refinement set in, it was outraging an ideal; it is shocking to think of a standard which denies reality and makes it hideous. Where did it come from—who first authorized it?

A person who is literary and imaginative reads a book about psychoanalysis—accepts the ideas, gives them his approval, and begins to apply them to all his friends. He sees their motives much more clearly than before, and even perhaps to himself, consequently thinks he knows all about psychoanalysis. But reading about it, and grasping it imaginatively and intellectually, is just as different from undergoing the experience of psychoanalysis as reading about somebody taking a bath is different from taking a bath yourself, or watching a tennis game is different from playing in a tennis game, or observing somebody else get drunk is different from getting drunk. It is a great temptation to people who have mind and imagination to substitute the *idea* of the thing for the *experience* of the thing itself.

ACTIVE RESPONSE

WHAT if every fresh burst of creativeness is to balance or overcome a blow? There are passive and active experiences ... I am hurt. One can't stand being victimized; one can cancel it by a creative action ... to make equilibrium between passive and active.

Development of the psychology and the moral of hitting back when you have been hit—something *active* is *necessary* after something passive—something to balance the having "*been hit.*" One must *hit*—but this is not considered good by modern nice people. Still, one gets all poisoned if the passive experience is not answered by an active one. ... Therefore, after an injury, one must *do* something, not to the person who injured you, but make an *action* as strong as the action which injured you and proving your strength as much as retaliation would. Creative, if possible, but anyway active. Then you will be all right without any poison.

Warren toward a person he loves takes what he enjoys and discards the rest—either ignores it or treats it as if it were something he regrets to be obliged to deplore. He doesn't love it.

A person to whom an injustice has been done—terrible feelings—especially because of the apathy and inertia of others—nothing less than hunger strike will impress them. That feeling of impotence and brooding over the matter—making the wound deeper and deeper—fatally warping the spirit—the only solution is to turn away from it—not feeding on it any more but turning away to the sun and air, and creativeness *out* of one's self, increasing one's own powers, calling on *faith*. Otherwise one is destroyed, eating a dead carcass—the stuffy air of a family row. ...

There is innocence to be found in the world, and those who have innocence and maintain an innocent attitude toward life are mostly artists and children. Among artists and writers, however, it is rare, because they are very subject to corruption. There is a definite seeking for innocence in the new spirit of the world ... Sherwood Anderson ... Gertrude Stein. ...

The effect of psychoanalysis: smashing the shell which has been growing for years. Age is thickness of shell. Men fall in love with people who are young because they are shell-less, soft, close, yet virginal, unaware.

An American wife who doesn't like being scolded and beaten by her French husband—why not accept this as something real and be thankful for it? Better than the utter negativeness of some husbands...Everybody has said that Americans are idealistic and French realistic; the connection not always detected. Connect with the funny feeling that I have when I am sick in France—misgiving, not because there aren't good doctors, not because I am away from home, but because of mysterious underlying something which is lacking. They do not really believe they haven't really got faith in what they are doing. *"C'est la vie!"* If somebody dies ... *"Que voulez-vous!"* The value of human life. They don't believe in miraculous effort being efficacious outside of church miracles. Their cynicism prevents the thing from happening. Just as in love they know less than anybody. You can never see it—love—in the face of anybody. They laugh—they don't believe in any other love than physical love.

They have, the French, the constant menace of war—for that they must summon up all their strength. How can they bother about anything else very much?

THE LITTLE LOCKSMITH

I RARELY talk intimately about things that I care seriously about, to any except the few intimate friends who I think will understand me and feel as I do. The most precious thing I have, the thing which flows into me when I write, I keep hidden very jealously for the ones I choose to have see it. But what right have I to act as if I were the proprietor of this thing? It isn't mine. I haven't any right to include some and exclude others from the enjoyment of any gift that comes from God. I am not the owner of it. I am a part of it, that is all. If anybody wants it, it is his.

In telling this whole story, why not very simply tell the

truth? There is nothing to be ashamed of if one tells the whole truth. Don't try to conceal one's badness; don't pretend to be better than I am. This arrogance of people who pretend they are not human . . .

This book will try to express Christianity. Grace: Jacques: without malice . . . without revenge . . . the badness inside which is inside all of us. The doctor of Sallanches was a wicked creature.

What is the harm in telling these things? You can see that I am a good person. This is a plea for honesty and innocence. I have done bad things—and yet I am not a bad person. Some better education—better equipment—or one has to break through with frightening honesty and innocence.

When my book is published, perhaps people will read it out of curiosity, many people; but I am afraid that of those who read it, not more than five or six will catch their breath and say, "Oh, that is how I felt, too!" or "That is what I thought!"

If there are any to whom this happens in the world, they will be so few that I shall never hear of it or know that my book has reached any such responsive ones, unless they do me the honor to communicate with me themselves, if they feel the desire to do so. It is impossible for me to express how welcome any such communication would be.

In writing an autobiography your readers' total impression after finishing the book is the essence of you—what you can't help betraying. Will it be "grace"? Grace is the glass slipper of Cinderella. The ugly stepsisters can't get it on, no matter how hard they try. Will the essence be worth anything? One after another steps out onto the stage. It is like Amateur Night in the Vaudeville Theater. It is a test. What a reason for being a successful writer! Why is it that talent alone isn't enough? Thousands of people have enough talent to become famous. It is the *need* to use it which is lacking.

I have come to the period of life when it is time to write memoirs. If I were in prison, I couldn't be better situated to write a great book. Cervantes—John Bunyan ... My husband, home, daily life, all suited to this composition. Moreover, the *nonbili*, laughing tranquillity, tempers the intensity, passion, inspiration, too much self, of youth. . . .

I wish my writing may be alive—not just in texture, but like an organic, live thing in itself, like a branch of a living tree, startlingly alive like a bough of apple blossoms that somebody breaks off and carries into the house. Language is so stale, I have to keep pruning, cutting out deadness, letting it lie for a while, then pick it up again and see where it is dead, prune it and prune it, let it grow, then let it lie.

Clichés are like a cat's fleas. The work in progress is the cat, a living, beautiful creature, but the fleas hop automatically onto its body, and there must be a constant warfare against them. Nothing less than a catlike biting hunt can rid a piece of my writing of its clichés.

Semantics, like my own magic—the thing becomes its opposite. The thing semantics proves is more than the deceptive power of words, it is the deceptive power of one's own attitude toward things making them good or bad, which proves that opposite things can be true. This tempts one to believe that everything can be good and there is no moral sense, really—which is the very bad thing about semantics, which proves that even semantics can be both good and bad.

Not able to talk, or think even, unless lying down with pencil and paper. I am in other circumstances like a medium when out of touch with her control ... stupid, ordinary, limited.

This chronicle for whatever may be its final significance, if any, is expanding, growing in accordance with its own laws—intrinsic quality—the story—the climax of it in Castine in the next volume.

The cycle of a person's work is bigger than the cycle of the person's life ... only a segment of the work can be accomplished in that case.

Early morning joy, innate joy—unreasonable joy.... Woo this joy and encourage it; it will be creative—it will bring all kinds of treasures ... *cf.* despair, which doesn't bring treasures.

Volume I. In whole book this play between—balance—atmosphere of place coming through, yet obscured still by ignorance and idealism in human relations. To evade the latter and lose oneself in the impersonal, not satisfying. How they play into each other—all through—the slow realization and fullness of experience and awareness.....

As there is design and symmetry in nature, I believe there is also design and symmetry in human experience if we will learn to yield ourselves to our destinies. Maybe in life certain mysterious forces being liberated, through some fortunate conjunction they work out their true harmony—you will find a cluster of experience, a short period of six or seven years, when all experience contributes to a symmetrical whole—the pearl in the oyster—the crystal in the rock or the quarry.

The idea of law—a law for happiness—rising out of human nature's elemental qualities and fulfillment—like laws of health—of growth and decay—etc.

People evolving—they are supposed to evolve when young and up to middle life, then one is just as evolutionary but external forces against it grow stronger and stronger because one's life has become more intricately attached to other lives, and evolving is liable to disrupt others. Therefore one hesitates—see all those older people soggy . . . tragic ones whose forward-going movement has been destroyed. . . .

The secret on the breath which enrages all those who also have a secret . . . it is like a defiance . . . insulting the others.

Money—how I felt about spendthrifts . . . immature . . . rebellious . . . ungrateful . . . given certain material to use creatively . . . moral obligation to learn conservation—*but* for the sake of being lavish—not in order to hoard and cling.

This business of irritation and temper . . . not to *waste* energy—I suffered from sense of guilt from *not* expressing temper—sense of danger compelled trying to express *everything* crossing t's and dotting i's—*let it alone!*—drop it, skip it. I acquired the awareness of being most unfamiliar before—now overindulged, worked over too much.

The Little Locksmith—thinking about this title. . . . As a child I was not going to be like the little locksmith. I felt superior to him, lucky and safe. But is anybody lucky and safe and superior? How can I separate myself and assume that I am to have special privileges, special protection against the evils of the world? Yet I always did assume it . . . And if others were hurt in tragic accidents or died at the wheel driving through the Sumner Tunnel, it was—well, their destiny. *We* had escaped. Anyhow, things were better for us, for some reason, perhaps because we had more sense or something; special protection anyhow. It came over me all of a sudden the other night, after saying my prayers on my knees, that this obsession to save *one's self*, protect one's *self* and be satisfied as long as that succeeds fairly well, is not enough. As long as the other little locksmith exists, I cannot be satisfied. If there is a little locksmith, everyone must be him too. It can't be for one and not for another, this safety, luck, special privilege, special protection.

The panic fears of then and now. The constant apprehensiveness of the danger, cruelty, wickedness, accident, hatred, and evil in the world. Always afraid, apprehensive. There *are* those bad things—especially now. They are a part of life, we can't pretend otherwise. And we can't fight them alone. If I make my bed in Hell, behold thou art there! Even the little locksmith is safe. Even the soldiers, sailors, lost children, broken and torn. We must make them safe—work for it and pray for them. Since these things *are*, it isn't enough to try to avoid and escape them. I must help somebody else to bear them. We must face it together.

My attachment to things—animism—putting self into object—life-long habit—once—after dream of death, sudden intuition as to the harm of putting so much into love of things—attempt to chasten this—then gradual falling off —St. Augustine. How about this animism? Does it take away from spiritual life?

Laughing at S. E. Morison because he went on with his Columbus cruise after England had declared war. What folly it was to laugh—not to realize that a historian is different from other people—like Columbus.

On waiting for something . . . playing solitaire . . . the influence of the cards . . . fear . . . superstition . . . Methodist distrust of cards well-founded. How to wait for something and not fall into despair and horror.

377

Highbrows have scorn of these things. You often find a highbrow as immature as a child up against a moral problem—myself last summer.

If I could only again be mending the clothes of one I love, or getting tea for him. It is idiotic to pretend that anything else matters or that anything else can give that marvelous joy. If you find a woman really content as an artist or professional person of any sort, you may know she has never had that other joy. This may sound like the most awful mid-Victorianism, but it is devilishly true.

I ought to accomplish some good writing but at present I prefer to commit to the Devil all poetic warmth or fervor. I can imagine myself writing a dictionary or putting up a rail-fence with a good deal of satisfaction. My desire for painting is quite on the side; there is no need of lyrical emotion there. I feel like flaunting a fine cold, unemotional and soulless savoir faire—the word soul has been crammed down my throat until I am nauseated, and as for the physiological functions of the male and female, I am done with them. And yet it isn't the real thing that has been my dose—it is a childish, mawkish, maudlin, drunken imitation. I have never been before in such a condition of clear sanity.

The phonograph is almost identical with the human voice, and is actually *more* moving to me. It is the human voice in miniature, perfect in its own proportions. In a way it seems to me the essence of the bare soul of the music one hears at the opera or concerts. You are not distracted by the sight and color or any other thing. In a dark room you sit and hear a most perfect, delicate, thrilling voice, disembodied from all material. It is truly tear-compelling. It is so excitingly beautiful that you find yourself in the clouds, breathless. Surely with such a medium one can achieve truer music than with such primitive thing as a mandolin. It is an everlasting miracle to me—almost more thrilling than a sewing machine.

In certain human experiences one has a feeling of absolute well-being, complete fulfillment, as in sexual intercourse, also in creative writing, painting, or any other creative activity. In these experiences the cause of happiness seems to be the complete surrender of self which occurs at such times. But in practical matters we don't get this happiness, or expect to find it, nor do we ever use the method of surrender. We are too much in awe of practical matters, of money and arrangements for our shelter and subsistence, to think of surrendering them to the unknown force which we allow to govern sexual love and art.

Hit or miss we have found that happiness in a moment of reconciliation after an estrangement from someone we love, in losing ourselves in adoration of the stars, and the earth's beauty.

In a profound article on *War and Peace*, Clifton Fadiman points out Tolstoy's historical theory that individuals are not the makers of history, but that history is made by great unseen forces which merely use individuals as tools. If Napoleon had never been born, another man would have come forth in the same period, as the inevitable child of the period and the expression of it. The same thing has been said of Hitler.

Since the intellectuals are always insulated against any religious movement, it is forced to come through other sorts of people at first, until it is recognized by a superior mind who can see things without prejudice or aversion.

Truth is an irresistible force. It pushes its way at last through every obstruction. It travels like lightning from one part of the world to another. It is like a fire—it burns up the dead wood of falseness, it cleans as it goes. In times like the present times it burns even more fiercely. For now is the time of great cleansing and purifying of the whole world. For a little while the truth seems to be embodied in one great person, a figure who speaks to the world, one round whom the eager fighters can rally, for those words of truth they can rush into battle.

Now [in 1942] for many multitudes it is Madame Chiang Kai-shek. For others it is Gandhi. For some it is President Roosevelt. For many others it is Prime Minister Winston Churchill. The truth can only stay with the man or woman who values it above everything. As soon as he begins to allow his words or his acts to be even so secretly polluted with self-interest, the fire of truth will overwhelm him instead of issuing from him, and he will be burned like a piece of dead wood and his leadership will pass to another.

I heard a French voice speaking for the human race, from Cairo. It was Easter Sunday and the voice was General de Gaulle's. As soon as I heard it I realized suddenly, and afresh, that there is still hope for the human race in the test which it is now undergoing, for the simple reason that a few people, and perhaps many more people whose voices we cannot yet hear or whose martyrdom we shall never know about, value their own incorruptibility more than they value their lives.

They value incorruptibility, and they would die for it! They would fail, if necessary, in everything else, but they would not fail in incorruptibility. They believe in the human spirit, they believe in the essential need of the human spirit to be free so that it may follow God's guidance and not man's.

A fanatic is a person to whom ideas are more important than people or than personal relationships. There are periods in history when ideas *are* more important. Then certain people are *used* by great forces—they are like radio receivers ... certain ones are sensitive—sense of prophecy. ... If they are true to themselves, they allow themselves to be used—history has known their names ... to their little experiences they are strange and unpleasant usually.

Ideas like seeds ... over and over and over—repetition —repetition ...

There are some of us now who find inescapable—sense of obligation ... find ourselves out of harmony with our own immediate past, and with our immediate environment. Sudden change—conversion ... be brave enough to follow this ... families are divided as they were in the Civil War ... conscience ... morality ... it is a choice between corruptibility and incorruptibility ... we see how many of the nicest people we know are shameless about telling lies —believing lies in ourselves. We have made marriages— we have used religious ceremonies as decoration—disregarding the promises, the sacrament described in them. Hitler is possessed, he believes, by a power of intuition— second sight which guides him. We laugh at that, but perhaps it is true. He is our dragon. God is directing Hitler, as he directed Chamberlain, because the world needed Hitler. Why? Look at what we were before he came into power.

Gaiety, happiness, warmth ... marriage ... I torture myself. Every now and then I drive myself away out of my safe happy harbor. Something in me desires hazard, loneliness—peril, hideous suffering. My mind goes on those terrible nightmare voyages—far away—lonely—seeking an absolute truth—nonhuman, noncompromising ... lacking complete truth in myself ... *chez moi*, fear. You can't proceed—make progress—get anywhere—develop and grow—

381

unless you tell the truth all the way. You discover that in another human being who is truthful you have infinite possibilities of hell and heaven. Changing—as infinite and various as Nature. If you respect yourself, you express yourself always without shame or fear.

NOTES FOR MERRILL MOORE

I THOUGHT something was really wrong with me this A.M. because I was thinking so fast, or rather receiving impressions so fast and so vividly. Something was *rushing* inside of me! I felt *too bright*—manic. Like Kitty, "I am in a bother. I am in a hurry—I am as wild as a fox. I want to get on to other things that are whirling around in my head." (Kitty is my niece, she is not manic; but once, aged eight or nine, she sat up in bed drawing and writing, and she described her feelings in the lines I quote.) Then, having written my rude letter to Mr. Weeks, I thought I was perhaps getting like Jack when he told everybody the truth about themselves, and I felt scared. Then I went to the darling cafeteria, which is beyond words delightful on a cold Sunday morning—the Greeks waiting on us. Young man in glasses asks for oatmeal. "Utmeat," says the counter man. "Utmeal," says the man at the back. Then the young spectacled one, who reminded me of Jack, told the Greek about making pancakes out of the leftover oatmeal and eating them with maple syrup. "At home, when you have some left over, that's what my mother does. You do it at home—not here. It wouldn't do for here—but you do it at home." Then in came the wonderful old lady . . . the little thin wispy figure . . . feet in rubbers . . . far apart . . . straight long coat . . . wispy hat . . . hollow wispy face and squashed hat . . . strange cracked voice . . . and such love and affection, asking the counter man if he was better, sorry to hear he was sick. He

said, "I wasn't sick. I can't be sick." The tall, fancy Juno-
esque girl came in white blouse like a slightly dirty
sweater, embroidered with pearls across the front ... ring-
lety bangs ... head held very high ... the neck and face
beginning to show battle scars, yet still young and power-
ful-looking, especially beside the little hollow, wispy old
lady who looked up at her with a polite and respectful
smile as they stood at the counter. The fancy one ordered
her salad in a torch-singing voice, very casual, off-hand
like Harriet. A handsome boy came in and sat facing me.
He was drawing or making a plan of something on a piece
of paper as he sat at his table. Each of these persons and
several others who came in seemed extraordinarily heightened for me in their significance. It was like a play in
which each did his part to perfection—the spectacled
one after telling about the oatmeal pancakes apologized
jocosely for his "crazy ideas." Later, when some of his
acquaintances came in, I heard a tag end of humorous
conversation in which the spectacled one remarked that
he himself was crazy enough anyway. I think he is, probably.

I began to say that this feeling of intense impression-
ability which I have now, and the excitement of it, is
maybe a result of the narrow life in Blue Hill, and my almost drunken way of talking to M.M., insatiably talking and
telling *everything* about myself, is because, alas! I practice so much repression at home.

The word *spate* describes it ... like the bridge at Blue
Hill Falls when the tide is rushing out. Too many ideas,
rushing too fast toward the chance to escape in talking—
all pent up and gathering too fast. So I am afraid there
will be a flood, and it will carry the bridge away. Floods
of spring, the great melting after winter—"*Sacré du Printemps*"—the great upheaval and renewal. That wild Stra-

vinsky music, how excited I was the first time I heard it! When I heard it, I first realized that the sweetness and softness of spring is really a huge violent force in action.

I woke up this morning *Ça val—Ça va* is what it is. After all my horrible dread and anxiety all is well ... *Ça va* ... *God within me!* I have just discovered that when I say God within me, it gives me a sudden sense of maturity, equality inside me. This is something that psychiatry strives for. Christianity creates in people a wonderful combination of maturity and humility—*childlikeness* and *boldness*—not afraid of anything or anybody—yet with an overwhelming sense of obedience to the Will of God.

I felt the need last night, yesterday afternoon, St. Valentine's Day, when I had such happiness, of a church. I need a church to go into and kneel down and be humble and grateful and pray to God to keep me humble and grateful. A person might say, "Why do you need a church? Why can't you pray anywhere?" Well, you create a room with a special atmosphere for other purposes—why not a place with a special atmosphere for the most important purpose, the purpose of God's guidance and our humility toward God?

Crazy moths skittering like ballet dancers. It is nearly midnight. I am lying on my back in the dark. My knees are drawn up, my hands are clasped across my forehead. I am lying in bed thinking about God. The night is very still and dark. At first there is no air moving, then in the stillness suddenly there comes a soft motion of air. A sweet coolness flows for a moment across my bed. What is it? What is this invisible presence that touches my face? The wind bloweth where it listeth. The wind or night—I do not know what it is. I do not know who gave me my life—who gave me this body, this breath, this beating heart, this thinking mind, and this sense of deep happiness. My humility, my ignorance, and my sense of wonder make me know there is God. I feel myself held in His hand. Feeling this thing is absolutely necessary for me to feel gratitude—therefore gratitude makes me have to surrender the circumstances of my life also.

INNER STRUGGLE

WHEN I wake up suddenly in the night with a feeling of intense despair, with my heart beating fast and hard, I must remember then that my despair is only my resistance to suffering. It is my despair at feeling despair, which prolongs and increases itself. I must remember then that I am a child of God. I must surrender myself to whatever suffering He sends me, take it as a gift, as a friend, even, sent to me for some reason. The reason why I resist it so bitterly is because I cling stubbornly to my own idea of my life, my idea being that I should be exempt from suffering—that I should be always functioning happily—that I should be allowed to work and produce my book. What good is my book if I don't know enough to be humble at all times, in all things? God is with me—controlling me, filling me just as much when I am suffering as when I am joyous.

Why I believe in anonymity—Merrill Moore stresses the person as being wonderful, a genius, etc. That is bad. I keep trying to get away from that and to lose myself in God. I am not remarkable—neither is M.M.—except in our receptiveness and obedience to God. It is the truth itself which is remarkable as it may come through us, by the grace of God—by our humility and selflessness. I believe we need to return to the idea of the Middle Ages in which artists were nameless, working for the glory of God, not for themselves and their fame. I distrust my own ability to receive fame and not be corrupted by it.

This age is so corrupted that the truth is not recognized as such unless it comes from an individual recognized—or rather unless it comes in a form which could belong to an accredited person...Oxford Group members are laughed at by intellectuals...

Obedience is necessary to happiness, to spiritual peace. In marriage you surrender to episodes which have not intrinsic merit or claim, but great claim and merit because they are part of the marriage which was destined for you. And out of them, surrender to them, acceptance of them, a harmony is arrived at, very deep and valuable, instead of flouncing and flinging away from those episodes because of a false sense of one's own personal value and right to independence. Obedience to God rather than to a person —how to distinguish. U. S. A. defied George III—the founding fathers obedient to God—religious freedom. Now the nervous breakdowns.

CHRISTIANITY

The Psalter...Evening Prayer—25th Day....
Peabody, Mass.

Thy hands have made me and fashioned me.
O give me understanding, that I may learn thy commandments.
They that fear thee will be glad when they see me, because I have put my trust in thy word....
I know, O Lord, that thy judgments are right, and thou of very faithfulness hast caused me to be troubled....
O let thy merciful kindness be my comfort, according to thy word unto thy servant....

O let thy loving mercies come unto me, that I may live;
  for thy law is my delight....

Let the proud be confounded, for they go wickedly about
  to destroy me, but I will be occupied with thy commandments.

Let such as fear thee, and have known thy testimonies,
  be turned unto me....

O let my heart be sound in thy statutes, that I be not
  ashamed.

I opened mother's little book of common prayer the
first night I arrived here, and opened it upon the evening
prayer for the 25th day—on the opposite page—which is
amazingly apropos of what I am feeling and of the reason
why I have come away.... This morning Kitty (who is
sleeping with me) and I were waked by the music box,
which suddenly started to play at 6 A.M. all by itself.
This is an omen—of a new beginning—a new happiness—
my little music box that I got on a famous day in Haute
Savoie. *Je commence encore.* Kitty read me some of her
poems last night before we went to sleep. Very beautiful,
with the sound of Emily Brontë.

CREATIVE BREATH

SOMETHING wonderful is happening to me. It is like the
time when I first bought my house—that same feeling of
surprised, delicious excitement. Almost too much....

To be humble, submissive to universe, selfless, yet make
of one's self the poem, the lovely interpretation, medium
for mysterious heightened sense of life—a flower—flexible
—sensitive—*honest—true.* Always praying for simplicity—
for receiving God.

I receive this miracle, I lie in the sun, I breathe, I am happy. Yet I must fulfill this gift, or else it will rot on me. I must *give* it again, myself. The gift of life is fulfilled, fully experienced and received and lived, only when it is handed on. It cannot be hoarded, saved. I must give my life away, never try to protect or save myself. What a sterile life it is that is selfishly hoarded.

Every action is good or bad in the sense that it is fruitful or sterile, according to whether or not it is a true action. Examples of untrue action, society, etc., caused mostly by what people will think. Amiability, kind deeds, devotion to parents, husbands or wives, or children—confused with the extraordinary beauty of these when they are true.

Imitation instead of reality—of imitation due humble with the hope of achieving the reality which imitation does just for effect.

Highly important quality is fruitfulness—out of one action grows the next, the whole tenor of a life. The happiness or unhappiness of a life depends on its fruitfulness.

The way things grow—slow accomplishment—the magic of transformation—chemistry of bacteria in soil—this compost—one thing becomes its opposite—you accomplish something when you take part in this magic instead of resisting it; follow and do as it does. A life follows a lead and (this compost) the rich life builds out of evil—good. Untoward circumstance becomes great good fortune. The little locksmith's Happiness. . . .

The Spirit of the Lord God is upon me; because the Lord hath anointed me to preach good tidings unto the meek; he hath sent me to bind up the brokenhearted, to proclaim liberty to the captives, and the opening of the prison to them that are bound. To give them beauty for ashes, the oil of joy for mourning, the garment of praise for the spirit of heaviness.

Sunday afternoon. Brown room, open window, the soft almost imperceptible breeze yet so fresh, soft and of the sea—delicious to the lungs, to the nose. It is very still here, one of those brooding, rich afternoons, cloudy sky with dim, golden light. I am thankful that I live here where I can hear seagulls at any time of day. They are mewing and crying now, faintly, softly, out over the harbor. Near in tops of apple trees there are little summer chirpings of birds, so domestic-sounding compared to those crying gulls, and the soft sound of somebody hammering or pounding out of doors, across the cove. Everything seems contented. Downstairs, Toupsie lying wide and fluffy and motionless on the wooden floor of the little back porch. Sunday afternoon, calmness and satisfaction, the wonderful, graceful looping branches of the bleedingheart, and against the light the lower pendants of the flowers look as if they were made of crystal. I don't care how unkempt the grass and the unpruned trees look. There is everything, every possibility here; every reason for utter contentment and fulfillment. Be patient. Make haste slowly.

Miss Nelly Townes came to the back door Saturday night when Dan was making an omelette in the kitchen and gave him a rose for me, a large half-open pink rose on a very long stem with a great many sprays of leaves on the stem all up and down, a very handsome rose. I shall have an excuse to go to her house and see the Chinese statuette again.

It is Sunday morning—raining, heavy showers mixed with the sound of church bells pealing loud for church... sound of church bells and sound of rain.... Thinking of Miss Nelly Townes and her roses.

Still life
    pink beads—
    zinnias in pewter jug—
    playing cards—
    farmer's almanac
    coffee-milk
    spectacles—
    opera glasses
    knapsack
    egg-dish with eggs—

A joyously beautiful day—the water is running deep, deep blue with white caps. Such air! The rose geraniums in the window—their spraying leaves sparkle with growth —soft, velvety in the sun. A set of portraits of Blue Hill characters. Draw for a month instead of writing. No snow at all—springlike wind.

Dan and I were saying how nice it is to have had one's adventures and settle down in contentment to meditate and enjoy—the brick wall of our house—the southern side is a beautiful color—the brick wall is such a comfort, reassuring, permanent, solid.

In the evening, sitting on the terrace at Sarn in June or early July 1942, it is twilight. The sun has set, but the sky is still full of light—high, clear sky. And the earth is full of light and color. We are sitting on the second terrace. It is the moment when the chimney swifts come

out into the air. They are darting around our heads, five or six together. They are like the links of a little chain which is being flung round and round in the air just above the house by an invisible hand. Every time they come swinging round into sight and sound over the west corner of the roof we hear their cries, and it is like the shrill sound of a metal chain being violently shaken, whirling through the air. They sound, too, rather like a handful of quite young children just darting out of school and screaming with fun and uncontrollable laughter and play.

The sound of oars, rowlocks, and water on a beautiful August morning. Mira barking, 8:30 A.M. I put my head out of the window in my workroom and look down at her lying in front of the dahlia bed. See nothing but kitten and Trouvée for her to bark at. Admire the wonderful dahlias from top window and cosmos and calendulas in bloom. Wonder if Mira is barking from stomach-ache. Then hear oars in rowlocks and plashing water and see man rowing dory away from our shore. Object of Mira's suspicion and severity. I think of the sound of Warren's canoe paddle in Ipswich River. I didn't speak of that in my book, but it was a thing I always noticed and enjoyed.

THE BELOVED HOUSE

I have taken care of it with my hands—
Many times opening the doors
Closing the doors
Standing in the entrance to each room before leaving—
Coming back in the damp spring with the creak of the
  floor in the silence
I have closed the windows before the bright storms
The shutters when the force of wind would come—
I have tied back the blind that sprang loose in the night
And in the spring a branch that throbbed at the pane in
  the long room
I have stood in the dark at the East doorway—
I have stood in the dark at the West doorway.

It was done before they say
Over and over it was done
And there, but I was not there
It was done to me
I was not there
It was not I who said
This is the way it has to be
I must go away—
From the house and the grass and the trees
That was not anything I ever said—
That was not me.
Many bodies are buried
And I am dead
Should I know how it is, now
To be dead?
Let them be kind to us after this
Because we suffer
And there is no color to show the grief
And there is no touch

From the Journals

And no sound
No taste, no smell, sharp bitter fresh enough
To tell that the pain is the pain
Of the ground
And there are no words, no sounds
No sounds can say
The bursting strain as the soul pulled away—
Only only finish the pain
Never know it, hear, smell, taste, touch it again.

                    —*A poem by Catharine Huntington*

THIS BOOK HAS BEEN DESIGNED BY
CARL PURINGTON ROLLINS
AND SET IN CALEDONIA TYPE
WITH DECORATIONS ADAPTED FROM
OLD STENCILS